W9-ABJ-646

Date: 12/6/21

BIO PARKS
Mace, Darryl,
Rosa Parks : a life in
American history /

Rosa Parks

Recent Titles in Black History Lives

W.E.B. Du Bois: A Life in American History
Charisse Burden-Stelly and Gerald Horne

Thurgood Marshall: A Life in American History
Spencer R. Crew

Barack Obama: A Life in American History
F. Erik Brooks and MaCherie M. Placide

Harriet Tubman: A Life in American History
Kerry Walters

Zora Neale Hurston: A Life in American History
Stephanie Li

Rosa Parks

A LIFE IN AMERICAN HISTORY

Darryl Mace

Black History Lives

 ABC-CLIO®

An Imprint of ABC-CLIO, LLC
Santa Barbara, California • Denver, Colorado

Library of Congress Cataloging-in-Publication Data

Names: Mace, Darryl, 1975– author.
Title: Rosa Parks : A Life in American History / Darryl Mace.
Description: Santa Barbara, California : ABC-CLIO, An Imprint of ABC-CLIO, LLC, [2021] | Series: Black history lives | Includes bibliographical references and index.
Identifiers: LCCN 2020021993 (print) | LCCN 2020021994 (ebook) | ISBN 9781440868429 (hardcover) | ISBN 9781440868436 (ebook)
Subjects: LCSH: Parks, Rosa, 1913–2005. | African Americans—Civil rights—Alabama—Montgomery—History—20th century. | African American women—Biography. | Civil rights workers—United States—Biography. | African Americans—Michigan—Detroit—Biography. | African American political activists—Michigan—Biography. | Montgomery (Ala.)—Biography. | Detroit (Mich.)—Biography.
Classification: LCC F334.M753 P385537 2021 (print) | LCC F334.M753 (ebook) | DDC 323.092—dc23
LC record available at https://lccn.loc.gov/2020021993
LC ebook record available at https://lccn.loc.gov/2020021994

ISBN: 978-1-4408-6842-9 (print)
        978-1-4408-6843-6 (ebook)

25 24 23 22 21   1 2 3 4 5

This book is also available as an eBook.

ABC-CLIO
An Imprint of ABC-CLIO, LLC

ABC-CLIO, LLC
147 Castilian Drive
Santa Barbara, California 93117
www.abc-clio.com

This book is printed on acid-free paper ∞

Manufactured in the United States of America

Contents

Series Foreword

The Black History Lives biography series will explore and examine the lives of the most iconic figures in African American history, with supplementary material that highlights the subject's significance in our contemporary world. Volumes in this series will offer far more than a simple retelling of a subject's life by providing readers with a greater understanding of the outside events and influences that shaped each subject's world, from familial relationships to political and cultural developments.

Each volume includes chronological chapters that detail events of the subject's life. The final chapter explores the cultural and historical significance of the individual and places their actions and beliefs within an overall historical context. Books in the series highlight important information about the individual through sidebars that connect readers to the larger context of social, political, intellectual, and pop culture in American history; a timeline listing significant events; key primary source excerpts; and a comprehensive bibliography for further research.

Preface: Rewriting Rosa Parks in Collective Memory

> For a long time, I had been very much against, as far back as I can remember myself, I had been very much against being treated a certain way because of race. . . . [A]nd for a reason that over which I had no control, had always been taught that this was America, the land of the free and home of the brave, and we were free people. And I felt that it should be actual in action rather than just something that we hear and talk about. And as my reason is a little hard to explain to most people, but I just feel that I was being mistreated as a human being and I wanted to in this way make known that I felt that I should have the same rights and privileges. (Parks, Horton, and Nixon 1973)

The indelible Mrs. Rosa Parks offered this quote to radio host Studs Terkel during an interview broadcast in 1973. Highlander Folk School founder Myles Horton and labor organizer Edgar Daniel (E. D.) Nixon joined Parks for this dialogue. Both men were integral leaders in the fight for racial justice, and both men worked closely with Rosa Parks. Terkel brought the group together to discuss how the Highlander Folk School and the Montgomery Bus Boycott influenced the Modern American Civil Rights Movement. Parks's influence on these men and their work is immeasurable, as the interview and other communications attest. Conversely, Parks's time with Myles Horton at Highlander Folk School and her work with E. D. Nixon, former president of the Montgomery, Alabama, chapter of the National Association for the Advancement of Colored People (NAACP) had a profound impact on her actions and activism.

When ABC-CLIO approached me with this project, I wondered why we needed another book on Rosa Parks. Parks was a household name, and I remembered reading about her in much of the scholarship on civil rights. Diving deeper into the scholarship, I learned an important lesson that drove my desire to write this book. Although Rosa Parks was a central, even foundational, figure in the narrative of the Modern Civil Rights Movement, there was very little scholarly analysis of her life and her life's work. She appears in nearly every, if not every, book written about the Civil Rights Movement, yet authors often focus exclusively on her December 1, 1955, stand on the Montgomery Bus Line that signaled the start of the famed Montgomery Bus Boycott of 1955–1956. Much of the body of available children's literature also limited the scope of Rosa Parks's role in the black freedom struggle. Three books however stand out as more comprehensive approaches to Rosa Parks and the Montgomery Bus Boycott, Nikki Giovanni's *Rosa*; Dee Romito's *Pies from Nowhere: How Georgia Gilmore Sustained the Montgomery Bus Boycott*; and Russell Freedman's *Freedom Walkers: The Story of the Montgomery Bus Boycott*. Still, more work needs to be done to illuminate for young people Rosa Parks's lifetime of leadership and activism.

For too long, Rosa Parks's own autobiographical work stood alone as a testament to her engagement with and influence on U.S. history. Recently, biographers and other authors have begun to foreground Rosa's lifelong activism and service to black liberation. Douglas Brinkley published a biography of Rosa Parks in 2000 that started to explore her role as an activist leader. In 2010, Danielle McGuire's work, *At the Dark End of the Street: Black Women, Rape, and Resistance—A New History of the Civil Rights Movement from Rosa Parks to the Rise of Black Power*, opened the doorway to a wider analysis of Rosa Parks and her impact on America. Through McGuire, we learn how active Rosa was battling for justice in cases where black women experienced rape and other sexual violence. Three years later, Jeanne Theoharis's political biography, *The Rebellious Life of Mrs. Rosa Parks*, expanded further Rosa's lifelong activism, and Theoharis shed much-needed light on Parks's life after the Montgomery Bus Boycott. Included in her analysis are the years of economic neglect that Rosa and her family endured as Americans refused to hire the symbol of the Montgomery Bus Boycott and failed to offer adequate financial support to this activist leader. Theoharis further explicated, particularly in the newer 2015 edition, how Parks's image, a symbol of black triumph, was frozen in time much like her likeness is frozen in stone in Statuary Hall within the U.S. Capitol building. Triumphant heroes cannot experience poverty, cannot live in destitution, and cannot feel neglect, because any sense of struggle overshadows the successes and runs counter to an American progress narrative.

This work adds to the recent scholarship on Rosa Parks by speaking to audiences less likely to gravitate to the works of McGuire and Theoharis. This book, and this series, offers a synthetic analysis of existing literature and aims to reach a nonscholarly audience. Of particular note, this work offers a structure and a level of analysis written for high school and college students. The goal is not to replace the excellent work of predecessors; rather, this work aims to pique the reader's interest so much that they want to read the other recent scholarship. Moreover, I hope that reading this work will drive them to read Rosa Parks's own accounts of her life, particularly *Rosa Parks: My Story*, and visit the Library of Congress where the Rosa Parks papers now reside on a ten-year loan. The collection is expertly curated and largely digitized. It is a treasure trove of information, and the Rosa Parks Collection proved invaluable to my work. I wrote this work to pay honor to the excellent recent scholarship on Rosa Parks, to captivate the minds of people who might not gravitate to those works, and to offer an homage to the stunning courage, astounding political foresight, and stalwart leadership of Rosa Louise McCauley Parks.

You will find in these pages that Rosa Parks's story is a story of American culture. Her life as an individual teaches us about U.S. society and American cultural norms, yet her legacy as the mother of the Civil Rights Movement is incomplete as it exist in much of the collective memory of the United States. Her life highlights the complexity of gender roles within American society and within the black freedom struggle. Parks's courage and activism underscore the profound difficulty of the civil rights movement within the context of white supremacist America, and Rosa's life as a whole embodies the cultural framework of black protest.

Rosa Parks came from a long line of race resistance pioneers. She put to work the lessons learned from her family, particularly her mother and maternal grandparents. In subtle—and not-so-subtle—ways, Rosa Parks lived a life of resistance that began long before and lasted long after her December 1, 1955, refusal to give up her seat on a Montgomery, Alabama, bus. Sadly, much of the collective memory of Rosa Parks confines her activism to that singular moment, and even in that moment of defiance, too often we remember Rosa Parks as a quiet activist whose "tired feet" kept her from following the unwritten rules of racial segregation. Rosa Parks determined to defy the segregation laws in that moment, and in other moments before and after her arrest, because she was an activist leader in her core. She rose to the occasion by sitting down for racial justice, and her immobility moved a city, a race, and a nation.

Acknowledgments

In times of trouble and despair, Rosa Parks would recall her favorite scripture: "The Lord is the strength of my life. Of whom shall I be afraid?" (Psalms 27:1). When I agreed to write this biography, one of two projects I contracted with ABC-CLIO to complete, I had little idea of the trials I was about to encounter in my personal life. Yet, the Lord sustained me and helped me bring both projects to completion. He surrounded me with overwhelming support from family and friends and made this writing process a bonding experience between my sons and me.

Before I even started writing, I read Rosa's 1992 biography with my two sons, James and Chris. I am so grateful for that time shared with them and for their patience with me throughout this process. As I stated above, dynamic books from Jeanne Theoharis, Danielle McGuire, Douglas Brinkley, Rosa Parks, Jo Ann Robinson, Joseph Fitzgerald, Paula Giddings, and many others made this synthetic work possible. Your scholarship and biography inspired me and fueled this text, and for that, I owe a debt of gratitude.

Cabrini University supported my work as well, and I am grateful to President Taylor, Provost Ugochukwu, and Dean Filling-Brown for their encouragement. Special thanks goes to my mentor and dear friend Mark Kiselica for leading me through tough times. My department has shown me unwavering support throughout my career and through this project. James Hedtke and Jolyon Girard gave me my start in academia and in publishing, respectively, and I am forever grateful. Courtney Smith, who is writing the book on Jackie Robinson for this series, has been a stalwart advocate. Joseph Fitzgerald has been my dear friend since my first year of graduate school, and I am so blessed to be able to call him colleague, confidant, and friend. Nancy Watterson read multiple drafts of this work and offered me the expert critique and caring support necessary to bring it to completion. Laura Groves was there to pick me up and encourage me through all of the difficulties I faced during the writing of this book. She shared her confidence in me even when I was in the midst of so much doubt. She was a solace and a support in the midst of the storms. In more way than I can explain, this work exists because of Laura. I am grateful for your love and support, and I appreciate so much the times of rest and comic relief you and Caroline provided as I wrote.

My mother, Jackie Mace, also read chapters of this book, and it is such a joy to discuss all of these experiences with her. I adore you, Mother Dearest, and feel so blessed by you. Your love of life, history, and the Lord inspire me daily. Mom and Tracy, among other things, the Christmas trip to D.C. in December 2018 was a salve that helped me heal and begin to write again. I love you both. Most of all, I want to thank my grandmother, Elizabeth Trotter, for inspiring my love of history, storytelling, and Rosa Parks. For as long as I can remember, when I thought of Rosa Parks, I pictured my grandmother. Both were models of unfailing faith and unwavering determination to fight for what was just and right in this world. Mommom, you didn't live to see this book sitting on your bookshelf, but I dedicate it to you because the work I do is in honor of you.

1

The Roots of Race Consciousness

Parks was born Rosa Louise McCauley on February 4, 1913, to James McCauley and Leona (Edwards) McCauley. Born in Tuskegee, Alabama, Rosa came into the world in a center for education and uplift for black Americans. Rosa was named after her maternal grandmother, Rose, and her paternal grandmother, Louisa. Her brother, Sylvester, was named after his maternal grandfather by the same name. Family names were commonly passed down across generations. Naming practices among African American children during the period of enslavement show the importance of passing on family names. Cheryll Ann Cody notes that "the rules a society uses in the selection and transmission of family names indicate the value that the parent or individual selecting the name attached to the preservation of ties to the namesake" (Cody 1987, 564). This practice, which was so important in the early stages of American enslavement, and which often involved the preservation of traditional African names, reemerged in importance after the turn of the nineteenth century, when the increased profitability of the Deep South's cotton production replaced the Upper South's tobacco crops as the dominant cash crop in the American South. To meet the exploding need for labor to satisfy Deep South demands, many enslaved people, especially men, found themselves "sold down the river," which means sold or transported from tobacco lands in the Upper South to cotton plantations in the Deep South. This process separated families and made the continuity of names and naming all the more important. That is not to say that fathers being sold down the river created the only need for naming conventions: "Some cultures express continuity by linking the child to the grandparents or extended kin." Rosa Parks's parents had some sense of, or connection with, this tradition, and both Rosa and Sylvester bore names that connected them to their ancestors (Cody 1987, 564). At times, as was the case with Rosa, naming practices "hint at ties to families of both parents" rather than indicating "'unilateral descent'" (Gutman 1976, 197). For her mother, at least, passing down a sense of history, both familial and of the race, was an important part of how Leona socialized and acculturated her children to the harsh realities of racism and racial oppression surrounding them in their everyday lives.

Parks's mother, Leona Edwards, came from Pine Level, Alabama, a town in Montgomery County outside the city of Montgomery, Alabama. Leona was a teacher who instilled in her daughter the importance of education as a means of uplift. The Edwards family all lived in and around Pine Level, and Rosa spent the majority of her childhood in Pine Level. Rosa's father, James McCauley, hailed from Abbeville, Alabama, the county seat of Henry County, Alabama. Rosa remembered her father as a highly skilled brick and stone mason as well as a carpenter and builder. Owing to the limited employment opportunities for African Americans, even skilled blacks like her father traveled often for work. From McCauley, Rosa learned the value of hard work, and her dexterity as a seamstress might very well have been inherited from her father.

Rosa's parents met in Pine Level, where her mother grew up. Her father had a brother-in-law, husband of Rosa's paternal aunt Addie, who was the pastor of Mount Zion African Methodist Episcopal Church in Pine Level, and that was where Rosa's parents met. Wed in Pine Level on April 12, 1912, the two moved to Tuskegee in pursuit of more work for James. Tuskegee, the county seat of Macon County, Alabama, offered James lots of work opportunities in and around the county, and Tuskegee was the home of the aforementioned Tuskegee Institute. As Parks tells it, "both black and white leaders call the town of Tuskegee a model of good race relations" (Parks 1992, 6).

James McCauley's work kept him on the road a lot, and Leona, who was used to the comfort of having lots of friends and family around her while she was in Pine Level, found Tuskegee to be lonely and isolating. These feelings intensified when she became pregnant with Rosa. Pregnant women did not spend much time outside of the house, and Leona had to quit her teaching job during her pregnancy. With her husband on the road, and isolated from her family in Pine Level, Leona had some very unhappy days in Tuskegee. Still, according to Rosa, her mother felt Tuskegee was a good choice for a place to settle because "Tuskegee was still the best place in Alabama for African Americans to get an education" (Parks 1992, 8).

The ready availability of educational opportunities and the potential for work at Tuskegee appealed to Leona McCauley. She harbored hopes that her husband, Rosa's father, would get a job teaching at the Institute. These teaching jobs came with the benefit of housing, and Leona envisioned her new family enjoying the security of housing and the benefits of a Tuskegee education for her children. However, Rosa's father did not share his wife's dreams. James wanted to continue his work as a contractor, work that paid more than any teaching position at Tuskegee. These disagreements about the direction and future of the family would put a strain on the McCauleys' marriage.

Though Leona's hopes for her husband to teach at Tuskegee never came to fruition, the family did benefit from the Institute. Shortly after Rosa was born, James's younger brother Robert came to live with the family. He aided in taking care of Rosa, who was quite sick as a baby, and he took some courses at the Tuskegee Institute. Robert was also a builder, and he spent some time studying the trade at Tuskegee. Leona later told Rosa that Uncle Robert knew more about building than his teachers, and they deferred to his superior knowledge.

The McCauley family's stay in Tuskegee was short-lived. James decided he wanted to head back to Abbeville to be with his family, so Leona and baby Rosa left with him. In Abbeville, Rosa's family moved in with her paternal grandparents. Her father came from a large family—at least ten children—and Rosa had many aunts and uncles of varying ages. Her father's youngest brother, George, was just eight years old when Rosa's family moved to Abbeville. Rosa was less than two at the time (Parks 1992, 8–9).

James McCauley continued his construction work, a trade he learned from his father, after moving back to his hometown. In her biography, Rosa recollected that she knew relatively little about her paternal ancestors, and what she did know came from her Uncle George. What she learned was that her father's grandfather (likely his paternal grandfather) was unknown and may have been a Union soldier stationed in the South after the Civil War. Her father's grandmother (again likely paternal) was formerly enslaved, and she had some Native American heritage. Census records show that James's father was Anderson McCauley, and his mother was Louisa McCauley (U.S. Census Bureau 1900, 1910).

During their time in Abbeville, Leona became pregnant with Rosa's younger brother, Sylvester. James determined that he wanted to move to the North to pursue more work. Leona was not willing to move with him, and she decided it was best to move back to her family home in Pine Level rather than remain with her in-laws in Abbeville. James later joined his family in Pine Level, and he lived with them until Rosa was two and a half, but he soon left to pursue work elsewhere. He returned to the family for a brief stint when Rosa was five, but after that, she did not see her father again until she was an adult. Her father later wrote to Rosa, apologizing:

> I kept thinking of writing you and still putting it off. It was in view of the
> fact that I was over shadowed. With open shame that I and I alone allowled

[*sic*] the Evil spirit to lead me completely out of myself for these many years in grose [*sic*] desertion of a good wife and two of the sweetest children ever lived. (Theoharis 2013, 2–3)

Without paternal support or even a paternal presence, Rosa's mother was left to raise the two children as a single mother. She received tremendous support from her parents and other relatives in Pine Level, but financial strains played an important role in Rosa's life.

Laws that existed during Rosa's formative years did little to hold her father responsible for supporting his offspring. The 1910 Uniform Desertion and Nonsupport Act had many problems that made it relatively unenforceable. The primary issue in the McCauley situation was that the law did not offer provisions for fathers who left the state in which his family lived. In short, Leona had no recourse to collect money from her husband once he left the state of Alabama. Adding to her woes, prosecutors were hesitant to enforce the law even when fathers remained in the state. It was not until the 1950 passage of the Uniform Reciprocal Enforcement of Support Act that the government could prosecute fathers who left the state, and this was well beyond the time when Rosa and her family could have benefited from support for dependent children (U.S. Department of Justice 1950). In fact, it was in 1950 that her father sent the letter to Rosa apologizing for his neglect, and perhaps it was the passage of this new law that prompted his attempts to reach out to his daughter.

Despite financial issues, Rosa and Sylvester received lots of love and support in Pine Level. In fact, much of Rosa's personality was shaped by her time in Pine Level with her maternal grandparents. As Rosa put it, contrary to her time with her father's family, "my memories of my mother's parents are very clear" (Parks 1992, 11). Living with her maternal ancestors for so long, Rosa learned a lot about her heritage. She learned that her grandmother's father had the surname Percival, recorded in the 1870 census as Pursavill (U.S. Census Bureau 1870). According to Rosa, her maternal great-grandfather, James Percival, was a Scotch-Irish immigrant who came to the United States as an indentured servant, although the 1870 census entry for the family lists him as African American. Erroneous census records abound, particularly from this era, and census takers could have assumed James Percival was a black man because the enumerator only spoke to his spouse who was obviously black. Whatever the reason for the seeming error, Rosa Parks recounts that Percival arrived through Charleston, South Carolina, and was later transported to Alabama. This change in location corresponds somewhat with the census records, as James Percival's place of birth is recorded as Charleston, South Carolina. In Alabama, he was indentured to a family named Wright, but he was allowed to keep his name. Parks points out in her biography that this was one of the major differences between enslaved Africans and indentured Europeans. The enslaved rarely had the opportunity to keep their names, whereas European servants often maintained that right. The process of enslavement was a process of "social death," and the goal was to strip enslaved people of any remnants of their identity, including their names, in order to indoctrinate them into a life a servitude that would extend to their descendants. As such, enslavers gave names to the enslaved to stake a permanent claim of dominance and control over their lives and the lives of their children. Percival, as a white man who would eventually earn his freedom, did not endure such oppressive restraints on his humanity.

Percival married an enslaved woman by the name of Mary Jane Nobles. It is unclear how the state of Alabama characterized this union, but it is likely that the marriage was not sanctioned by the governing body. Though the state of Alabama did not have formal laws banning interracial marriage before Reconstruction, enslaved people were barred from entering into legal contracts, including marriage. By 1852, the Alabama legislature had moved to limit marriage to unions between white people or free people of color. The union of James and Mary Jane Percival did not meet this standard, both because James was white and Mary Jane was black and because Mary Jane was enslaved. Regardless of the legality, James and Mary Jane lived as husband and wife. They had three children, including Rosa's maternal grandmother and namesake Rose, before the end of the Civil War, and they had six other children after the end of the conflict. As Rosa notes in her biography, these last six children were born free (Parks 1992, 12).

Freedom was a tenuous notion for recently freed people, and the Percivals, like many others coming out of enslavement or other forms of servitude, remained on the land where they had previously served. Rosa recounted, "My great-grandparents stayed on in their small log house on the [Wrights'] land and continued to work for the family" (Parks 1992, 13). James Percival continued to build furniture for the Wright family in the postbellum period, but Rosa noted that he felt empowered enough after the war to build a table for his own family home. Rosa's grandmother Rose, despite her young age, took a position caring for the young children of the Wright household, thus keeping her away from the grueling field work.

Although freedom looked a lot like servitude for the Percivals, the end of the Civil War and the passage of the Thirteenth and Fourteenth Amendments did bring certain rights, including the right for all people, regardless of previous condition of servitude, to purchase land. Armed with these rights, the family at some point purchased twelve acres of land that was previously part of the plantation on which they labored. In this fact, Rosa's family was relatively unusual; by purchasing land, the family ensured a level of stability and security in the coming decades (Parks 1992, 13).

On her maternal grandfather's side, Rosa also learned of interracial relationships and imbalance-of-power relationships. Her grandfather's father was a plantation owner who raped an enslaved woman working in the house, Rosa's great-grandmother. Jeanne Theoharis, in her biography of Rosa Parks, identified this great-grandfather as the son of the plantation owner. The product of this nonconsensual sexual relationship was Sylvester Edwards, a man who had "no discernable features of black people" (Theoharis 2013, 3). Able to "pass" as white, Sylvester Edwards took liberties regarding race relations that darker-skinned black people were often more hesitant to take. Severely mistreated as a child, Sylvester was led to capitalize on his ability to "pass" as a way to exert some of the power and control stripped from him in his youth. His mother died when he was young, and his father died as well, and then an overseer by the name of Battle took control of the plantation. He frequently beat and deprived

---

White Supremacy

White supremacy reached full maturity at the same time that some white Southerners attempted to bring economic growth to the region. How did the South reconcile a burgeoning capitalist economy with a feudal labor system? The industries that developed, such as textiles, tobacco, and lumber, were perfect for low-waged workers and an abundance of natural resources. The desire for cheap labor led to factory development in rural areas and stifled the development and growth of large urban centers. Of course, this created even more differences between the North and South.

It was not until the second decade of the twentieth century that Southerners began to embrace true economic and urban expansion. Military mobilization for World War I helped to jumpstart this evolution. The desire for growth, at least among Southern elites, a group to which most Southern mainstream newspaper publishers belonged, continued throughout the first half of the century. New Deal programs poured money into Southern economies, and the mobilization for World War II represented the largest push for economic advancement.

After World War II, Northern industrialists embraced the idea of moving their operations to Southern states. The companies enjoyed cheap land, cheap labor, and tax breaks, and they used the favorable climate as a way to entice current employees to move south. All of this changed on "Black Monday," the name white Southerners gave to the 1954 *Brown* decision. The Southern backlash to integration slowed the pace of industrial development and led some industrialists to seek out new homes for their businesses. Therefore, white Southerners' dual personas manifested in an insistence on a tradition of segregation and white supremacy, which hindered significant and prolonged industrial growth.

Sylvester of basic necessities like food and clothing. This treatment instilled in Sylvester a deep-seated hatred and mistrust of white people, and therefore he refused to be cowed by white supremacy. Growing up in the presence of her maternal grandparents, Rosa learned the values of self-reliance and self-worth—values essential for activists in the struggle against white supremacy.

Rosa recalled with a sense of adoration how her grandfather would challenge existing racial norms in his everyday life. Sylvester had very light skin and straight hair, so he would act every bit their equal when he encountered white people he did not know. He would introduce himself by his last name, Edwards, and shake their hands. He called white men by their first names or full names, and he would not use the honorific "Mister." Even with white men who did know him, Sylvester would challenge their preconceptions of race relations by not acting intimidated or inferior. As Rosa told it, "Any little thing he could do, he did. It wouldn't be anything of great significance, but it was his small ways of expressing his hostility towards whites" (Parks 1992, 16–17).

Sylvester forbade Rosa and her brother, his namesake, from playing with white children, even the white kids on the Hudson plantation. Sylvester Edwards also vowed that neither his children nor any of his relatives would have to work as domestics for white families. One of the most common jobs for black women, domestic work paid very little, and black domestics labored under constant fear of both violence from the families they served and unwanted sexual advances directed toward them. Sylvester himself was a product of these rape-conducive conditions, and he did not want that for anyone in his family.

Sylvester and Rose Edwards had three daughters, Fannie, Bessie, and Leona. Bessie died in her teens, leaving Fannie and Leona as the only surviving direct descendants. Despite Sylvester's aversion to his children taking domestic work, Fannie moved to Montgomery and took a job in the home of a white family. Leona, however, remained in school and earned her teaching certificate from Payne University in Selma, Alabama. Teaching was a very respectable position for black people, and despite the fact that black teachers did not make as much as white teachers, it was much more lucrative than domestic work.

Leona, Rosa's mother, taught in Pine Level before marrying James McCauley and moving to Tuskegee. She also taught there until she had to quit during her pregnancy with Rosa. Leona may have taught for a time when the family moved in with James's parents in Abbeville. Once they all settled back in Pine Level, Rosa's mother again looked for teaching positions, but the one in the Pine Level black school was already filled. Black teachers, no matter how qualified, could not teach in white schools, and all of the schools were segregated. The closest teaching opening was in a village called Spring Hill, so Leona McCauley took a job there. Spring Hill was too far away for her to travel back and forth from Pine Level each day, so, during the week, Leona stayed with a family close to her job. This left Rosa and Sylvester under the care of their grandparents. The 1920 Census lists Rosa's great-grandfather, James Percival, as a member of the Edwards household along with Leona, Rosa, and Sylvester. Another relative, recorded in the 1900 and 1910 census as Lora and Cora, respectively, who was a niece of Rose Edwards and her husband, lived in the family home for a time before Rosa and her family went to live there (U.S. Census Bureau 1900, 1910, and 1920). All of this shows the importance the Edwards elders placed on family and supporting family members. These values were passed down to Rosa, and she made important decisions throughout her life that underscored her dedication to family.

Even at an early age, Rosa showed this dedication to family in the ways she cared for her brother. With her father out of the picture and her mother away most weeks teaching, Rosa felt responsible for her brother, Sylvester. In return, her younger brother adored and idolized his big sister. Rosa recounted in her biography that Sylvester would follow her around everywhere and repeat everything that she said. Sylvester was mischievous, and he often got in trouble with their grandparents, who took on the role of primary caregivers. Rosa remembered a time where her grandmother was about to give Sylvester a whipping, and Rosa said, "Grandma, don't whip brother. He's just a little baby, and he doesn't have no mama and no papa, either." Moved by Rosa's protection, Rose Edwards spared the rod that day, but Rosa remembered that she "got more whippings for not telling on things he did than I did for things I did myself" (Parks 1992, 20). Overall, however, Parks recalls that she "never did get out of that attitude of trying to be protective" of her brother (Parks 1992, 21).

Family stories like these stuck with Rosa Parks, and she recalled them often throughout her adulthood. In fact, history, including family history, was an essential element of her family time. As Theoharis noted, "At home, the McCauleys discussed the history of slavery, the situation of blacks in Alabama, and how 'to survive, not getting into trouble by confrontation with white people who were not friendly to us'" (Theoharis 2013, 6). This often meant standing up for oneself in subtle ways that did not directly mirror the blatant militancy of Sylvester Edwards; rather, Rosa learned "controlled anger . . . that balanced compliance and militancy" (Theoharis 2013, 6). Sometimes, this meant simply sitting back and watching white people challenge systems of racial oppression put in place by their own. One of the family's favorite stories occurred in 1919 when a white veteran, the son-in-law of Moses Hudson, who owned the plantation adjacent to Rosa's childhood home, came to Alabama to visit the Hudsons. Moses Hudson stopped by the Edwards farm with his son-in-law, and this soldier took a liking to Rosa. He patted six-year-old Rosa on the head and said she was "such a cute little girl" (Parks 1992, 3). As the family told it, the "Yankee soldier" treated the young Rosa Parks like "just another little girl, not a little black girl" (Parks 1992, 3). This was taboo, because white supremacist southern culture did not permit white people to treat black people as equals, or even as human beings. As such, Moses Hudson took issue with his son-in-law's treatment of Rosa, and the plantation owner's face "turned red as a coal of fire" (Parks 1992, 4).

The year 1919 brought other revelations for Rosa Parks. The end of World War I saw the return of hundreds of thousands of black soldiers from the war effort. The violence that erupted that year was unprecedented, and Rosa learned that at the heart of this was a white supremacist effort to show black soldiers who felt "as if they deserved equal rights because they had served their country" that nothing could be further from the truth in the minds of most white people. Red Summer, the name given to this most violent of seasons in a year full of vigilante violence, saw the eruption of over thirty race riots across the United States of America, resulting in hundreds of deaths (overwhelmingly of black people) and the rampant destruction of black properties in segregated black neighborhoods. James Weldon Johnson, then field secretary for the National Association for the Advancement of Colored People (NAACP), who in 1920 became the organization's first executive secretary, coined the phrase "Red Summer" to highlight the senseless and callous snuffing out of black lives throughout 1919. All of this death and destruction had a permanent effect on Rosa Parks, and she worried about racial violence in her hometown of Pine Level.

Violence did come to Pine Level, as it did across the country. In fact, the thirty-six recorded race riots during Red Summer do not accurately capture the scope of racial oppression that reared up across the country in the wake of World War I. Although Pine Level is not one of the places on record for having a race riot in 1919, Rosa Parks's recollections of that year show that a full-blown race riot was not necessary in order for black people to feel the oppressive yoke of white supremacy. In fact, Rosa Parks notes that "by the time I was six," which corresponds with 1919, "I was old enough to realize that we were actually not free" (Parks 1992, 30). She recalls, "The Ku Klux Klan was riding through the black community, burning churches, beating up people, killing people. . . . At one point the violence was so bad that my grandfather kept his gun—a double-barreled shotgun—close by at all times. And I remember we talked about how just in case the Klansmen broke into our house, we should go to bed with our clothes on so we would be ready to run if we had to" (Parks 1992, 30). Faced with the constant fear of violence, Sylvester told his family, "'I don't know how long I would last if they came breaking in here, but I'm getting the first one who comes through the door'" (Parks 1992, 30).

Mercifully, the family did not have to endure such violence, but the events of 1919 and the family's armed response shows the importance of armed self-defense for Rosa's family (Fitzgerald 2018). Rosa's reaction to her grandfather's words is telling. Contrary to the collective memory of Parks as a quiet, passive woman, Rosa recalls, "I remember thinking that whatever happened, I wanted to see it. I wanted to see him shoot that gun. I wasn't going to be caught asleep. I remember that at night he would sit by the fire in his rocking chair, and I would sit on the floor right by his chair, and he would have his gun right by just in case" (Parks 1992, 31–32). At that moment, and throughout her life, Rosa Parks's actions demonstrate her training in the cultural context of black protest—a protest methodology that at times employed violence as a form of defense. Not only was Rosa Parks eager to see her grandfather defend his space—something that flies in the face of the image of a passive, docile Parks—but these events also show that as a family, they were committed to standing up for their rights, no matter the cost.

RACE RIOTS

The violence in Rosewood, Florida, the Tulsa, Oklahoma, race riots, the Scottsboro Case, and the Wilmington and Atlanta race riots were only a few of the incidents in which accusations of a black man raping a white woman sparked rioting, violence, and death. Often, the accusations were false, and the majority of the dead had black faces. Emmett Till's lynching was just another in a long line of white men objectifying and, in their minds, protecting their "prized possession," the white woman. Southern black men learned the lesson quickly, and most avoided even looking at a white woman, but Emmett Till, a Chicago boy, did not understand the depths of fear and hatred that existed in the South.

Tensions that working and housing discrimination engendered naturally led to a rise in Northern race riots. However, early in the century, Springfield, Illinois was a classic example of factors that would eventually lead to middle- and upper-class whites leaving urban environments and class conflict and solidarity across racial lines. Better-off whites in Springfield, Illinois, incited the lower classes to riot by projecting the ills of society upon the entire black community. They convinced the lower classes that the two black prisoners, one accused of rape and the other accused of murder, in the Springfield jail were symbolic of the morality of all African Americans. When the riot broke out, better-off whites and the local newspapers lauded the riot as a righteous effort to clean up society. Once they realized they could not stop the rioters, these white inciters turned their attack on the very people they once praised. They distanced themselves from the rioters, calling them riffraff and highlighting the fact that they were predominantly lower-class men and that there was a strong Irish presence. After the riot ended, and the guilty parties were rapidly convicted, the better-off whites again praised the riot's social cleansing benefits. The projection of social ills is a common theme behind race riots.

One of the rights they enjoyed was land ownership, something uncommon for black people across the country and particularly difficult for blacks in Alabama. In fact, Rosa's grandparents were the only black family in the area to own their land. Black landownership was so rare that the 1900 and 1910 Censuses listed the Edwards family as renting rather than owning their homestead (U.S. Census Bureau 1900; 1910). In truth, the Edwards family inherited the land from James Percival, who purchased twelve acres after the end of the Civil War. James's daughter, Rose, Rosa's grandmother, had served in the house of the then plantation owners, the Wright family. For her service, Rose was given six acres of land along with a house on that property. As such, the Edwards family, headed by Sylvester and Rose, owned eighteen acres of land adjacent to, and formerly part of, the Wright plantation (later known as the Hudson plantation once the Wright daughter married Moses Hudson).

This eighteen-acre farm served as an important base for the Edwards family, both in terms of growing food to eat and also in terms of a sense of security that land ownership offered. The family was able to raise their own chickens and cultivate a garden on the land. The farm had fruit, pecan, and walnut trees that provided further sustenance, and the family even raised a few cows. Rosa recalls, "We didn't have to buy many things at the stores" (Parks 1992, 33). The sales of the animals and the eggs from the chickens allowed the family to buy much of the necessities they did not grow on the farm, mainly cloth for garments—Rosa's mother would sew all of her clothes. Still, even with the freedom of landownership, the Edwards family struggled financially. The farm just barely met their needs in good years, and any extra money the family possessed came from her mother's teaching and the work the family did on other people's land.

Rosa picked cotton on the neighboring Hudson plantation from the age of six or seven. At that young age, she was expected to pick one to two pounds of cotton a day. As she grew older, the expected yield increased, and she took on other responsibilities, including "chopping cotton." Field hands harvested (or picked) cotton in the fall once the crop was ripe. In the spring, they chopped the cotton, meaning clearing the weeds from around the plants and thinning the plants to make them stronger. She earned fifty cents a day for chopping cotton and one dollar for every hundred pounds of cotton picked. Rosa worked in the fields as long as there was enough sunlight to work, or from can see in the morning to can't see at night. It was hot and grueling work, and Rosa remembered how the "sun just burned into me" (Parks 1992, 35). On top of that, the sandy soil burned her bare feet because "didn't nobody have shoes on but the hoss [horse] and the boss" (Parks 1992, 35).

Working on the Hudson plantation offered Rosa a rich perspective on the state of race relations. A man by the name of Sherman Gray served as foreman for the field laborers. Everyone called him Mr. Sherman or

Mr. Gray, despite the fact that he was half black, because he was respected by the laborers. Above Gray was the white overseer, Mr. Freeman. Rosa recollected this frequent exchange between the two men:

> Mr. Sherman Gray would go up to Mr. Freeman and ask, "What would you all white folks do if you didn't have us niggers to work for you?" suggesting that a compliment was in order for the high-quality work the field hands were doing. Mr. Freeman would answer in an authoritarian manner, "Sherman, if I didn't have you all working for me, I'd have some others. I would have some more damn-fool niggers working." (Parks 1992, 35–36)

Rosa and all of the other black laborers who witnessed this oft-repeated banter learned so much about their worth in the eyes of white Alabamians. They were considered easily replaceable and thus not seen as worthy of any compliment or consideration. The meager wages for back-breaking work and the constant disrespect from Mr. Freeman and other whites challenged the sense of self-worth that her family instilled in her.

Still, Rosa maintained her dignity and sense of self, even when the racists around her told her with every word and deed that she was worth nothing. Due to these conditions, her grandfather wanted to be sure that his entire family avoided acting cowed or inferior to anyone. His deep sense of dignity and self-reliance led him to the messages of Marcus Garvey and the Universal Negro Improvement Association. A native Jamaican, Garvey immigrated to the United States in 1916. He developed a significant following among African Americans who gravitated to his message of economic self-determination and black-nationalist pride.

It was a constant and conscious effort to counteract the message of black inferiority that confronted Rosa every day. Education played an essential role in her house, particularly with her schoolteacher mother. Leona taught her daughter how to read and write before she entered school, and Rosa became a lifelong avid reader. Even the text she read, however, carried racist messages that left indelible impressions on her. At the age of eight, she read *Is the Negro a Beast? A Reply to Chas. Carroll's Book Entitled "The Negro a Beast"; Proving that the Negro Is Human from Biblical, Scientific, and Historical Standpoints*. This text, intended to counter the idea that black people were subhuman, still "maintained the idea of black inferiority," according to Parks biographer Jeanne Theoharis (Theoharis 2013, 4).

Theoharis elaborated, "The impact of the book on young Rosa was immense and devastating as she 'didn't have any idea that there would ever be a way to protest'" the belief in black inferiority. She found hope, however, in the political activism and resistance in her family and in the black history text (scholarly and popular) that she encountered throughout her adolescence and adulthood. She wanted a counternarrative to challenge the racist messages enveloping her in her daily life, and she gravitated toward people like her future husband, Raymond Parks, who reminded her of her grandfather and his refusal to accept inferiority. Rosa found the history of African Americans, written by African Americans, an additionally comforting counternarrative, and "she saw the history of black survival, accomplishments, and rebellion as the ultimate weapon against white supremacy" (Theoharis 2013, 4). Amid all of the miseducation, Rosa found ways to educate herself about the true history and legacies of power, self-worth, and perseverance of her race; and although life circumstances initially prevented her from gaining the level of education she hoped to obtain, Rosa found solace and uplift in her schooling and education amid the pervasive miseducation surrounding and enveloping her.

2

Miseducation and Reeducation

"I remember that when I was very young they built a new school for the white children not very far from where we lived, and of course we had to pass by it. It was a nice brick building, and it still stands there today. I found out later that it was built with public money, including taxes paid by both whites and blacks. Black people had to build and heat their own schools without the help of the town or county or state" (Parks 1992, 26–27).

At a very young age, Rosa McCauley began to understand the pervasiveness of white supremacy and how the culture of black inferiority affected her life. She was quick to identify injustices, and they left a negative impression on her. Black people confronted a daily miseducation that relegated them to second-class citizenship—or no citizenship at all. It was "a complete and solid pattern as a way of life" (Theoharis 2013, ix). Though she did experience some kindnesses from white people that left her feeling like "not all white people in Pine Level were hostile to us black people," she had a general mistrust of whites (Theoharis 2013, ix). Her maternal grandfather, Sylvester Edwards, fueled this mistrust, not even letting Rosa and her brother Sylvester play with the white neighbors, but the most affirming evidence that whites could not be trusted came in the ways white people treated black people as inferior. The system of white supremacy and the whites who benefited greatly from it forwarded a narrative where white people should, and did, hold all the power, whereas black people must remain in, and be content with, their place of subjugation.

Rosa's family worked tirelessly to counter this miseducation with messages of resilience and self-worth in the face of racial oppression. At home, her mother and grandparents taught Rosa about her family heritage. She learned that she was part of a family of landowners—a source of pride that was rare for black people across the south. She saw her grandfather repeatedly standing up for his rights and refusing to be intimidated by white people. Sylvester Edwards experienced constant abuse and neglect as a child, and in his adult life, he refused to let himself or his family expose themselves to such harm.

Rosa's mother, Leona McCauley, an educator, taught Rosa the importance of education as an accessible pathway for uplift. Leona admired Booker T. Washington and George Washington Carver, men who challenged existing ideas of what black people could achieve. Washington, known as the "Wizard of Tuskegee," drew the ire of many black people when, in his 1895 "Atlanta Compromise" speech, he urged black Americans to accept their current position in life and strive for uplift by making sure whites viewed their labor as essential to the well-being of the nation. Having secured a great deal of goodwill and financial support from prominent white Americans who embraced his message of patience, Washington went on in later years to modify his message to one of black advancement and uplift. He called for educational advancements for both blacks and whites, and he identified education as a shared purpose and a shared potential for uplift that transcended racial barriers. Washington noted a common citizenship regardless of race, and he highlighted the need for equality of opportunity so that every citizen might help improve the collective experience of the nation. Leona's other hero, Tuskegee Institute professor George Washington Carver, largely stayed out of politics, choosing rather to promote agricultural and scientific advancements that made him one of the most prominent African American scientists of his time. Both Washington and Carver carved their place in American history and their legacy as black American heroes through subtle assertions of their humanity and worth. These subtle methods resonated with Leona McCauley, perhaps because that was the way her mother trained her to challenge existing racial norms.

Rosa's namesake, her maternal grandmother Rose, showed her how to resist white supremacy in ways that did not require risking her life to stand up for what she knew was right. Rosa recalled one specific incident where her grandmother stepped up and scolded her for taking actions against racial injustice that could have endangered her life. She recounted, "One day when I was about ten, I met a little white boy named Franklin on the road. . . . He said something to me, and he threatened to hit me. . . . I picked up a brick and dared him to hit me" (Parks 1992, 22). Such actions could have put Rosa in grave danger. There are countless reports of African

---

MEDIA REPRESENTATION OF BLACK PEOPLE

With the March 16, 1827, publication of the first edition of *Freedom's Journal*, Samuel Cornish and John Russwurm ushered in a new era of journalism and fomented the mission for black-owned and -operated periodicals. The two editors promised readers that the new paper would be a source of uplift for black people. Cornish and Russwurm founded *Freedom's Journal* because, as they put it, "we wish to plead our own cause," an act they saw as necessary because the public were "deceived by misrepresentations" of black people. Although this first black periodical lasted only two years, subsequent black newspapers and magazines answered the call put forth by *Freedom's Journal*'s founders.

For the better part of the next century, publishers and editors of black journals shone a light on stories that failed to grace the pages of mainstream newspapers. Collectively, the black presses emerged as a transcript of the black public sphere, where "conversations about Black publicity, rights, and interests take place and are transformed into strategies to counter the oppression of White supremacist rule." The persistence of black press owners and employees, combined with increased agitation throughout the first third of the twentieth century, led to a profound shift in public spheres, in which, by the 1940s, exposés on segregation, lynching, rape, and general poor treatment of African Americans, historically reserved for the pages of the black press, began to seep into the mainstream press and generate discourse within white public spaces.

Americans, even children, who were kidnapped, beaten, and even lynched for much lesser acts of boldness. When she learned of this encounter, Rose Edwards scolded her granddaughter. "I had to learn that white folks were white folks and that you just didn't talk to white folks or act that way around white people" (Parks 1992, 22). Although this reprimand did not sit well with Rosa initially, she eventual came to see that her grandmother "was scolding me because she was afraid for me. She knew it was dangerous for me to act as if I was just the same as Franklin or anybody else who was white. In the South in those days[,] black people could get beaten or killed for having that attitude" (Parks 1992, 23). Rosa's future responses to similar injustices combined her mother's contemplativeness, her grandmother's sense of self-preservation, and her grandfather's defiant militancy.

Like her family, the black community in Pine Level also worked to create spaces where black children could understand their humanity and embrace their rights as citizens. In essence, they had to "make the best of a bad situation" (Theoharis 2013, x). Rosa saw in her family the multiple ways black people had to exist and exert power within America's white supremacist culture. Black people had to be nimble, and blacks responded to each oppressive situation in ways that maintained their dignity while still preserving their safety and lives. In Pine Level, as in many places in the country, education about the culture of black resistance to white supremacy came through a united effort of home, school, and church. Rosa began school when she was around six years old. She attended the one-room schoolhouse on the church grounds of Mount Zion AME (African Methodist Episcopal) Church in her hometown. This school educated around fifty-five students at the time Rosa attended. Students sat in rows according to grade level. Miss Sally Hill was Rosa's first formal teacher, although she recounted in her biography that her mother was her first teacher. Leona taught Rosa how to read at a very early age, around four or five, and Rosa was very prepared for school. Rosa liked Miss Hill, and she recalled how the teacher would comfort her when she was sad about the other students teasing her. Miss Hill also encouraged Rosa in her reading. She remembered, "No matter what Miss Hill gave me to read, I would sit down and read the whole book" (Parks 1992, 25). This love of reading served her well throughout her life, and she was well versed in both history and current events.

After a year, Miss Hill left, and Mrs. Beulah McMillan took over as teacher in the one-room schoolhouse. Miss Beulah, as the students called her, was an experienced educator. She had taught Rosa's mom, and Rosa treasured a particular photograph from the time her mother was a student. Miss Beulah also encouraged Rosa's love of reading, and Rosa recalled her second teacher fondly. What Rosa did not enjoy were the blatant inequities between the white schools and the black schools. For instance, the older boys in her school were responsible for managing the wood used to heat the building. Some of the wood came from parents who brought supplies to the school because the government refused to build or supply black educational institutions. It was up to members of the black community to sustain the schools in their neighborhoods.

Adding to the inequities in education, black schools remained open four months, whereas white schools offered nine months of classes (Parks 1992, 27–28). Deeply entrenched economic inequalities were at the root of this policy. Black children often needed to work their family's land, so many black families could only afford to have their children in school for the four-month period. However, almost all of these black families were working the land as sharecroppers or tenant farmers. They did not own the land where they worked and lived; rather, they rented parcels from white landowners. In return for working the land, sharecroppers receive a share of the crop, hence the name. Tenant farmers had similar labor relationships, with the primary difference being that they received monetary payment instead of a portion of the crop. Both sharecropping and tenant farming contracts were heavily weighted in favor of the landowner. Often, these agricultural laborers rented tools and livestock in addition to the land.

Whenever tools broke or livestock died, the laborers bore the responsibility for fixing or replacing the goods. Sharecroppers in particular had a difficult time with this arrangement because their labor contracts rarely left them with any disposable income from year to year. Without cash or goods on hand to pay or barter for the cost of broken equipment, sharecroppers had to pledge a portion of their meager share of the harvest to compensate for these inevitable equipment failures. The result was an ever-deepening cycle of debt as sharecroppers and tenant farmers signed away future gains. Laws prevented sharecroppers and tenant farmers from securing more favorable contract on other farms if they owed a debt to their current landowner. Thus, many African Americans in Alabama and across the South were held captive on the land they rented in a system of debt peonage, or forced labor to pay off a debt. Moreover, often the land belonged to the plantations on which they and their ancestors were formerly enslaved. Very little changed for black people even after the abolition of the institution of enslavement.

Rosa Parks's family owned their land, and they did not have to enter into sharecropping or tenant farming contracts. Even though Rosa's family owned their land, she still realized at an early age that "conditions for my family and me were in some ways not much better than during slavery" (Parks 1992, 28–29).

The climate of black poverty fueled by white supremacy proved an important and indelible education for the young Rosa Parks. She saw the inequity very starkly during her early school years. White schools boasted far superior resources and accommodations. Rosa remembered that white schools had glass windows, while the black school only had shutters separating students from the outside world. Inclement weather, oppressive heat, dust, and insects affected the learning environment for black students in ways that did not taint the experience of white students. Some white students rode buses to school, but black students all had to walk each school day. Black students traveling to and from school learned to walk a distance from the road because as the buses passed, the white pupils would launch trash and epitaphs from the windows. Any complaint on the part of African Americans carried with it the threat of injury or death. Much like during the institution of enslavement, "white people would get angry" if they saw black people complaining or acting unhappy (Parks 1992, 28). Rather than resorting to open defiance, black people often had to "sooth [themselves] with the salve of attempted indifference, accepting the false pattern set up by the horrible restriction of Jim Crow laws" (Theoharis 2013, x). Such was the state of black resistance in white supremacist America. Blacks had to be careful about how they spoke, behaved, and lived their lives, for the fear of violent repercussion was a real and ever-present danger.

Pine Level, a small town, did not have the segregated facilities found in many of the bigger cities across the South. Although this meant that Rosa and other black locals did not have to suffer the indignity of using "Colored" restrooms and drinking fountains, it also meant that white people were always around scrutinizing black people's every move. This is why Rose Edwards, Rosa's grandmother, always taught vigilance and proud deference as a survival strategy. Life for blacks in the South and across the country was a constant negotiation of tenuous, sometimes life-threatening, interpersonal interactions. They had to evaluate every encounter in a split second to decide how to react, when to stand up for themselves and when to appear cowed. Rosa described how black people had to "perform to their [whites] satisfaction or suffer the consequence if we get out of line" (Theoharis 2013, x). It was a "major mental acrobatic feat" (Theoharis 2013, x). Any wrong decision could result in violence or even death. Rosa recalled that "there was always violence, and you'd hear about it every time." Living through the heyday of Jim Crow, she "heard of a lot of black people being found dead and nobody knew what happened" (Parks 1992, 30–32). Violence and murder were commonplace, and the normalization of brutality had a profound effect on Rosa Parks, who recalled in her memoirs that "that was the only way I knew and Pine Level was the only place I knew" (Parks 1992, 32). Though normalized, the violence and abuse served to fortify Parks and other African Americans. Rosa did not dismiss the treatment of black people as acceptable; rather, she resolved to do her part to resist oppression directed toward her.

Black institutions offered spaces for African Americans to speak their minds, relax their vigilance, and organize resistance to white supremacy. In these spaces, black people found relief from life patterns where they had to "walk . . . on a tightrope from birth" (Theoharis 2013, x). Although inferior in almost every way to white schools in terms of facilities and supplies, black schools offered black youth the opportunity to learn empowerment away from the oppressive gaze of whites. Rosa found solace and support in her time with her teachers, Miss Hill and Mrs. Beulah. In the face of constant messages of black inferiority, her schooling provided positive messages that there was a refuge in the storm of white supremacy, that black people possessed the potential for and had obtained greatness, and that education was an essential vehicle on the pathway to racial uplift. These messages reinforced the race-positive education she received from her family, and Rosa treasured her schooling. All of these experiences guided Parks as she grew older, for she had learned the hard lessons of how to be black in America. This was the cultural framework of black protest at the time: live life with dignity and know how to survive amid constant oppression.

Closely linked to black schools in many areas of the South, including Pine Level, the black church offered additional separate spaces for black people to grow individually and as a race. In many ways, black churches, even the clandestine spiritual meetings of the enslaved, provided spaces for blacks to throw off the guises they put on in front of whites. Here, they did not have to pretend to be subservient. They could speak their minds much more freely. In black-only and predominantly black religious meetings, they could lead the services and tailor the messages in ways that spoke to the black community. Black church meetings served as breeding grounds for the revolts of people like Nat Turner and Denmark Vessey during enslavement, and they supported religion and social outreach projects that formed a basis for Reconstruction efforts in the wake of the Civil War. These churches established black educational, self-help, and social institutions that would enliven black communities throughout the Jim Crow era, and they served as organizing bases for the modern Civil Rights Movement.

Parks belonged to the AME church, and she gained vital lessons from the church that would serve her throughout her life. The AME church, a Christian denomination founded in 1794 at Bethel AME church with Richard Allen as the first pastor, is the first independent protestant denomination founded by black people. It took two separate lawsuits, in 1807 and 1815, for the AME denomination to exist as an independent institution. Throughout their history, the AME church has worked for the uplift of people of African descent. After the end of the Civil War, the church spread rapidly throughout the American South, and Rosa and her family attended one of these congregations, Mount Zion AME Church. For Rosa, the church offered a captivating space because preachers could incorporate "the West African culture passes down from generations of slaves to the sharecroppers of 1920s Alabama" into their sermons (Brinkley 2000, 28). In her words, "The church, with its musical rhythms and echoes of Africa, thrilled me when I was young" (Brinkley 2000, 28). So enthralled was the young Rosa that at a very early age, she strove to memorize scripture. She remained "a devoted member of the African Methodist Episcopal (AME) Church," a church "known as 'The Freedom Church' during the abolitionist movement,'" in part because of prominent abolitionist members like Frederick Douglass, Harriet Tubman, and Sojourner Truth (Brinkley 2000, 28). For Rosa, the church fostered her belief in "Christ as humanity's savior," a belief "developed after her baptism in the AME Church at the age of two" (Brinkley 2000, 28). Armed with this faith and the conviction that came along with it, Rosa Parks "was soon performing daily devotions, praying frequently, and going to church as often as possible" (Brinkley 2000, 28). She "was never pressed, against my will, to go to church. . . . I always wanted to go" (Brinkley 2000, 28). For Parks, the Bible and Biblical teachings she received in the church offered "such comfort and peace," and the lessons "became a way of life and helped me in dealing with my day-to-day problems" (Brinkley 2000, 28). The solace offered in the black church was a constant support for Rosa Parks throughout her life. For her, faith in the salvation of the soul and faith in the salvation of her people were both highly anticipated and intersecting realities.

Rosa's mother believed that education was the key to the salvation of the race, and she made sure her children received as much education as possible, even at times sacrificing both financially and in terms of her proximity to Rosa. Leona McCauley was already spending the weeks separated from her children working in a nearby town of Spring Hill as a teacher in order to provide for her family. Rosa's mother had to log continuing education hours in order to maintain her teaching license. This led Leona to the city of Montgomery from time to time so that she could take courses at Alabama State Normal, now Alabama State University. The school, founded in 1867, offered advanced educational opportunities for formerly enslaved individuals. In fact, the school's founders were formerly enslaved, and Alabama State University claims the designation of HBCU (historically black colleges and universities), and it is "one of the oldest institutions of higher education founded by black Americans" (Alabama State University n.d.). Black professionals like Leona McCauley gravitated to the school because it was one of the few places they could go to further their education and maintain their professional credentials. That is why McCauley spent the summer of 1921 in Montgomery, Alabama, renewing her teaching license. Rosa accompanied her mother on this educational endeavor. Initially, the two stayed with a cousin, Ida Nobles, who was a first cousin of Rosa's grandmother, Rose. Though unmarried, Cousin Ida, as Parks called her, had committed to raising her nephew, Gus Delaney, the son of one of Ida and Rose's other sisters who had died in a streetcar accident after she moved north to Chicago. Gus Delaney was around sixteen in 1921, and Rosa recalled seeing him as a "grown man" at her young age (Parks 1992, 39–40).

During her time in Montgomery, the young Parks enrolled in school at Alabama State Normal. The institution of higher education also offered schooling for youth, serving as a teaching lab for education students enrolled at the college. Often sick during the academic year due to chronic tonsillitis, Rosa benefited from the additional education she received during the summer program at Alabama State Normal. She recognized in her biography that she was sick much less of the summer than in the winter, and she rarely, if ever, missed a day of this summer school in Montgomery. By the time she and her mother got situated and Rosa enrolled in summer school, she only received a few weeks of education, but she enjoyed her experience. The educational opportunities available to Rosa spoke to her mother, and, throughout the summer, Leona considered ways to have Rosa stay in Montgomery for her schooling. One option that really appealed to Rosa's mother was to have Rosa stay with Cousin Ida during the school year. A Montgomery education was favorable for many reasons, but the most appealing aspect was that black schools in Montgomery ran for nine months, unlike the four months in Pine Level. Although Rosa was not privy to these adult conversations, Leona McCauley and Ida Nobles apparently discussed options. Ida agreed to take Rosa in, but she insisted that the arrangement include Ida taking over full legal guardianship, including Rosa changing her surname to Nobles. These ideas did not resonate with Leona McCauley, and, after a strong disagreement with Ida, Leona left Cousin Ida's house and chose to stay with other relatives in Montgomery instead, her first cousin Lelar Percival, his wife Saphonia and their three children, Pauline, Claud, and Morris. Judging by the family listing in the 1930 census, at the time Rosa and her mother went to stay with them, the children were around the ages of four, two, and less than one year of age (U.S. Census Bureau 1930). Rosa noted in her biography that Morris was a new baby, and this was her "first chance to stay in a house with a new baby, and I enjoyed that" (Parks 1992, 41). Overall, Rosa enjoyed her summer in Montgomery. She was in good health, and she was very impressed with Alabama Normal. Rosa recalled being struck with how much bigger the school was than her school in Pine Level. There were five buildings and an athletic field with bleachers. The facilities stood in stark contrast to the one-room Pine Level schoolhouse.

When Rosa and her mother returned to Pine Level at summer's end, they learned that the school there had closed. Further highlighting the racial inequities in education, Rosa and her brother Sylvester now had to walk eight miles each day to and from their new school in Spring Hill while white children rode school buses to the much closer local school that was reserved for whites. Leona McCauley was the teacher in Spring Hill, so, even with the injustice of having to walk so far to school, Rosa got the opportunity to see her mother and learn from her each day until the age of eleven. Leona still spent the weeks living in Spring Hill, because the work of running the school and preparing lessons plans for all of her students made traveling back and forth to Pine Level each day too onerous. She knew her two children were in good hands with her parents, and that allowed Leona to focus her attention on being the best educator she could be each day. Rosa remembered fondly how good a teacher her mother was, recalling how she incorporated exercise even though the school did not have a gym. Rosa also enjoyed the ways her mother integrated practical skills like sewing and knitting into the educational experience; her education was more than just "reading and writing and studying" (Parks 1992, 42).

When the young Rosa reached eleven or twelve years of age, her mother proposed a change in schooling. Spring Hill only offered education up to sixth grade for black children. Education was crucial to Leona McCauley, and she was determined to offer her children as much schooling as possible. In response to the limited education available, Leona sent Rosa to school in Montgomery at Montgomery Industrial School for Girls. Alice L. White and Margaret Beard had formed this school dedicated to the education of black girls from kindergarten through eighth grade in 1886. Both White and Beard, white women from the north, felt a calling to foster the education of black people in the years following Reconstruction. White and Beard were members of the American Missionary Association, an organization dedicated to establishing black schools in the South. The two joined forces in Macon and Quitman, Georgia, at another one of these schools, but the Quitman school burned in 1885, presumably as a result of arson. Many white people in the South hated the idea of black people receiving an education, and they balked further at the idea of Northerners coming in and disrupting their strict racial hierarchy by offering uplift for Southern blacks. Having cut their teeth in Georgia, White and Beard formed the independent school in Montgomery, Alabama. In honor of White, who served as principal of school, the Montgomery Industrial School was affectionately known as "Miss White's school," and Beard was a member of the school faculty (Harmon n.d.; Parks 1992, 42; Theoharis 2013, 7–10).

Miss White's school had a great reputation, and Leona McCauley felt it was the best place for Rosa. White and Beard subscribed to Tuskegee Institute founder Booker T. Washington's philosophy for educating black people, at least his publicly articulated philosophy. Washington emphasized industrial (or trade) knowledge for black people rather than education in the humanities in fields like English, sociology, or philosophy. This approach appealed to many white people because it framed black education as a process of preparing black people to work as laborers rather than as social, cultural, and economic innovators and revolutionaries. The "Wizard of Tuskegee" even praised Miss White's school for its work with young black women, saying the school was "doing good, practical work in that city" (Theoharis 2013, 8). At Miss White's school, Rosa learned these lessons through her training in sewing and clerical work. Both of these skill sets were seen as women's work at the time, and Rosa found herself limited by gender norms of the day. As was the case throughout her civil rights activism, her schooling taught Parks that women had limited access to many jobs and that their sex made women ineligible for leadership roles. During the Montgomery Bus Boycott in particular, despite the fact that Rosa's actions precipitated the mass protest efforts, she was neither offered a major leadership role nor invited to speak at the mass rallies that helped sustain the movement. Rather, Rosa Parks had to carve out leadership spaces of her own as she found ways to navigate the difficult terrain of gendered culture in civil rights organizations.

Through her schooling, Rosa also received a structured education in how to be a proper Christian woman, and that instruction included strict

Christian morality. During the daily devotional services, instructors discussed race as well. Miss White and her all-white and Northern staff were not racial progressives by many standards. They did believe in the right of black people to receive an education, but they did not take a race-forward stand against, for example, the absolute evil of enslavement. Jeanne Theoharis noted, "Rosa recalled once, when the topic of slavery came up, Miss White said, 'If there had not been slavery, and our ancestors had not been brought from Africa, we would probably still be savages climbing trees, and eating bananas'" (Theoharis 2013, 10). Remarks like this left a mark on the young Parks; they were part of the miseducation that surrounded her and made the self-edifying training she received from her family and from learning about black success stories so important (Parks 1992, 49).

Still, Rosa loved her time at Miss White's school, and she noted how much she appreciated the sacrifices these white women made. White and her staff endured constant alienation from local white people. The school battled arson, and the white community shunned the faculty and staff in every social context, including church services. As Rosa noted, "Any social life they had, had to be with blacks, and therefore they went to black churches and so on" (Parks 1992, 42). Receiving an education from white women who occupied a liminal status, ostracized by fellow whites and not completely welcomed by blacks, came with a potentially confusing mix of messages of self-worth along with at least the shadow messages of black inferiority. Overall, though, for Rosa, Miss White's school reinforced messages she had learned at home: that "[I] was a person with dignity and self-respect, and I should not set my sights lower than anybody else just because I was black. We were taught to be ambitious and to believe that we could do what we wanted in life" (Parks 1992, 49). These positive messages were important for sustaining hope in the face of seemingly insurmountable racism, and they offered a counternarrative to the persistent rhetoric of black inferiority. However, these messages did not take into consideration the social, political, and economic barriers that eventually stood in progress's pathway for Rosa Parks and millions of other African Americans.

Even during her schooling, Rosa felt these pressures. Her mother could not afford to send Rosa to Miss White's school, and she struggled in the early days of Rosa's time there. By her second semester, Rosa had received a scholarship that looked more like today's college work-study grants. In return for tuition relief, Rosa dusted, swept, and cleaned classrooms at the end of the school day. The school also benefited from wealthy benefactors, including Julius Rosenwald, part owner and president of Sears Roebuck and Co. (Parks 1992, 45). Rosenwald was a huge supporter of black education, establishing and supporting thousands of black schools. He was also a major contributor to the Tuskegee Institute and benefactor for Booker T. Washington. Parks recalled that at one point during her time at

Miss White's school, Rosenwald came to visit and observe the operations (Parks 1992, 45). Presumably the visit registered with her, because she remembered her mother talking about Rosenwald's efforts in black education, and it stands to reason that Leona knew of the philanthropist's support of Booker T. Washington and the Tuskegee Institute.

Although she was old enough to enter Miss White's school in the sixth grade, Rosa joined the fifth grade class instead. The days of school missed due to her chronic tonsillitis and eventual tonsillectomy, combined with the fact that Miss White questioned the rigor of education Rosa received in her rural schooling, fueled this decision. Rosa had suffered from chronic tonsillitis since the age of two, and rural doctors hesitated to perform the surgery with general anesthetic because they believed young Rosa's heart could not handle it. They did offer a solution that included only a local sedative, but her mother refused that option. Before beginning school with Miss White, Leona received a second opinion from the Montgomery doctors. They felt a comfort with the surgery that rural doctors did not, and so Rosa underwent a tonsillectomy before entering Miss White's school. The surgery brought an end to her chronic illness, and it was a relief to Rosa and her family. Yet, Rosa took a long time to recover from the surgery. She was so sick, experiencing swelling and temporary blindness, that she spent multiple days in the hospital before having to return to Pine Level for a time to recover. Rosa's cousin Thomas, who had the same surgery on a two-for-one deal, recovered immediately. After she finally recovered, Rosa was in much better health and she began to grow rapidly (Parks 1992, 42–44). The surgery had a holistic rejuvenating effect, and upon returning to Montgomery and beginning at Miss White's school, the staff learned how advanced she was. After the first term, they transferred Rosa to the sixth-grade class.

Parks began her time in Montgomery living with her Aunt Fannie. Fannie was a widow with four children. They lived a little ways outside of the city proper. Rosa remembered walking to school most days; however, they did take the streetcar when the weather was particularly bad. Fannie's children all attended public school; Rosa was the only one in the household that went to Miss White's school. Despite attending different schools, Rosa did walk to and from her aunt's house with the other children. This journey took her through white-only sections of the city, and Rosa recalled being taunted and harassed on the trips to and from school. At one point, she got into a shoving match with a white boy who was passing by on roller skates. When the boy's mother, who witnessed the incident, threatened to "put me so far in jail that I would never get out again," Rosa calmly responded that "he had pushed me and that I didn't want to be pushed, seeing that I wasn't bothering him at all" (Parks 1992, 48). Like her grandfather, Sylvester Edwards, Rosa knew how to take a stand for her rights, even at this young age. She learned self-respect from her family and from the black schools she attended. The dignity she showed in the face of threats against her person mirror acts of resistance, including her 1955 refusal to give up her seat on the Montgomery bus, that marked her response to blatant racism and disrespect. This and other incidents like it led her mother, Leona McCauley, to have Rosa move back in with Lelar and Saphonia Percival. Living with the Percivals meant Rosa did not have to pass through white neighborhoods in order to get to school. Rosa's defiance and her mother's efforts to circumvent further conflicts highlight the delicate tightrope that black people had to walk in a white supremacist world. Black people fought to maintain their dignity while also avoiding altercations that would lead to physical harm or even death. The line they walked was narrow, guided by unwritten and constantly changing rules that were impossible to follow with any degree of certainty, and it depended almost solely on the whims of white people, who could violate or kill blacks with impunity. Rosa learned her lessons well. She embodied the fighting spirit of her grandfather, the cautious reserve of her grandmother, and the calculating mind of her mother (Parks 1992, 45–48).

The three terms that she spent at Miss White's school reinforced these familial lessons. Rosa was able to complete eighth grade before the aging Alice White and her staff closed the school in 1928. White was in failing health, and none of the faculty felt capable of stepping in and running the operation. It was very difficult to recruit new teachers and administrators to the schools because of the constant threats of violence levied at the school and the staff. Moreover, for many whites in 1928, the idea of black educational uplift was ludicrous, if not offensive, to their ideals of white supremacy (Harmon n.d.; Parks 1992, 49–50).

For Rosa, though, opportunity for furthering her education came through the newly established public black junior high school in Montgomery. The school, Booker T. Washington Junior High, was her educational home for the ninth grade. That year Rosa also moved back in with her Aunt Fannie. Fannie and her children had relocated, and Rosa could live there and not have to go through white sections of the city to get to school. While living with her aunt, Rosa did some work at the local Jewish country club. This work took her into the white neighborhoods, but she worked alongside her aunt and cousins, so she was not traveling alone. Even with her companions, Rosa still encountered threats and intimidation in the white neighborhood. She recalled that her brother also experienced vicious threats once he came to go to school in Montgomery. White youths threatened to throw Sylvester in the creek; they attacked him with rocks; and at least once, a white man flashed a pistol, threatening to shoot Rosa's brother for standing up for himself. These were but a few of the egregious acts of racism that faced Rosa and the black people of Montgomery on a daily basis (Parks 1992, 50–52).

Yet, Montgomery was still the best place for Rosa and her brother to further their education. With no public senior high schools for black pupils, Rosa returned to Alabama Normal School for tenth and eleventh grades. By this time, the school was called Alabama State Teachers' College for Negroes—"Negro" being the polite terminology of the day. She intended to finish out her education and graduate from the laboratory school, but she dropped out in September of her eleventh-grade year to take care of her ailing grandmother. When her grandmother died a month later, Rosa moved back to Montgomery and began working in a denim shirt factory. She returned to school for a short time before having to drop out again when her mother fell ill. Though unhappy to have left school twice, Rosa was dedicated to taking care of her family. They had taught her so much about self-respect, dignity, and navigating the treacherous waters of white supremacy, and she committed herself to caring for them in their hour of need. Sylvester also dropped out of school, taking a job to earn money for the family while Rosa tended the farm and cared for their beloved mother. It wasn't until after she married that Rosa Parks finally graduated from high school; however, the education, formal and otherwise, that she received in school and from her family shaped her into an activist and leader in the struggle for human rights, and her sense of justice led her to fall in love with her eventual husband, Raymond Parks (Parks 1992, 53–54).

3

The Reality of Rape Culture

"So many African Americans felt that you just had to be under Mr. Charlie's heel. . . . Parks believed in being a man and expected to be treated as a man" (Parks 1992, 59).

With her grandparents gone and her mother having health issues, Rosa Parks settled into work and caring for her family. She had hoped to be a nurse, a social worker, or any other job where she could "'help people to be relieved of suffering,'" and in her late teens and early adulthood, her family was the focus of her caring heart (Theoharis 2013, 10). Now, in the midst of the Great Depression, Rosa, like so many other African Americans, struggled to find sustained work. She cared for her mother, endeavoring to "make things light as I could for her"; tended the family farms; and worked as a domestic in the homes of white families (Theoharis 2013, 10). The McCauley family benefited from the fact that they owned their own land—something rare for black people in general and nearly unprecedented in Pine Level, Alabama, where Rosa grew up. Rosa's great-grandparents, James and Mary Jane Percival, managed to purchase twelve acres of land. The family later added six additional acres, complete with the permanent family home, as a bequest to Rosa's grandmother Rose from the Wright family, who owned the plantation where the Percivals labored prior to the end of enslavement. Rose helped rear the Wright children, and it appears she endeared herself to the family in some way; however, sometimes such bequest came as repayment for the awful abuses endured during time of service. White guilt existed even during the institution of enslavement and the years of Reconstruction, and at times whites chose to offer land and other gifts to assuage their guilt. There is no record of this happening in the case of Rosa's family, but the specter of rape and other assaults hung heavy within the atmosphere of white supremacy that characterize this time period.

Rape—and the fear of rape—haunted black people, particularly black women. That was one of the reasons Rosa's grandfather, Sylvester Edwards, pushed education and didn't want any of his family members to engage in domestic service. He had experienced brutal violence from white people, and he wanted to spare his family, particularly his daughters, from that fate. Rosa's Aunt Fannie, Sylvester and Rose Edwards's eldest daughter, however, left home and worked in Montgomery as a domestic, despite her father's objections. Financial constraints, exacerbated by the Great Depression and general economic oppression of black Americans, forced Rosa into domestic service in her early adulthood. Though she rarely spoke of this time in her life, Rosa did write a short story, found in her personal effects archive in the Library of Congress, that recounted a near-rape experience.

Whether allegorical or biographical, this story underscored the intersecting powers of white supremacy and the patriarchy in affecting the physical, social, and psychological lives of black people in general and black women in particular. Black women negotiated a tenuous terrain of gender role and female subservience in white America, and the patriarchal system of male dominance left little space for black women to assert their autonomy. Women's bodies, too, were subject to male rule, and black women, who were viewed as doubly inferior because of their race and their gender, endured countless assaults from men. Given the context of the patriarchy, rape culture, and gender norms of the time, it is likely that Rosa Parks's short story is in part or completely autobiographical. Parks's biographer, Jeanne Theoharis, noted that there is no evidence that Rosa wrote fiction; that the account accurately identifies Parks's favorite Bible verse; and that the timeline of the story corresponds with the period in history when Rosa was engaged in domestic work (Theoharis 2013, xi). She began this narrative with one of her favorite Bible verses:

> "The Lord is the strength of my life. Of whom shall I be afraid?" This portion of Psalms 27 came in my mind as in answer to my prayer of "Lord what can I do?" when I found myself trapped with a white man with a Negro man acting as procurer, without my knowledge or consent. (Parks ca. 1956–1958)

Often, whites would secure the help of black men and women as they perpetrated unthinkable crimes. Holding all the power, white people would entice blacks with prizes like added power and preferential treatment. During the antebellum period, black men on plantations often held "managerial" roles over the other enslaved black people, and plantation owners and overseers charged these black men with the task of driving the field laborers to work harder. These arrangements continued to exist even after the end of the institution of enslavement. In her autobiography, Rosa recalled that during her childhood, Mr. Sherman Gray served in this role, noting that many called him the "top nigger" (Parks 1992, 33). Accounts of the 1955 lynching of fourteen-year-old Emmett Louis Till offered a similar dynamic where two black men, Henry Lee Loggins and Levi "Too Tight" Collins, who both worked for one of the murderers, J. W. Milam, assisted in the kidnapping and beating of the Chicago youth (Mace 2014, 83). In Rosa Parks's handwritten narrative, "Sam" was the black man who offered her up for the pleasure and domination of the white man she called "Mr. Charlie." Rosa continued her story with background information that corresponded with her own biographical information, adding further evidence that this story was historical rather than allegorical.

As she wrote:

> In the late spring of 1931, I was past my 18th birthday. I was out of school before getting the high school diploma because poverty kept me from paying tuition to continue. It was during the depression and I was quite lucky to have a maid of all work job in the home of a couple who paid me $4.00 weekly for 7 days a week and nights for 50¢ extra or a cost off article of the white lady's clothing.
>
> A small child, in the home, a little boy, 1 year old made it necessary for me to be on duty many nights until early morning hours (some times all night). (Parks ca. 1956–1958)

At this time, Rosa was engaged in work similar to that taken on by her maternal grandmother, Rose Edwards. In return for her dutiful service, the family she served granted her six acres of land and the house where Rosa spent many of her formative years. Neither Rosa nor her grandmother made any reference to sexual relations between Rose Edwards and any member of the Wright family she served; however, the power dynamics of the day and the fact that the family bequeathed land and a house to Rose raises the question of whether or not that bequest was an effort to assuage guilt about some rape or other coercive experience perpetrated against Rose Edwards. Whatever the case, in Rosa's story, the protagonist certainly dealt with unwanted sexual advances from a white man, and a black man acted as a go-between attempting to facilitate this rape attempt, for:

> The porter at the place of business also was the cleaning man at the home for heavy spring cleaning. He worked with me all this particular day, leaving in the late after noon.
>
> I prepared and served dinner. The Mr. and Mrs. were off for their night of pleasure. The baby was put to bed by me and he was sleeping. It was a typical

hot, Alabama night. All doors and windows were open wide only the screen doors of the house were fortified. I was washing dishes before going to the living room to read the newspaper or the den to listen to the radio or phonograph records. They had an old fashioned up right hand operated victrola. No electric record player.

How tired I was. After a long day of cleaning, cooking, baby tending, I really anticipated eagerly getting some rest and relaxation for a part of the night before they came home. A knock at the back door broke my reverie and I hurried to answer. I was not at all alarm to see Sam standing, so I spoke to him at the same time unhooking the screen door and inviting him to enter.

He did not come inside, but asked me to look for his coat, he said he had forgotten. I went to a side screened porch where several garments were hanging along the wall. A quick glance revealed no coat. So I looked again more carefully the second time. Sam's coat was no where in sight.

On my way back to tell him I could not find a coat, I saw Mr. Charlie standing in the kitchen. He smiled as I spoke to him. I asked if he had seen Sam. He said "yes, he is out in my car." I said, "He didn't wait for me to try to find his coat. I didn't see his coat. Maybe he left it some where else."

Mr. Charlie poured himself a drink from the whiskey bottle on the table as I went back to my dish washing. He stood near me, sipping the drink, talking about nothing in particular that I can remember. He declined my request that he take the whiskey and be seated in the living room. I said the folks may be coming back soon if he wanted to wait for them. (Parks ca. 1956–1958)

This "Mr. Charlie" took the liberty to pour drinks and make himself comfortable in another white family's home. Clearly he did not feel any fear that the family Rosa served would have any issues with him being in the house. Nor did he worry that the sexual advances he perpetrated would offend Rosa's bosses. Also of note is the fact that he did not begin his most aggressive advances until all the distractions of dishes were complete and all of the sharp implements were stowed away. Rosa made it clear that:

As I put away the last piece of kitchen cutlery, a large, sharp, butcher knife, and was about to leave the kitchen, he said he was there to see me, not the Joneses.

He offered me a drink of whiskey, which I promptly and vehemently refused. He said I shouldn't be afraid to take a drink. Jones wouldn't miss it. I told him I didn't drink whiskey and I didn't want him there to visit me. He moved nearer to me and put his hand on my waist. I was very frightened by now (or just plain scared nearly to death[)]. At his touch, I jumped away as quickly as an unbridled filly. He was a bit startled and asked me not to be afraid. He would not hurt me. He liked me. He didn't want me to be lonely and would I be sweet to him. He had money to give me for accepting his attentions. (Parks ca. 1956–1958)

Keeping with the theme of offering black people rewards for unthinkable services, "Mr. Charlie" proceeded to try to buy Rosa's affections. First he offered her a drink, as if their relationship was cordial and casual. He proceeded to touch her without any consent. When Rosa resisted, Mr. Charlie resorted to trying to comfort her with a statement that he did not want to hurt her. His final ploy at this point was to offer Rosa money. Coercion is the theme underlying all of Mr. Charlie's efforts, and those attempts are grounded in the racialized and gendered power dynamics that existed between white men and black women from enslavement through the Jim Crow Era. Though "Sam" seemed to have bought into this system, Rosa did not live under the same presumptions. Her body was her own, and she did not believe she had to give over to sexual assault just because patriarchal white supremacist culture told her to do so. Rosa recounted:

> Now, I knew Sam's mission here was not a forgotten coat. I was trapped and helpless. I was hurt, and sickened through with anger and disgust. I had been tricked by one whom I trusted and thought was a friend. I felt filthy and stripped naked of every shred of decency. In a flash of a moment I was no longer a decent, self respecting teen age girl, but a flesh pot, strumpet to be bargained for and parceled as a commodity from Negro to White man.
> My puny 5 foot 2", 120 lb frame could not possibly be pitted against this tall, heavy set man. He seemed at least 6" [sic] tall, weighing possibly 200 pounds. HE was young, strikingly handsome, with very black hair, and dark, swarthy color of skin. He was fast becoming intoxicated on alchohol [sic] and lustful desire for my body. (Parks ca. 1956–1958)

Not only was Rosa at a physical disadvantage compared to Mr. Charlie, but she was at a clear power disadvantage, established and maintained by the patriarchal white supremacist culture in which she lived. White men possessed all the socially assigned power, and Mr. Charlie felt free to exert that power without fear of repercussions. The alcohol is also significant. Whites espoused the belief that black people were inferior and that sexual relationships between blacks and whites were unacceptable; however, these nonconsensual relationships abounded. Mr. Charlie's drinking spoke to the fact that he would need to be drunk to admit his sexual attraction to a black woman, and it provided him an excuse in case his white peers questioned his attempts to have sex with an African American woman. Whereas Mr. Charlie got drunk to assuage his guilt, the object of Mr. Charlie's desires relied on her own will despite the fact that:

> So many frantic thoughts raced through my mind. His strength. My weakness physically. The white man's dominance over the Negro's submissive subjection throughout the history of chattel-slavery-semi-freedom to this moment. I thought of my poor great grandmother who in slavery days could not do more or know more than to be used and abused by the slave owner.

She was bred, born and reared to serve no other purpose than that which resulted in the bastard issue to be trampled, mistreated and abused by both Negro slave and white master. It is said she was a rarely beautiful girl, skilled in finest sewing. She died young, leaving three small children—2 sons—1 daughter[;] my grandfather was her older son.

At this moment the state of Ala was doing every thing possible to electrocute 9 young Negro boys, the Scottsboro boys, for the alleged rape of two white women hoboes.

I stood still, breathed a prayer, "Lord what can I do?" Out of the shattered wreckage of my being came a sharp, clear and positive thought from the Bible, "The Lord is the strength, of whom shall I be afraid? The Lord is my light and my salvation whom shall I fear?["] (Parks ca. 1956–1958)

As was the case throughout her life, in this instance, real or metaphorical, Rosa turned to her faith as a source of solace and fortitude. She loved memorizing scripture, and this passage of strength and protection helped to buttress her against Mr. Charlie's advances. Rosa wrote:

I knew that no matter what happened I would never yield to this white man's bestiality. I was ready and willing to die, but give any consent, never, never, never. It was absolutely unthinkable. All my fear had been replaced by a hard as tempered steel determination to stand completely alone against this formidable foe as long as I drew the breath of life.

Without the least bit of quaking or quivering of my voice, I talked and talked of every thing I knew about the white man's inhumane treatment of the Negro. How I hated all white people, especially him. I said I would never stoop so low as to have anything to do with him. He had quite a sum of money. He asked me to give him a price. When I refused, he tried to give me the wallet to get what I wanted. I turned away and moved out of his reach. Saying I was not for sale and the U.S. Mint wouldn't buy me if he could offer it.

I asked him if the white women were not good enough for him, and it was too bad of something was wrong with them. He would get nowhere with me. I taunted him about the white man's law drawing the color line of segregation. I would stay within the law—on my side of the line. He conceded that he thought I was a nice girl, as why he was there to see me, and I said, "You may think it, but I know it." (Parks ca. 1956–1958)

Rosa went on the attack rhetorically, using the laws and customs created by white Americans to argue Mr. Charlie down. She refused to be bought of cajoled, and she held on to her sense of pride and her self-determination. She rejected the notion that she was a commodity to be bought, sold, or bartered according to the whims of either white of black men. While "the master's tools will never dismantle the master's house," as feminist scholar Audrey Lorde proclaimed, in this account penned by Rosa Parks, the protagonist used the patriarchal structures as the foundation for her resistance of Mr. Charlie's advances. This story and this stand would not bring an end to white sexual oppression of black women, but in the story, the black woman scored a personal victory over this one instance of unwanted sexual advances and the rape culture that dominated the lives of black women. Rosa noted:

> He asked why I was so particular when Sam had given his approval saying it was all right for him to be there with me. I reminded him that Sam had nothing to do with me or what I chose to do or not do. He did not own me and could not offer me for sale.
>
> I said I hoped to marry and live a decent respectable life rather than be a white man's tramp. He offered to leave and send Sam in to me. He said he could make him divorce his wife and marry me if I wanted a husband. (Parks ca. 1956–1958)

Once again, Mr. Charlie, apparently unaccustomed to hearing no from black people, tried another tactic to convince Rosa that she should have sex with him. When she spoke of her intent to marry, he offered up Sam as a groom, stating boldly, and perhaps even accurately given Sam's collusion in this rape attempt, that he could get Sam to bend to his will. As South African activist Steve Biko noted: "The most potent weapon in the hands of the oppressor is the mind of the oppressed" (Biko 1978, 92). Rosa Parks would not let her oppressor, Mr. Charlie, get into her mind. She was not going to act like an oppressed person; rather, she foreshadowed Biko's ideal of black consciousness, namely, rejecting "all value systems that seek . . . to reduce . . . [black people's] . . . human dignity" (Biko 1978, 92). Rosa show tremendous dignity and self-worth through this ordeal. Rather than being cowed by Mr. Charlie's repeated attempt, Rosa became angrier and more determined to ward off his advances.

As Rosa recounted:

> By now I was really livid with anger, a cold, cruel controlled anger. I said I hated Sam as much as I did him and I would not wipe my foot or spit on either of them.
>
> I refused to argue with him further. I had repeatedly asked him to leave me alone throughout the episode. I said there was nothing he could do to get my consent. He couldn't pay me, or fool me, or frighten me. He need not think that because he was a low-down dirty dog of a white man and I was a poor, defenseless helpless colored girl, that he could run over me. If he wanted to kill me and rape a dead body, he was welcome, but he would have to kill me first, and I would no longer be responsible for myself. But while I lived, I would stand alone in my belief. No matter who was against me. No matter how many Negro men's permission and sanction he could get would do no go[od]. "I don't care if you line them up, pile them or stack them. My answer is still No!" (Parks ca. 1956–1958)

For Rosa, as was the case for countless black women, the dual oppressions of white supremacy and male dominance intersected in the efforts of two men, one white and the other black, to rob her of her independence and her ability to control her own body. Disregarding the rules of the day, Sam set the trap, and Mr. Charlie attempted to spring it on young Rosa. The same white people who created and enforced the rules could at any time make the decision to break those rules when it suited their purposes. It was bad enough for black people to have to exist in a society where whites were able to make all of the rules. Such lack of power was demoralizing and destructive to the black psyche.

Knowing that following the rules created by whites did not always mean black people were safe from harm was worse, however, because there was no way to avoid conflict if a white person chose to change or disobey established laws. In essence, white people could ignore or break any rule of race relations with impunity, but black people could find themselves at the end of a rope even if they toed the line and followed all of the written rules. White supremacy was so heinous precisely because there were no ways for blacks to ensure their personal safety even if they obeyed all traditions, laws, and customs of the day. The constant uncertainty and ever-changing codes black people lived under put tremendous emotional and psychological strain on blacks throughout their lives. Such was the case in Rosa Parks's near-rape narrative. As she recounted:

> He said the color of a person didn't matter to him if he liked the person. I said it would not matter to me if there was no color line and all people could be respected equally. I would not be intimate with a man that the law did not permit me to be married to and respected by. At this he proposed that I marry Sam. At long last Mr. Charlie got the idea that I "No, very definitely No."
>
> He said he would not bother me any further. All this time we were standing and walking around the living room. A large piece of furniture between us most of the time.
>
> I was so tired and spent physically that I sat in the large upholstered chair with an ottoman. He wanted to sit on the ottoman, so I moved it away from the chair and told him I would rather he leave but I didn't care what he did as long as he didn't bother me. I didn't want to see him. It made me sick to look at him.
>
> I picked up the newspaper, opened it wide, holding it where I couldn't see him and started reading. (Parks ca. 1956–1958)

Recounting her first meeting with her eventual husband, Raymond Parks, Rosa noted that she "wasn't very interested at that particular time because I'd had some unhappy romantic experiences" (Parks 1992, 55). The unwanted sexual advances from Mr. Charlie were not "romantic," but it is likely Parks used that terminology as a euphemism for experiences that were sexual in nature, coerced or otherwise. Assuming her near-rape account is at least in part biographical, it is reasonable to assume Rosa was referring to that narrative as one of her "unhappy" experiences. Adding weight to this speculation is the fact that Rosa initially rejected her future husband in part because he was too light-skinned and reminded her of a white man. In her words: "When he [Raymond Parks] saw me, he wanted to come and call on me, but I thought he was too white. I had an aversion to white men, . . . and Raymond Parks was very light skinned" (Parks 1992, 55).

A mutual friend introduced Rosa and Raymond, thinking that the two would be fond of each other. Raymond had recently ended a relationship, and this mutual friend saw an opportunity to make this connection. Unlike Rosa, Raymond was very interested in this connection. Raymond was ten years older than Rosa, so he was in his late twenties and she in her late teens when the two met. Raymond was a barber by trade, and at that time, he was working a barber chair in a Montgomery shop owned by O. L. Campbell (Parks 1992, 55). When they met, Rosa was polite to him but did not show interest in him. Still, Raymond later tried to find Rosa. He traveled to her neighborhood and sought her out, asking her neighbors if they knew Rosa McCauley. As she recounted in her biography, some of her neighbors thought he was white and refused to acknowledge that they knew any Rosa McCauley. Most certainly, this feigned ignorance occurred because black people across Montgomery—and across the United States—had either known of or experienced the type of unwanted sexual violence that Rosa detailed in her near-rape experience. Whereas some black people, like the "Sam" in Rosa's account, chose to expose black women to sexual assault, many more went to lengths to prevent white men, or those they saw as white men as in the case of Raymond Parks, from getting any access to black women.

Raymond would not be dissuaded, however. On his first trip to Rosa's neighborhood, he eventually came across her house. Rosa's mother Leona encountered Raymond, and he asked after Rosa. Understanding that he was not a white man, Leona invited Raymond in, and Rosa and Raymond spent some time talking. She was still not interested in him; perhaps she was not interested in any relationship at this time, given the abuses she experienced with Mr. Charlie. When Raymond came back to her house for a second visit, Rosa refused to even see him, choosing rather to go to bed. Respectfully, Raymond Parks said, "If she's gone to bed, I won't stay," and he left (Parks 1992, 56). Presumably, this respect of her space had an impact on Rosa, and she agreed to spend time with Raymond on his subsequent visits to her. Mostly, they went on rides in his car. It was a rare thing for a black man in Montgomery to own a car, and Rosa definitely took notice.

She was even more impressed once she began taking rides with Raymond and hearing his life story. Like Rosa, Raymond had spent time in his younger years caring for his relatives. He "looked after his ill mother and grandmother until they died when he was in his late teens" (Parks 1992, 57). Like Rosa, Raymond's father left the family when he was very young.

Raymond grew up in an all-white neighborhood, and his family was the only black family there. Despite being able to pass as white, Raymond was denied access to the white school. With the white school off limits and the black school out of reach due to proximal distance from the Parks home and Raymond's family obligations, he was homeschooled by his mother. She taught him basic skills, and Raymond received very little formal education. She, however, worked hard to educate Raymond, and he was an informed reader and staunch political activist.

Raymond left home in his early twenties after a conflict with his minister. After his mother died, he took a job as a sexton in a local white church, taking care of the church and church grounds. When the wife of one of the church deacons, Mrs. Jones, accused Raymond of neglect in his care of new shrubs in the churchyard, Raymond denied and vehemently challenged the charges. The pastor did not approve of this black man challenging the word of a white woman, and he threatened that her husband, Deacon Jones, would "sweep up this churchyard with you" (Parks 1992, 58). Raymond Parks did not act cowed in the face of white aggression, and this incident caused him to quit his job and leave town before he got deeper into an altercation. Rosa recalled of her husband, "Parks [as she called him] did his best to get along, but whenever white people accosted him, he always wanted to let them know he could take care of his business if he had to. They didn't bother you so much back then if you just spoke right up. But as soon as you acted like you were afraid, they'd have fun with you" (Parks 1992, 58). Refusing to back down in the face of the pastor's threats toward him, Raymond responded, "Mr. and Mrs. Jones will not wipe up the churchyard with me and neither will you" (Parks 1992, 58). Experiences like these, where Raymond stood up for himself, reminded Rosa of the examples of strength under fire exhibited by her grandfather, and they endeared her to Raymond.

Originally uninterested in Raymond Parks, Rosa grew to adore and love him as they went on drives together during their courtship. Raymond would talk to her about his life experiences, often hours at a time, and she treasured that time together. There is little doubt that Raymond, who was already enamored of her and actively pursuing her affection, loved Rosa's life stories and her desire for the uplift of black people. As they shared their experiences, Raymond likely felt Rosa's grandfather, whom she adored so much, was a kindred spirit, and he was almost certainly drawn to the legacy of that fighting spirit that he saw in Rosa. As they dated (or courted, as it was called at that time), Rosa and Raymond developed, through their accounts of white injustice and black resilience, a partnership that would sustain them throughout their life together. It was a partnership built upon respect, love, and protest of white supremacy. For Rosa, "I was impressed by the fact that he didn't seem to have the meek attitude—what we called an 'Uncle Tom' attitude—toward white people. I thought he was a very nice man, an interesting man who talked very intelligently. He could talk for hours at a time about all the things he lived through. Parks was also the first real activist I ever met" (Parks 1992, 59).

It was through Raymond that Rosa learned about the case of the Scottsboro Boys. In March 1931, nine African American youths were arrested in Paint Rock, Alabama. The nine, most of whom did not know each other, had been riding a freight train along with other drifters who were looking for work. The Great Depression, the greatest economic disaster in American history, brought with it tremendously high unemployment rates. In 1931, when the Scottsboro incident began, over 15 percent of Americans were unemployed. The lack of jobs led many to "ride the rails," hopping freight trains for free transportation from one town to another, in search of work. That is why the Scottsboro Boys were on the train that day. There were many "hobos," a term used to describe migrant workers, often homeless, on the train. The nine Scottsboro Boys got into a fight with a group of white drifters as the train traveled through Alabama. When the train reached Paint Rock, an armed white mob stopped the train and confronted the nine black youths. Two white female drifters, Victoria Price and Ruby Bates, emerged from the train and falsely accused the nine youths of raping them. The white mob, who intended to arrest the boys on the charge of assault, immediately added rape to the list of offenses. The mob transported the nine to the jail in Scottsboro, Alabama; hence the name Scottsboro Boys. When other local whites learned of the charges, they came together, intent on lynching each of these nine black boys accused of raping white women.

Rumors of what happened on the train spread like wildfire. As historian Danielle McGuire detailed: "By late afternoon, their accusations had been transformed into a lurid tail [where] . . . 'nine black brutes' had 'chewed off one of the breasts' of Ruby Bates. The incensed white mob stood outside the Scottsboro jail, reportedly shouting 'Give 'em to us,' 'Let those niggers out,' and 'If you don't [let them out] we're coming in after them'" (McGuire 2011, 10–11). The threat of extralegal violence led Alabama Governor Benjamin Meeks Miller to call out the Alabama National Guard to protect the nine.

Within five days, a grand jury indicted all nine boys, meaning the members of the grand jury agreed there was enough evidence for the defendants to be brought to trial. Over the course of the month of April 1931, eight of the nine Scottsboro Boys were tried, convicted, and sentenced to death. Only Roy Wright was spared the death penalty, and that was because he was only thirteen years old. Still, eleven jurors voted to put Wright to death, while only one juror voted for life imprisonment.

The International Labor Defense (the legal arm of the Communist Party) and the National Association for the Advancement of Colored People (NAACP) stepped up to defend the convicted boys through their

LYNCHING

There were numerous instances of mobs storming Southern jails and dragging prisoners to their deaths; however, the prisoners had black faces, and the mob was full of Southern white people. Victims of such violence include, but are by no means limited to, the following: Sam Johnson, Henry Askew, Ed Rush, Elijah Clarke, George Reed, John Henderson, "Prophet" Smith, F. D. McLand, Eugene Carter, Godley, Dudley Morgan, David Wyatt, Charles Evans, Grant Richardson, Belle Hathaway, John, Moore, Eugene Hamming, "Dusty" Crutchfield, J. C. Williams, Richard Puckett, Virgil Swanson, Marie Scott, Charley Jones, Caesar Sheffield, Mallie Wilson, Oscar Martin, Jesse Washington, Jesse Hammet, John Foreman, Mary Conley, Frank Dodd, Will and Jesse Powell, Jim McIlherron, Lloyd Clay, Will Brown, Isaac McGhie, Elmer Jackson, Nate Green, Edward Roach, Irving and Herman Arthur, Harry Jacobs, John Henry Williams, Alexander Winn, Will Turner, Charles Atkins, "Shap" Curry, Mose Jones, John Cornish, Lindsey Coleman, Demon Lowman, Clarence Lowman, Bertha Lowman, Henry Choates, George Hughes, Henry Argo, Willie Kirkland, Nelson Nash, Norris Bendy, George Armwood, Joe Love, Isaac Thomas, Andrew McCloud, Claud Neal, Ellwood Higginbotham, Lint Shaw, Roosevelt Townes, and "Bootjack" McDaniels. These men, women, and children were all taken from the protection of Southern law enforcement and brutally murdered. From 1882 to 1959, an estimated 4,733 black people were killed by white lynch mobs. In contrast to popular images, lynching does not always involve a faggot and a rope. Many of the victims listed here were burned alive, drawn and quartered, riddled with bullet holes, or bled to death. The latter was often unintentional. The mob would have rather killed the victim in another manner; however, a victim sometimes died of wounds inflicted as people in the mob sliced off parts of the victim's body to keep as souvenirs. The most popular "keepsakes" were ears, noses, teeth, and sometimes even testicles.

appeals processes, but the national office of the NAACP made the decision to back out of the appeals in early 1932. The sexually explicit nature of the accusations, the involvement of the Communist Party, and the interracial rape narrative led the national office to distance themselves from the fight; however, local NAACP members, including Raymond Parks, worked vigorously to raise awareness of and funds for the Scottsboro Boys appeals. All of these efforts put Raymond in grave danger. Rosa recalled that her future husband would not even share with her the names of the people he worked with on these justice efforts, recalling in her memoir that Raymond "used to say that all of their names were Larry" (Parks 1992, 60).

The fight for justice for the Scottsboro Boys was an uphill battle, and these young men, all falsely convicted, spent over a decade in prison fighting the miscarriage of justice. Portions of the appeals went all the way to the U.S. Supreme Court, and that court issued rulings that were important for the Scottsboro Boys and for countless future defendants who faced biased and unsympathetic courts. In *Powell v. Alabama*, the court ruled that defendants in the Scottsboro case must receive adequate counsel from defense attorneys and that they must have sufficient time to consult with their attorneys before standing trial. These rights were denied the Scottsboro Boys as the state of Alabama rushed to secure conviction and sentencing of the falsely accused youths. The Sixth Amendment to the Constitution of the United States guarantees a citizen's right to counsel, and in *Powell* the Supreme Court determined that a lack of adequate legal counsel was a violation of a person's right to due process under the law dictated by the Fourteenth Amendment. The Supreme Court followed up on this 1932 ruling in 1935 with *Norris v. Alabama*. In *Norris*, the Court ruled that the exclusion of black people from the jury was a violation of the defendants' civil rights because the practice denied a person equal protection under the law as dictated by the Fourteenth Amendment.

Despite these high court rulings, it wasn't until 1950 that all of the Scottsboro Boys were released from prison. During the appeals process, one of the women alleging rape, Ruby Bates, testified she and Victoria Price had lied about the rape, but the white supremacist legal processes in Alabama continued to steamroll these black youths because black males, even as young as thirteen, were demonized as hypersexual beings intent on raping white women. The narrative of rape that these two women spun fit existing stereotypes, and many whites were looking for any opportunity to slaughter black males, for they believed all black men fit into this rapist mold.

Rosa Parks became captivated with Raymond during this time period. He was willing to stand up for justice in the face of certain white retaliation. Historian Jeanne Theoharis framed it this way: "Raymond was 'willing to defy the racists and stand up to the establishment.' What impressed her was 'that he refused to be intimidated by white people—unlike many blacks, who figured they had no choice but to stay under 'Mr. Charlie's' heel" (Theoharis 2013, 13). Raymond joined the Scottsboro fight early on, and his courage impressed Rosa and reminded her of her maternal grandfather's determination to stand up to white people on a consistent basis.

Raymond had sought Rosa ever since he first met her. Perhaps because of her young age compared to Raymond, or because of the unwanted sexual advances she experienced as detailed in her near rape experience, Rosa was less interested in commitment than Raymond. She recalled that they talked marriage as early as their second date, but it was Raymond doing all the talking. Rosa admitted, "I had never given marriage a thought at all" (Parks 1992, 64). Still, Raymond persisted, intent on winning Rosa over and marrying her. Eventually, his persistence worked. On a day like any other, Raymond said to Rosa, "I really think we ought to get married," and

Rosa agreed (Parks 1992, 64). Adhering to formalities in terms of family consent, the next day Raymond approached Leona McCauley and asked her for permission to marry Rosa. Leona agreed. Thus, Raymond and Rosa got engaged in August 1932. They wed in December 1932 in Pine Level, Alabama. The wedding took place in Rosa's mother's house. The betrothed did not send out invitations, and only family and close friends attended the ceremony (Parks 1992, 64).

Rosa and Raymond Parks settled their newly formed family in Montgomery's east side, close to Alabama State. Their marriage was a strong partnership grounded in mutual respect, and after they wed, Raymond encouraged Rosa to go on and finish her high school education. Rosa earned her diploma in 1933 at the age of twenty. This accomplishment put Rosa in the minority in terms of education of African Americans. In Alabama at this time, only 7 percent of black people held a high school diploma, yet, Rosa still had a tough time finding employment. Eventually she took a job at St. Margaret's Hospital while sewing to supplement her income (Parks 1992, 65).

In 1941 the U.S. economy had recovered significantly from the Great Depression, due in large part to the growing war against fascism and the U.S. effort to supply its allies. That year, Rosa got a job at Maxwell Airfield. She recalled how different some things were on the base than in the rest of Alabama. For one thing, the base was not segregated. On the base, Rosa rode the buses and trolleys and sat in public places alongside whites. Other than the actual military service, the base was integrated. These arrangements left a mark on Rosa Parks. She would coexist peacefully among white people while on the base, but as soon as she left the property, she returned to segregated buses and a life on the margins of white society. White people did still belittle and demean black people on these bases, sometimes leading to massive outbreaks of violence and even murder, but the law of the land on these bases was one of integration. Rosa never felt any personal attacks; however, Raymond, who later took a job as a barber on the same base, did experience discrimination and white hostility.

President Franklin Delano Roosevelt, through Executive Order 8802, had barred segregation and discrimination by federal agencies and all unions and companies engaged in war-related work. This order did not integrate the military—that would not happen until President Harry Truman signed Executive Order 9981—but the order did break down many barriers of discrimination that kept black people out of lucrative military contracts and labor opportunities. President Roosevelt did not sign the order of his own will; rather, agitation on the part of black people forced his hand. In September 1940, black rights activists, including Asa Philip Randolph (labor leader), Walter White (NAACP), and Thomas Arnold Hill

(National Urban League), met with President Roosevelt and his advisors to protest the segregation in the military.

Discontent with the administration's slow pace of action, in January 1941, Randolph joined forces with Bayard Rustin to plan a protest march on Washington, D.C. Known as the March on Washington Movement of 1941, the effort gained tremendous support among black Americans. President Roosevelt did not want hundreds of thousands of protestors descending on the nation's capital in a period when he was trying to distinguish American freedom from fascist oppression, so he acquiesced and signed Executive Order 8802 desegregating the war industry and establishing the Fair Employment Practices Committee to oversee this desegregation. Buoyed by the success of this movement, Randolph and Rustin would continue for over a decade to organize March on Washington Movements, and these agitations led to monumental changes in racial policies in the United States. Most notable of these movements was the March on Washington for Jobs and Freedom in 1963 when Dr. Martin Luther King Jr. delivered his "I Have a Dream" speech. An amazing orator, Dr. King dominated that 1963 day in American memory, but the March on Washington Movement efforts across more than a decade left an indelible effect on American society and culture. Every step of the way, A. Philip Randolph and Bayard Rustin led these efforts for racial justice.

These movements resonated with Rosa and her husband, Raymond. Raymond continued to advocate for the Scottsboro Boys through the 1930s. Rosa recalled her husband religiously attended local meetings, and on one occasion that meeting occurred at their Huffman Street home. What stood out to her were the number of guns present. She said, "This was the first time I'd seen so few men with so many guns. The table was covered with guns" (Parks 1992, 67). These men came ready for action, because black people have always been ready to act in their self-defense against racial oppression. Although the scene shocked Rosa—she recalled "sitting on the back porch with my feet on the top step and putting my head down on my knees, and I didn't move throughout the meeting"—she gained admiration for her husband through the evening. He was taking a stand, something that her grandfather taught her was so important. As Rosa noted, "I was very, very depressed about the fact that black men could not hold a meeting without fear of bodily injury or death. Also I was reminded of the time I was a child and I sat next to my grandfather waiting for the Ku Klux Klan to ride down on us" (Parks 1992, 67). Fortunately for Rosa, white supremacist did not intervene on either occasion, but the fear of white vigilante justice clearly was a factor in her adolescence and adult life. She addressed these palpable fears with a resilience and a faith that buttressed her through the deepest storms of her life.

Rosa was not one to run from a conflict, and neither were many other black women, but it is clear that black women did not participate in the early meetings Raymond held. The level of danger, combined with the gender conventions of the day that relegated women to passive, subservient roles, meant women often did not engage at the same level of danger as men. Yet, women were as integral to resisting white supremacy as men. Often serving as domestics in close proximity to white men, black women were frequently place in more compromising and dangerous positions than black men ever endured. Like Rosa's account of the near-rape experience, black women worked constantly to fight off white oppression and hold on to a sense of dignity and self-respect in the face of constant threats, intimidations, and violations. These factors, and likely the near-rape experience, led Rosa into a life of activism that formalized the things she and countless other black women had already been doing to assert their rights and humanity. For Rosa Parks, these efforts during her life in Montgomery came largely through her work with the local NAACP.

4

Black Voter Registration Efforts

"Hope is wanting something that means a lot to you. It is like wanting something that you do not have. Hope is something we feel in our hearts. When we hope for something with our hearts, it becomes an expectation. Hope is also something we believe in. Many people I have known believed in ending racial segregation in this country, and their hope that it could happen influenced their actions and brought about change. A friend of mine, the Reverend Jesse Jackson, says, 'We must keep hope alive.' I agree. You can help keep hope alive by believing in yourself. Your hope for yourself and for the future can make this world a better place to live" (Parks 1996, 32).

Rosa Parks learned about hope and the power of hope at a young age from her family. Although they struggled financially and with the oppressive racial system, the McCauley family held hope for a better life in their hearts. This hope drove her grandmother, Rose Edwards, to nurture and protect young Rosa. Her mother, Leona McCauley, channeled her hopes for her children, Rosa and Sylvester, into support of their education, and she endured many financial sacrifices to ensure that her children received as much education as possible. Sylvester Edwards, Rosa's grandfather, maintained his hope through his refusal to back down in the face of white aggression. Rosa Parks was a product of all of these familial lessons, and she embodied the lessons she learned in her youth as she moved into adulthood.

Not only did Rosa continue to embrace hope throughout her life, but she also gravitated to others who shared the same visions for the future and dedication to seeing these hopes come to fruition. That was what brought Rosa together with her husband, Raymond Parks. Parks, as she liked to call him, was already engaged in clandestine racial uplift work in support of the Scottsboro Boys, nine black youths falsely accused of raping two white women. Raymond attended and held secret meetings to organize fundraising and other efforts aimed at freeing the Scottsboro youths. The men at these meetings—and they were all men—kept constant watch for whites who might try to attack this group, and firearms were always present in large numbers. The sight of these guns did not turn Rosa off, for it reminded her of her youth when she would sit up with her armed grandfather, who was poised to shoot any "Ku Kluxer" who dared attack the Edwards home (Parks 1992, 67). Having experienced so much as a child, Rosa recalled, "It didn't bother me being married to Parks. He was doing the same thing before we got married; and I knew how dangerous it was" (Parks 1992, 68; McGuire 2011, 11).

On a daily basis, Rosa and Raymond Parks busied themselves with building a life together after their marriage in December 1932, but the two "believed in ending racial segregation in this country, and their hope that it could happen influenced their actions and brought about change" (Parks 1996, 32). The two settled into a routine, living in the home of Mr. King Kelly, a deacon at the Dexter Avenue Baptist Church where Dr. Martin Luther King Jr. would eventually become pastor. King Kelly did not approve of Raymond Parks's agitation around the Scottsboro case, so Raymond never held meetings while they lived with the Kelly family. Rosa speculated that Kelly feared losing his job, so he did not want to get involved in the case in that way. It was common for many middle-class blacks to shy away from the type of open resistance that Raymond and his fellow activists embraced. These tensions, both in tactics and causes, that often-separated black people along socioeconomic class lines would be a constant theme in Rosa's life and in the struggle for black liberation.

Throughout the early years of the Scottsboro fight, white police sought out activists like Raymond and his group. Rosa recalled multiple incidents when she feared her husband would not return home from his evening meetings. She would see police patrolling up and down her block, looking for clandestine Scottsboro meetings, and, on at least one occasion, Raymond had to enter their home through the back door to avoid being spotted by the authorities bent on rooting out these activists.

Raymond Parks was a lifelong agitator, but the fame his wife received because of her December 1, 1955, arrest overshadowed his work. When leftist activist Esther Cooper Jackson recounted to friends her interaction with Raymond Parks, those friends remarked that they "didn't even know she [Rosa Parks] had a husband" (Theoharis 2013, 16). By the time Rosa sprang into the public spotlight, Raymond had moved away from organized protest efforts. When the two met, however, Raymond, not Rosa, was out front in the battle for civil rights. Activism was never a competition for Rosa and Raymond, though. There was plenty of work to go around, and battling white supremacy required everyone to do their part in the fight. In the 1930s, during the Scottsboro trials, Raymond would carry food to the nine boys, in addition to organizing efforts for their defense. In those days, Raymond discouraged his wife from active participation in the dangerous Scottsboro defense efforts. Rosa recalled that her husband believed "it was hard enough if he had to run [;] he couldn't leave me and I couldn't run as fast" (Theoharis 2013, 15). The fever pitch of racial tension in 1930s Alabama put Raymond Parks—and all those working in support of the Scottsboro Boys—in constant danger, and the police could send activists running for their lives at any time. That is why "the committee would meet at odd hours—before daybreak and in the middle of the night" to avoid discovery, unlawful arrest, or worse. In addition to the clandestine organizing, Raymond also belonged to the Montgomery chapter of the NAACP (Theoharis 2013, 15). He was active early in his adulthood, but in the 1930s and at times during Rosa Parks's NAACP involvement in the 1940s, black elite led the chapter. Fear of losing their lucrative jobs and other intimidations lorded over them by Alabama white supremacists led these black elite to take a gradual approach to civil rights that frustrated and infuriated Raymond Parks. Fed up with the slow pace of progress and the relative ineffectiveness of the Montgomery NAACP, Raymond stopped attending meetings. In the coming decade, Rosa would turn to this organization as she entered publicly into the fight for racial equality.

In her daily life, Rosa confronted countless incidents of racism and discrimination; it was such a part of life that she didn't bother to tell others, including her husband, about every offense. One such instance occurred when she was accompanying some of the Kelly family to the train station, seeing them off on a train ride. Rosa recollected that she "was walking a little behind them . . . when a policeman approached" and asked if she was a ticketed passenger. Unlike the hypervigilant restrictions on transportation that came into vogue after the September 11, 2001, terrorist attacks, generally anyone could accompany passengers all the way to the train doors throughout the twentieth century. Despite this freedom of movement, on this occasion, a police officer stopped Rosa as she was accompanying the Kellys, telling her that if she did not have a ticket, she could not proceed. The Kellys did not witness this encounter, because they were walking in front of Rosa and did not notice that she was no longer with them. The policeman pushed Rosa against the railing and blocked her progress. What galled her even more was the fact that another African

American woman, close to Rosa's age, witnessed the event and began joking and flirting with the officer. In Rosa's words, "she seemed rather familiar with him" (Parks 1992, 70). Doubtless, this encounter with the white police officer and the flirting young black woman brought to mind her narrative of the near-rape experience found in the Library of Congress archives. Buoyed by her faith, Rosa used every tool in her arsenal to fend off the advances of the white man, Mr. Charlie, as he tried to buy, bribe, coerce, and force her into a sexual liaison. In contrast to Rosa's determined defiance, the black woman she encountered during this experience of police intimidation openly flirted with and tempted the white officer, who would never see her as more that a sexual object and a toy for his pleasure. Rosa was not willing to "play the game" of racial and sexual subservience, and, in the racist and patriarchal system in which she lived, she was constantly under the oppressive hand of white men angling to control her, either through her perceived acquiescence or their abusive domination.

Although she did not tell her husband about this particular encounter, Raymond and Rosa Parks frequently discussed incidents of racial and sexual oppression. Regarding the Scottsboro case, Raymond told Rosa that he could not rest until they were freed (McGuire 2011, 11). The Scottsboro case was unresolved for all the defendants for nearly two decades, but this was not the only effort taken up by the Parks family. Both Rosa and Raymond took up the cause of voting rights for blacks in their hometown. Rosa recalled, "After the Scottsboro Boys were saved from execution, Parks got involved in voter registration, which was something he was interested in even before we met. He was very discouraged about how few blacks were registered to vote" (Parks 1992, 71).

The Fifteenth Amendment to the Constitution of the United States, ratified in 1870, guaranteed all men the de jure (by law) right to vote, but millions of African Americans, like the Parks family, suffered de facto (by fact) limitations on this most fundamental right. Rosa Parks noted in her biography, "The right to vote is so important for Americans. We vote for people to represent us in government. If we do not like the way they represent us, we can vote for someone else. But in those days, most black people in the South could not vote" (Parks 1992, 71). That is why countless black people, including Rosa and Raymond, fought against disfranchisement.

Since the ratification of the Fifteenth Amendment to the Constitution of the United States, whites, especially white Southerners, engaged in concerted efforts to keep black people from voting. This disfranchisement took many forms, from revision of state constitutions to prerequisites for voting and outright violent voter suppression. The ratification of the Nineteenth Amendment, granting the franchise to all women, enhanced further the potential African American voting base, and white supremacists ramped up efforts to keep all black people from exercising their right to the franchise. Rosa recalled, "The segregationists made it very difficult for black people to register to vote." In fact, in her experience, "[I]n order to get registered, blacks had to have white people to vouch for them" (Parks 1992, 71). Without white support, individual African Americans could not register to vote in Montgomery, Alabama, and the Parks couple were among those who felt this restrictive hand. Rosa Parks did note, "A small number of blacks who were in good favor with white folks did get registered in that way," but the overwhelming majority of black Montgomery had no say in formal political processes. This stratification of black voters led to increased hostility among black people in Montgomery, and that hostility often fell along lines of socioeconomic class. According to Rosa, "when the white people vouched for and approved of them that put them on a different level from the rest of us" (Parks 1992, 71).

White Southerners worried that a large number of black voters would lead to elected officials sympathetic to the plight of African Americans. Black Southerners, like Rosa and Raymond Parks, worked tirelessly to carve out a niche of independence in the face of this unbridled oppression; however, the harder black people fought, the whiter Southerners resisted. Between the 1890s and 1965, Southern states engaged in systematic efforts to keep black people from voting, thus embodying James Silver's argument that whites valued control over the black population above any other goal. The ceaseless and brutal attacks on the black vote left some African

---

BLACK VOTER SUPPRESSION

The fact that there were very few black people registered to vote was not due to lack of effort. Charles and Medgar Evers, native Mississippians, World War II heroes, and college graduates, attempted to register black voters beginning with the election of 1946. When African Americans went to the polling stations, armed white citizens met and repelled them. Undeterred, both men continued to lobby for the franchise through organizations like the NAACP. Mississippi was the quintessential example of voter suppression. Part of the reason African Americans were prevented from voting was the fear that by sheer numbers, they would dominate Mississippi politics. Blacks outnumbered whites in the state until 1940. By 1950, there were 986,494 African Americans, or just over 45 percent of the population. By 1960, the number dropped to 915,743, or just over 42 percent of the total citizens. Thus, in this period, the black population was consistently dropping as push and pull factors led them to leave the state. Regardless of this fact, whites still kept black people from voting. On the eve of the 1964 Civil Rights Act, only 6.7 percent of African Americans in Mississippi were eligible to vote. However, there were still black majorities in many of the counties in the Delta.

Americans afraid to challenge the system of racial oppression, but many found ways to resist (Parks 1992, 72).

Voting rights activists like the Parks family employed various means of battling against these oppressive systems. When Southern states instituted poll taxes, which attempted to exclude poor black voters by requiring them to pay a tax before they could vote, African Americans raised funds in local organizations and churches in order to pay the taxes and increase the black franchise. Southern states also developed literacy tests, where white election officials asked black voters detailed questions about documents like the U.S. Constitution. Refusing to yield, numerous black people memorized the Constitution so that they could pass the literacy tests.

Black Montgomerians who wanted to vote faced additional obstacles, including fear of retribution for the franchise efforts. As Jeanne Theoharis wrote, "The application for voter registration required potential voters to identify their employer, their business and educational background, and any drug or alcohol use" as well as pledging "not to 'give aid and comfort to the enemies of the United States Government or the government of the State of Alabama'" (Theoharis 2013, 20). This is significant because answering these questions meant that the voter registration office had a record of which African Americans attempted to vote and where they worked. Employers could then punish their black workers who tried to exercise their right to the franchise. People also had to inform the registration office if they had tried to register previously, thus offering another potential disqualifying factor to the voter registration process.

Because whites administered and graded the test, even Black people with doctoral degrees were told they failed the test. John Dittmer outlined all of these mechanisms of control, arguing, "The most effective way to keep blacks from voting had been to prevent them from registering in the first place" (Dittmer 1995, 6). When resilient African Americans found ways around all of these traditional disfranchisement methods, the Southern wing of the Democratic Party created white primaries. Essentially, black people were excluded from voting in primary elections, because the state Democratic Party was a private organization that could grant membership to whomever it pleased. Naturally, no African Americans were eligible for membership. This was the most difficult fight for southern blacks; however, in the 1944 Supreme Court ruling *Smith v. Allwright*, a legal effort led by NAACP attorney Thurgood Marshall, the Court deemed white primaries unconstitutional.

For the Parks family, the ability to vote, both for themselves and for their community, was a major priority. The two were leaders in the Voter's League, a Montgomery group dedicated to registering black voters, and the League members often met in the Parks house. The Voter's League kept a detailed log of black Montgomerians who were able to vote; the list in the early 1940s consisted only of thirty-one names, and the total black population was over thirty-four thousand (Parks 1992, 72). Despite the abysmal success rate of black people trying to register, Rosa and Raymond joined with other black Montgomerians, including Edgar Daniel (E. D.) Nixon, who founded the Voter's League in 1940 (Theoharis 2013, 21).

E. D. Nixon was one of the most prominent African Americans in the city of Montgomery. Nixon founded the Montgomery chapter of the Brotherhood of Sleeping Car Porters (BSCP) during the 1920s, and he served multiple terms as the president of Montgomery's NAACP. New York attorney Arthur A. Madison, a native Montgomerian, made frequent trips to Alabama to assist the likes of Nixon and the Parks couple in registering black voters. Defying existing practice, Madison assured black registrants that they did not have to "wait until some white person approved" of black voters, choosing rather to march black Montgomerians down to the registration office and vouching for them himself (Parks 1992, 73).

Raymond Parks especially connected with Madison's message that black people did not require white people vouch for them in order to attempt to register to vote. Raymond made multiple attempts to register, but white voting officials continually thwarted his efforts. He refused to have a white person validate his effort to exercise his constitutional right; rather, Raymond rightfully felt that black people had as much right to the franchise as anyone else. It was not until after the couple moved to Detroit, Michigan, after the Montgomery Bus Boycott that Raymond successfully registered to vote (Parks 1992, 72).

Adding to difficulties black people found as they attempted to register, voter registration did not run on a regular basis. Blacks encountered very small registration windows, and registration officials would not announce when these windows opened and closed. As Rosa Parks recalled, "they

---

ASA PHILIP RANDOLPH AND THE BROTHERHOOD OF SLEEPING CAR PORTERS

Organized in 1925 by Asa Philip Randolph, the Brotherhood of Sleeping Car Porters was a major political, social, and economic force in black communities. It was made up of railway workers employed by white railroad magnet George Pullman. The Pullman Palace Car Company manufactured and staffed luxury rail cars and dominated the passenger train industry throughout the first half of the twentieth century. A. Philip Randolph organized the maids and porters, almost exclusively African American, into the first African American labor union sanctioned by the American Federation of Labor (AFL) and the first black organized union to sign a collective bargaining agreement with a major U.S. corporation.

might decide to have registration on a Wednesday morning from ten o'clock until noon, when they knew most black working people couldn't get there." Moreover, "If noontime came, they would close the doors, no matter how many people were still standing in line" (Parks 1992, 74).

Rosa Parks's first registration attempt came in 1943. She recalled that many African Americans—a number reaching 750, according to Jeanne Theoharis—including her mother and one of her cousins, attempted to register around that time, assisted by E. D. Nixon and Arthur A. Madison (Theoharis 2013, 21). Rosa's two relatives received voter certificates in the mail signifying that their attempts were successful. It was not long before local officials decided to take issue with Madison's voter registration efforts. Police arrested Madison on fabricated charges, and the state of Alabama eventually disbarred him. Madison returned to New York and his successful law practice, and black Montgomerians lost a powerful ally in their efforts to vote.

Unlike white registrants, who received their certificates immediately after taking the voter registration test, black people had to wait anxiously to see if they could vote. Essentially, whites gained automatic registration for simply attempting the test, whereas black voter registration, regardless of whether or not they passed the test, rested on the whims of white voting officials. Compounding these issues, all registered voters had to pay poll taxes in order to cast a vote in any given election. Rosa recalled, "The poll tax was $1.50 a year, and every registered voter had to pay it. But it was mostly black people who had to pay it retroactive" (Parks 1992, 75). Unlike white voters, who could vote each year by paying only $1.50, black voters had to pay $1.50 for every year since turning twenty-one years old, the legal voting age at that time. Rosa, who did not successfully register to vote until she was thirty-two years old, owed $16.50 ($1.50 times eleven years) before she could cast her first vote (Parks 1992, 76).

Parks recalled that on her second registration attempt, she witnessed the blatant white privilege in the voter registration process. Contrary to convention, the registration office was serving black and white registrants at the same time on that day. Generally, blacks and whites had separate registration windows so that black registrants could not witness the fact that voting officials allowed white registrants to pass the voter screening without resistance. However, on this day, Rosa was in the office with two white women. One of the women asked the voter registration official if she would provide the answers to the registration exam. The official, not so discreetly, asked the white women to wait until Parks left the office. It was unheard of for black people to receive service ahead of whites, so the logical explanation was that the voting official wanted to get Rosa out of the way so that she did not witness the officials providing exam answers to these white women or simply pass them because they were white. Perhaps there was something in Rosa's demeanor signaling to this official that she would protest if she witnessed such blatant favoring of these white women, or maybe Rosa's reputation preceded her. Either way, Rosa left the office that day knowing that those two white women faced no obstacles to their registration process (Theoharis 2013, 21).

It took Rosa three attempts before she successfully registered to vote in 1945. Prior to the third attempt, she considered bringing a lawsuit for violation of her constitutional rights; however, Rosa faced the obstacle of securing legal counsel and paying the attorney fees. The closest African American lawyer was Attorney Arthur D. Shores from Birmingham, Alabama, and Rosa was unsure he would take the case. Shores had represented some black Montgomerians in the past, but, Rosa recalled, he only took periodic trips to Montgomery, and he did not take on every case presented to him (Parks 1992, 76). Unsure of her ability to secure legal counsel, Rosa still took the initiative and copied down her answers to the exam questions. She wanted to have solid proof that she passed the exam in case she again faced denial of her voting rights. The registration official took note of Parks's actions, and that might be why she received notification in the mail of her successful completion of the registration process (Theoharis 2013, 21).

Interestingly, Rosa's attempts to register to vote brought to light the egregious conditions on Montgomery's bus system. She recalled that on her second attempt to register, she "was put off a Montgomery city bus for the first time" (Parks 1992, 76). The complex set of unwritten rules that existed on the Montgomery public transportation system often made it impossible for African Americans to be in compliance. One of the main issues was that so much was left up to the discretion of the bus driver. What counted as suitable behavior for one driver might not meet the demands of another driver. Moreover, drivers could change their own rules depending on their whims that day.

On this particular occasion, Rosa Parks encountered a driver who "treated everybody black badly" (Parks 1992, 78). This driver, whom Parks described as "tall and thickset" and "rough-looking" with a "mole near his mouth," was one who felt black people and white people should enter the bus using segregated entrances. Most of the buses had a front door and a back door. Some drivers maintained strict segregation in that white people could enter the front door, pay their fare, and proceed to their seat. Conversely, black passengers had to enter through the front door, pay their fare, and then exit the bus and walk to the back door, only to enter again through the back door and proceed to their seat. As if being forced to sit in the rear of the bus was not enough, this unwritten policy enforced by some drivers compounded the injustices already felt by the black passengers on Montgomery buses. Moreover, the practice of making black passengers enter, exit, and then reenter the bus caused a logistical nightmare that only served to delay the buses along the route. Black passengers exiting through the front door after paying their fares created a traffic jam at the front door as other passengers tried to enter behind them. Some of the drivers also made a practice of driving off before the black passengers who had paid their money could make it to the back door to reenter the bus.

When Rosa Parks made her second attempt to register to vote, she planned to take the bus to the registration office. Having paid her fare, Parks began to walk through the bus to the back where black people could sit. She turned back to see the bus driver standing close behind her telling her she needed to get off of the bus and enter through the back door. Parks responded that she was already on the bus and that the crowd of black passengers standing in the back stairwell of the overcrowded black section of the bus made it nearly impossible for her to enter the bus through the back door. The bus driver would not relent, and he proceeded to grab Rosa by her coat sleeve. She did not resist, choosing rather to march to the front of the bus in order to exit. Parks, however, was not planning to reenter the bus. Like other blacks determined not to tolerate such blatant disrespect, Rosa decided waiting for the next bus was better than riding with this exceptionally intolerant driver. On her way to the front door of the bus, she dropped her purse. Rather than bending over to pick it up, she sat down in one of the front seats reserved for white passengers and reached down to recover her bag. The bus driver stood right over her and demanded, "Get off my bus." Parks recalled, "He looked like he was ready to hit me." Rosa defiantly responded to the intimidation, "I know one thing. You better not hit me." No one hit Rosa Parks that day, but the displeased murmuring hurled in her direction from black passengers struck a chord. For Rosa, the black response, which foreshadowed how other black passengers would respond in 1955 when her refusal to give up her seat launched the bus boycott, proved that black "people took a lot without fighting back" (Parks 1992, 79).

Rosa Parks did fight back, in both subtle and blatantly obvious ways. She came from a line of determined, defiant activists who refused to be cowed in the face of disrespect. She sat up with her grandfather while he wielded a firearm ready to defend his home and family against the Ku Klux Klan. Her mother sacrificed daily to ensure that Rosa and her brother Sylvester gained as much quality education as possible, and her grandmother enforced the defiant dignity that was a model for Rosa throughout her life. When it came time to date, she gravitated to Raymond Parks, already a prominent activist by the time the two met. Rosa's successful registration effort put her in rare company. As Jeanne Theoharis noted, in 1951 black people made up 37 percent of the population of Montgomery, Alabama. Despite making up such a large segment of the populace, only 3.1 percent of eligible black voters successfully registered to vote.

Raymond Parks, for example, had multiple unsuccessful attempts. As a black man, he represented a greater threat to the white establishment than his wife did, and registration officials made it particularly difficult for him during his registration exams. However, even if he answered all of the questions correctly, it is likely that registrars would fail him simply because he was a confident black man who refused to act deferentially in the face of white supremacists. Raymond also worked with his local social club, the Men's Social Club, to raise funds to pay back poll taxes for black voters. Many of the club members refused to join in this effort out of fear of retribution from local whites (Theoharis 2013, 22). In the end, Raymond ceased his registration efforts and focused his attentions on other black uplift work. Together Rosa and Raymond Parks jumped into causes that promoted black uplift. From the Scottsboro Boys to voting rights, the Parks family was at the forefront of the civil rights effort in Alabama and beyond.

5

Public Activism

"At the time, of course, Highlander didn't come into my mind. But to go back to my firm belief, as far back as I can remember. Of course I want to give a great deal of credit to my mother and especially my grandfather, my mother's father, for giving me the spirit of freedom and to instruct me in the idea that I should not feel because of my race or color inferior to any person. But I should do my very best to be a respectable person and respect myself and expect respect from others. And to learn what I possibly could for self-improvement coming on through my early adulthood with work with the NAACP and other organizations. And trying to become a registered voter under hazardous conditions, such as being denied a number of times, and feeling that there was a threat just to become a registered voter and cast my ballot to elect offices" (Parks, Horton, and Nixon 1973).

Having successfully registered to vote in 1945, Rosa Parks exercise her right to the franchise freely for the rest of her life. Rosa knew that voting was essential to effecting change in the black condition in Montgomery, and she continued to work for black uplift. By 1945, Rosa was already a member of the Montgomery chapter of the National Association for the Advancement of Colored People (NAACP). She attended her first meeting of the organization in December 1943 (Theoharis 2013, 17). Her husband, Raymond Parks, was an active member of the organization in the previous decade, but he had decided to dedicate his time and efforts to other organizations by the time Rosa ventured into the NAACP.

The NAACP started in 1909 as an organization dedicated to securing racial equality. In their words, they sought people to answer "the Call" to renew the struggle for civil rights. Among the first members in the interracial organization were Ida B. Wells, W.E.B. DuBois, Henry Moscowitz, Mary White Ovington, Oswald Garrison Villiard, and William English Walling. Since its inception, the NAACP led the fight for black equality. In 1910, the organization established itself as a source of legal representation. The NAACP leadership dedicated themselves to fighting legal battles. At the time Rosa Parks attended her first meeting, the NAACP boasted some major legal victories. In a 1917 legal victory in *Buchanan v. Warley*, the Supreme Court conceded that states could not engage in residential segregation. In 1935, the organization succeeded in getting a black student admitted to the University of Maryland.

However, the NAACP was involved in more than just court cases. The organization and its members were at the heart of major racial developments in this country, including protesting when President Wilson segregated the federal government and when the racist film *The Birth of a Nation* was released; forcing Wilson to issue a statement against lynching; taking out antilynching advertisements in newspapers; ensuring adequate enforcement of President Franklin Roosevelt's Fair Employment Practices law; and forcing the integration of the military. The NAACP, both at the national and local levels, worked in concert with local black newspapers, and the tandem proved a formidable force in the face of white supremacy.

One of the NAACP founders, Ida B. Wells embodied this union of black press and black uplift organizations. Wells was an ardent race warrior who captivated the nation and the world with her gripping exposé of lynching. Born in July 1862 into enslavement in Mississippi, Wells moved to Memphis, Tennessee, in her late teens. There she found her "first experience in living in an urban black community" (Giddings 2008, 40). Wells thrived in the city, working as a teacher and continuing her education. Many elements of Ida B. Wells's life paralleled experiences in Rosa Parks's life. For instance, in September 1883, she defied racial conventions by refusing to give up her seat on the Chesapeake and Ohio Rail Line. Wells was seated in the first-class "ladies' car," having purchased a ticket to ride there; however, railroad operators often enforced segregation on the rail lines, and a conductor asked Wells to vacate her seat. When she refused, three men dragged her from her seat and Wells, refusing to sit in inferior accommodations, left the train. Refusing to let the offense go unchallenged, she secured legal counsel and sued the rail line. Her stance against segregation and white supremacy gained her notoriety (Giddings 2008, 60–63).

Wells, like Rosa Parks after her, documented accounts of racial injustices on the pages of the black press. She wrote for local black newspapers, and she would go on to be editor and co-owner of the *Memphis Free Speech and Headlight.* It was here that Wells protested lynching following the ghastly People's Grocery murder. In 1892, three men, including her friend and People's Grocery owner Thomas Moss, were lynched by a white mob after a series of altercations between whites and blacks at the black-owned and -operated grocery store. The mob dragged the three men from the jail cells and brutally murdered them while white reporters documented the event. Ida B. Wells published a pamphlet, *Southern Horrors: Lynch Law in all its Phases*, to significant acclaim. She lobbied the federal government for antilynching legislation, and, during her time as director of the NAACP Youth Council, Rosa Parks worked with members to write "letters to Washington to ask for a federal anti-lynching bill" (Theoharis 2013, 27). Wells also toured the nation, raising awareness of the plight of black Americans in the South, much as Rosa Parks would do half a century later. Economic pressures and threats of bodily harm levied by white Southerners led Wells to leave Memphis and she settled in Chicago. After the Montgomery Bus Boycott, the threats on her economic well-being and life that confronted Rosa Parks led her and her husband to follow a path similar to Wells, relocating from Montgomery, AL to Detroit, Michigan (Giddings 2008, 177–183).

BLACK PRESS

The Emmett Till trial showed the important role the black press served in the black community. These outlets followed the calling of Samuel E. Cornish and John B. Russwurm. In 1827, these African Americans founded the weekly *Freedom's Journal*, challenging, blacks should "plead our own cause" (Cornish and Russwurm 1827, 1).

The black press fed off this communal atmosphere, and printed articles that uplifted the entire black population. They spent time looking at individual African Americans and their achievements. This was particularly important because the mainstream media ignored key black figures. Additionally, highlighting success stories served as an important form of uplift in an oppressed society. Seeing that an African American succeeded in winning praise from the black community and "recognition" in the white community was empowering.

Black newspapers also made a concerted effort to report lynchings and other cases of violence perpetrated by whites on blacks. Especially important were instances of white men attacking black women. Focusing on the deviant nature of white America was a natural response to white efforts to project vices onto the black community. Projection of societal ills was a common theme in mainstream papers and in many white people's worldview. Frederick Detweiler acknowledged, "When anything evil is reported . . . the race of the culprit is not reported if the individual is a . . . member of some . . . white race; but when he is a Negro the fact of his race is played up. Then when a Negro does something praiseworthy the world never hears of it through the press" (Detweiler 1922, 150). The black press was critical in changing this process.

Theorists on the black press have focused on the importance of civil society and the public sphere. Civil society constitutes "the entire web of associational and public spaces in which citizens can have conversations with one another, discover common interests, act in concert, assert new rights, and try to influence public opinion and public policy" (Jacobs 2000, 2). Of course, in order to take advantage of this web, one must hold "citizen" status. This was impossible for African Americans during slavery and nearly unattainable once the institution ended. The specter of racism and hate forced black people to seek out alternate means of influencing "public opinion and public policy." The black press provided a source for such outlets by helping to define a new public sphere. The public sphere is defined as the "particular type of practice which takes place in civil society: the practice of open discussion about matters of common public concern" (Jacobs 2000, 22). The black press, by supporting black leaders, inciting civic discourse, inspiring the youth, and educating the public, fostered common public knowledge and concern.

Black newspapers provided social capital by fostering a "common stock of information and culture, which private citizens rely on in their everyday conversation with others" (Jacobs 2000, 3). The black press helped to define and make sense of reality. From 1900 to 1950, black newspapers enjoyed their widest readership and most influential period. During this time the black press evolved and strengthened. This newfound fortitude would serve them and the community well as they progressed into the 1950s. Black papers continued to be a valuable asset throughout the civil rights movement. They served as a source of information, outrage, expression, and uplift during one of the most turbulent times in American history. The plight of African Americans, which was so skillfully outlined on the pages of black newspapers, soon became headlines on the pages of mainstream papers. As Todd Vogel points out, "The black press redefined class, restaged race and nationhood and reset the terms of public conversation" (Vogel 2001, 1).

Wells would thrive in Chicago, continuing her race work and collaborating with many prominent progressives. Among her countless accomplishments, she was one of the founders of the NAACP, the organization where Rosa Parks cut her teeth in the fight for racial equality. Not surprisingly, Southern whites despised the NAACP because the organization led the battle for integration of Southern schools and vigorously challenged the disenfranchisement, Jim Crow segregation, and white supremacy that were the cornerstone of much of Southern culture. Many African Americans gravitated to the NAACP because of the inroads they made against Jim Crow segregation and because of their prominence in the black press.

Black newspapers, mostly published weekly so the operating costs were lower and there was no daily pressure to find the breaking story, were another foundational element in the battle for racial equality. In most cases, they were the only local sources of information from an African American perspective. As such, the black press followed the calling of Samuel E. Cornish and John B. Russwurm to present stories from a black perspective, as "we know our condition better than anyone" (Wolseley 1990, xiv). The black press fed off this communal atmosphere and the printed articles that uplifted the entire black population. They spent time looking at individual African Americans and their achievements, especially important because the mainstream media ignored key black figures. Highlighting success stories served as an important form of uplift in an oppressive white supremacist society. The plight of African Americans, which was so skillfully outlined on the pages of black newspapers, became headlines on the pages of mainstream papers, for, as Todd Vogel pointed out, "The black press redefined class, restaged race and nationhood and reset the terms of public conversation" (Vogel 2001, i).

As Jeanne Theoharis noted, Rosa originally thought the NAACP was an all-male organization, but when she saw a black newspaper article with a picture of her old classmate from Miss White's school, Mrs. Johnnie Carr, in an NAACP photo, Parks was intrigued. Carr was not in attendance at the December 1943 meeting, and Rosa found herself the only woman in a room of twelve men. Montgomery black women—and most black people in that city—stayed away from the NAACP meetings because of pervasive fears of retribution against any black organizing efforts. Raymond Parks harbored those concerns about his wife, and during his stint with the NAACP in the 1930s, he warned Rosa not to join the organization. Raymond felt it was "too dangerous, particularly in the years around the Scottsboro case." In fact, until Rosa joined, Johnnie Carr was the only female member of the Montgomery NAACP, and at the time, there were no youths participating in the organization (Parks 1992, 80–81).

That December meeting happened to include elections. Holding to gender conventions of the day, and highlighting the culture of gender within civil rights organizations, the men in attendance assumed the role of secretary should fall to a woman if one were present. Being the only woman at the meeting, Rosa was voted in as secretary. Recalling the event, Rosa noted, "I was the only woman there, and they said they needed a secretary, and I was too timid to say no. I just started taking minutes, and that was the way I was elected secretary" (Parks 1992, 81). Even among the most progressive race champions, gender roles and gender norms still circumscribed the roles women could take on in and out of the public eye. Much of the overshadowing of Rosa Parks during the Montgomery Bus Boycott came because of black men not wanting a woman out front leading a movement. Behind closed doors, as we see from this meeting of the local NAACP, women were expected to take on traditional female roles while the men served as the face of the organization. Case in point, the chapter secretary before Rosa was her old school friend Johnnie Carr, because Carr was the only female member the previous year.

When Rosa Parks joined the local chapter of the NAACP, E. D. Nixon served as president. He was much more militant than the NAACP leaders Raymond Parks encountered during his stint with the organization in the 1930s, and both Rosa and Raymond appreciated E. D. Nixon's approach to racial uplift. He brought to the presidency his leftist labor organizing mentality that called for black people to press the issues when it came to race relations and challenging white supremacy. Blacks who were more conservative still filled the ranks of the NAACP, and Nixon, now joined by Rosa Parks, fought many uphill battles to push the Montgomery NAACP into a more militant stance. Nixon's wife, Arlet Nixon, attended meetings on occasion, but Parks and Carr were the only women who were meeting regulars. As local branch secretary, Rosa recalled working hard to keep up with Nixon's correspondences. An unpaid position, the role of secretary was work on top of her regular employment. Parks enjoyed a strong working relationship with Nixon. It was Nixon who posted bond when Parks was arrested in 1955, and, once they returned to Rosa's home, Nixon immediately suggested her case could be the turning point of the bus segregation issue. Nixon recalled in an interview with Studs Terkel, "And now, after we got home, we had coffee and I talked to her, and I said to Miss Parks, I said, 'Miss Parks,' I said, 'Your case can be a turning point. We've got to have your case to change the situation'" (Parks, Horton, and Nixon 1973). Nixon saw how important Rosa Parks was to the movement for black uplift, but he also saw her as a woman who should take on traditional roles. In fact, Nixon and others bet that Rosa's sex, as well as other factors to be discussed later, made her nonthreatening and engendered sympathy rather than ridicule. Characterizing Nixon's views on gender roles, Rosa Parks recalled, "He used to say, 'Women don't need to be nowhere but in the kitchen.'" When Rosa would ask about her role, Nixon would demur, "But I need a secretary, and you are a good one." Although this banter remained friendly, and Nixon consistently praised Parks's work, the underlying gendered tone of the conversation shows how Nixon subscribed to traditional gender roles (Parks 1992, 82–83).

It is no wonder that Rosa said, "Going back to the late 1930s, or even earlier, and into the late 1940s, I really didn't know of that many women who were involved in civil-rights work" (Parks 1992, 81). "However, by the time you got to the late 40s and even into the 50s and 60s, women became more vocal and active." Rosa Parks was a trailblazer in this way. When most other women in Montgomery chose not to get involved in organizing and agitation activities, Parks leaped into the fight for racial justice. As Jeanne Theoharis described it, "Working with a handful of committed local leaders in Montgomery, Rosa Parks joined the cadre of Montgomery activists that would lay the groundwork for the civil rights movement in the decade before the *Brown* decision" (Theoharis 2013, 18).

Despite gender conventions of the day, Rosa Parks was not content to let the men around her do all of the work. In 1946, one of the Scottsboro Boys, Andy Wright, who had been released on parole in January 1944 and later left the state in violation of his parole, was rearrested and sent back to prison. Rosa Parks joined a five-person team, the defense committee, who met with the parole board in support of Andy Wright. Serving in that capacity with Parks were Zenobia Johnson, W. G. Porter, J. E. Pierce, and E. D. Nixon. Rosa remembered Zenobia Johnson fondly, partially because she was the only other woman in this group. Johnson and her husband ran the dining room at Alabama State Normal where Rosa attended school while her mother took classes to renew her teacher's license. The parole board did release Wright, and the committee helped him find a job. Sadly, Andy Wright's troubles with the law did not end with this parole. The physical and psychological toll of over a decade of imprisonment can wreak havoc on anyone, and Wright, who was nineteen years old when the Scottsboro case began, carried the wounds of his wrongful incarceration.

While housed in Kilby Prison in Montgomery, Alabama, Wright endured beatings from both guards and his peers. He was often ill, and there were times when others had to take on Wright's work detail. On one occasion, Charley Weems, another of the Scottsboro Boys, filled in for Wright and suffered a knife attack intended for Andy Wright. Of his incarceration, Wright wrote, "A colored convict's very best behavior is not good enough for these officials here. Every time they open their mouths it is ['] you black bastard.['] When we think we are doing right we be cursed at and kick around and beat like dogs" (Squires et al. 2005). Prison was a crushing experience for Wright, who wrote in 1939, "I am trying all that in my power to be brave but you understand a person can be brave for a certain length of time and then he is a coward down. That the way it is" (Squires et al. 2005). Broken down in prison, Wright struggled to adjust to life after his release. The specter of his imprisonment haunted him, and he rarely received the benefit of the doubt when accused of other indiscretions. This led to other arrests on trumped-up charges and other stints in prison. While the committee followed the developments in Wright's life, they could not reverse the damage caused by the initial false imprisonment and the brutality that he experienced as one of the Scottsboro Boys (Parks 1992, 84).

Rosa's experience with the Wright case and her role as secretary of the Montgomery NAACP place her on the frontlines of other legal battles. She recalled, "One of my main duties [as secretary] was to keep a record of cases of discrimination or unfair treatment or acts of violence against black people" (Parks 1992, 84). When reports of the rape of Abbeville, Alabama, resident Recy Taylor surfaced, Rosa traveled to support efforts to bring the perpetrators to justice. Taylor, a black woman, was on her way home from the Rock Hill Holiness Church on September 3, 1944, when a group of young white men accosted and gang-raped her. Taylor, who was married with one child, sustain such severe injuries that she was not able to have any more children. Her attackers left her in the middle of town and threatened to kill her if she told anyone of the assault (Parks 1992, 84–85; Theoharis 2013, 23). Historian Danielle McGuire offered the context, "After World War I, the Alabama Klan unleashed a wave of terror designed to return 'uppity' African Americans to their proper place in the segregated social order" (McGuire 2011, 28). The assault on Recy Taylor was but one example of white Alabamians trying put black people in their place. Viewing black people, and particularly black women, as inferior beings that could be possessed in every imaginable way, many white men felt justified in violating black women's bodies. Former South Carolina Governor Coleman Blease summed up these sentiments in his 1913 *Statement of Pardons, Parole and Commutations* when he wrote, "I am of the opinion, as I have always been, and have very serious doubt as to whether the crime of rape can be committed upon a negro" (Litwack 1998, 269).

Even with the pervasive denial of black women's humanity, there were some inklings that white Alabamians felt uneasy about the rape of Recy Taylor. In particular, the *Birmingham News* editorial staff published a piece entitled "Most Unfortunate" in the Wednesday, February 21, 1945, edition of the newspaper. The editorialist expressed concerns that the lack of grand jury indictment would further stain, having already been tainted by the Scottsboro case, outsiders' impressions of the state of Alabama. Rather than a case that would "languish in innocuous desuetude," the writer feared that "the whole state is now, or soon will be, under fire" (*Birmingham News* 1945, 6). Still, the governor, attorney general, and the residents of Henry County where the crime took place refused to act under the pressures of agitation from within and outside of the state of Alabama.

Pressure did mount. A group of activists formed the Committee for Equal Justice for Mrs. Taylor. The committee, headed by a white woman, Caroline Bellin, pressured the governor to convene a special grand jury, but that body refused to indict the rapists. Still, the committee gained the support of labor unions and black newspapers as they worked to raise awareness of white brutality against black women. The *Pittsburgh Courier,* one of the nation's most prominent black newspapers, ran an exposé covering the assault and injustice in Abbeville. Taylor, too, like countless black women before her, chose to agitate after her tragic assault. Although survivors of sexualized violence rarely received justice in Southern courts," McGuire noted, "black women like Recy Taylor who were raped by white men in the 1940s used their voices as weapons against white supremacy" (McGuire 2011, 39).

Many others came alongside Taylor, and the Committee for Equal Justice for Recy Taylor included prominent African Americans like W.E.B. DuBois, Langston Hughes, and Mary Church Terrell. Begun as a local chapter, the Alabama Committee for Equal Justice for Mrs. Recy Taylor had within a year become a national powerhouse that the *Chicago Defender* called "the strongest campaign for equal justice to be seen in a decade" (McGuire 2011, 13). Parks's recounting of her interview with Taylor moved the likes of E. D. Nixon (Montgomery NAACP and Montgomery Brotherhood of Sleeping Car Porters), Rufus A. Lewis (Montgomery funeral home director), and E. G. Jackson (editor of the black press the *Alabama Tribune*) (McGuire 2011, 13).

The original grand jury in the Recy Taylor rape case failed to issue an indictment, and the six rapists avoided a trial. Committee founders, together with other local and national members, flooded the governor's office with petitions and letters of protest. Rosa and Raymond Parks wrote, as did E. D. Nixon and Johnnie Carr. Under pressure from the Committee for Equal Justice for Recy Taylor and others, Alabama Governor Chauncey Sparks convened a special grand jury and appointed Assistant Attorney General William O. Harris to lead the case. This new group also failed to indict the six rapists, and the committee that Rosa Parks helped to form moved to investigate other cases. They did not, however, leave Taylor without support. Danielle McGuire clarified that "the Alabama Committee for Equal Justice moved Taylor and her family to Montgomery, where they provided an apartment and secured a job for her husband" (McGuire 2011, 36). Southern Negro Youth Conference activist Esther Cooper Jackson also kept close tabs on Taylor and advocated for justice in her case.

At that time there existed in the South, and throughout the nation, a culture of pardoning white-on-black crime. The pervasive belief was that black people were "on the order of lower animals" (McGuire 2011, 36). The more inroads black people made in society, the more the white backlash attempted to demean black lives. Rosa Parks saw this firsthand and noted, "Whites didn't like blacks having that kind of attitude. [S]o they started doing all kinds of violent things to black people to remind them that they didn't have rights" (McGuire 2011, 10). Sylvester McCauley, Rosa's brother, encountered this white paranoia when he returned to Montgomery after his tour of duty in both the European and Pacific theaters of World War II. Quoting Parks, Jeanne Theoharis offered, "Returning veterans . . . found that they were treated with even more disrespect, especially if they were in uniform" (Theoharis 2013, 22). The disgrace of fighting for his country only to return to segregation as normal drove Sylvester McCauley and millions of other black Southerners to seek greater opportunity in the north.

Still, millions of other African Americans remained in the South despite the conditions, and they worked to make the best of their lives. A growing number, like Rosa Parks, put themselves headfirst into the fight for racial justice. Justice was at the forefront of Rosa's mind when she traveled the hundred miles from Montgomery to Abbeville to interview Recy Taylor. Taylor, despite warnings from her white attackers, reported the rape to the local police, but they refused to act. Rosa spent time with Taylor and her family, no doubt having in mind her own near-rape narrative. Accounts differ as to what happened while she was in Abbeville, but as Rosa noted in her biography, "There wasn't much we could do" in the case of Recy Taylor.

Whereas black women's claims of rape went largely unheard, white women needed only to offer a hint of rape to send the lynch mob after any black male. Such was the case with the Scottsboro Boys and their decade-long efforts to clear their names after false accusations of rape landed them in prison in 1931. Those accusations robbed the boys of their innocence and haunted them for the rest of their lives. Danielle McGuire noted, "Unsubstantiated rumors of black men attacking innocent white women sparked almost 50 percent of all race riots in the United States between Reconstruction and World War II" (McGuire 2011, 26). There were over forty-seven hundred lynchings between 1882 and 1968 (Mace 2014, 149). Countless other black people faced incarceration and other forms of violence simply because of their race. Douglas Blackmon detailed how white Southerners and Southern states profited off these wrongful imprisonments, calling the convict labor system that dominated the south from Reconstruction to World War II "slavery by another name" (Blackmon 2008).

Jeremiah Reeves was but one victim of these practices. As a teenager, Reeves worked as a delivery driver. Reeves was having an affair with a white woman, Mabel Ann Crowder, to whom he made deliveries. In 1952 a neighbor of this woman caught the couple in the act. When Crowder realized she and Reeves had an onlooker, she cried rape. Authorities arrested Jeremiah Reeves, a sixteen-year-old high school student, and a jury convicted him of rape even though he and his lover were in a consensual relationship. When it came to black men and white women, the assumption was that white women would never consent.

Rosa Parks and the Montgomery NAACP worked to free Reeves. This case had a major effect on Parks. She recalled talking with a coworker about the case and telling the friend, "'I sure wish I knew where that woman lived, so I could go out there and see if she would tell the truth'" (Parks 1992, 86). Her friend replied that Rosa's mother and husband would never let her make such a trip, but Parks, moved by Jeremiah Reeves's plight, wanted to try anything she could to help. In the end, the state executed Reeves on March 27, 1958.

Before his execution, Rosa had frequent correspondence with Reeves. She also worked to get his writings—Reeves was a skilled poet—published in the local black newspaper. His poem "Condemned" captured the despair of his race-motivated incarceration and illuminated his faith.

Condemned before the eyes of the human race
Condemned to live a life of disgrace
Condemned with life as an open book,
So as to let the world take an onward look.

Condemned by the hand of sinful men
Condemned to live in a world of torture and sin,
Condemned to suffer loneliness, heartache and shame,
Condemned as an outcast with a scandalized name.

Condemned to suffer every pain and sorrow,
Condemned without any hope of tomorrow,
Condemned in a world of hatred and fear.
As I face the long and lonely dreary years.

Condemned—but I'm not ashamed
Condemned—but I'll bear the blame
Condemned as onward I trod
Condemned but eternally I'll trust in God.

This state of feeling "condemned to live in a world of torture and sin" was a sad reality for black people in Montgomery and across the world, yet many clung to faith, and as Jeremiah Reeves proclaimed, "eternally I'll trust in God" (Reeves n.d.). Rosa was one whose faith fueled her determination to keep fighting for justice. There were many roadblocks along the way, but, as Rosa saw it, "It was more a matter of trying to challenge the powers that be, and let it be known that we did not wish to continue being treated as second-class citizens" (Parks 1992, 89). She admitted, "Sometimes it was very difficult to keep going when all our work seemed to be in vain" (Parks 1992, 86). Rosa Parks did keep going, however, and her efforts were essential to the work of the Montgomery branch of the NAACP at this time.

The Montgomery NAACP worked in conjunction with the National Headquarters and with other civil rights organizations active on a local level. As secretary of the local chapter, Rosa Parks came alongside other race advocates throughout the 1940s, including Esther Cooper Jackson and her husband, labor activist James Jackson, and worked for racial justice in Alabama and across the nation. The two were often the target of anti-Communist attacks, and Jackson's work on the Recy Taylor case created such a backlash from white Alabamians that she was forced to leave the state (Theoharis 2013, 24).

Communist allegations plagued civil rights efforts in Montgomery. A labor organizer himself as the president of the Montgomery chapter of the Brotherhood of Sleeping Car Porters, E. D. Nixon felt the weight of these accusations. Elected president of the Montgomery NAACP in December 1945, Nixon ran on a populace agenda that promised to empower local citizens to steer the work of the local chapter. According to Jeanne Theoharis, the feisty Nixon wanted "black Montgomerians to 'wake up and . . . build it into a powerful organization'" (Theoharis 2013, 24). Membership in the Montgomery NAACP was low in 1945, but Nixon and Parks's rise to prominence signaled to the majority working-class black population in Montgomery that the local chapter was working for the people. Both leaders were from the working class and brought working-class ideology to the chapter.

Still, Nixon and Parks, as well as other "mainstream black activists," had to maintain an ideological and rhetorical distance from leftist activists in order to ward off accusations of collusion with Communists (Theoharis 2013, 24). "They did what was necessary to survive politically and continue their assault on Jim Crow," Danielle McGuire commented (McGuire 2011, 38). As Jeanne Theoharis and Danielle McGuire noted, Rosa never declared herself anti-Communist, and her collaboration with organizations like the Highlander Folk School show that she was eager to work in partnership with anyone who was like-minded when it came to racial justice.

The pragmatic Rosa Parks worked with E. D. Nixon to expand local NAACP membership in the 1940s. Within the first two years of Nixon's presidency, the local chapter grew from 861 to 1,600 members. Together, they push the Montgomery NAACP to challenge erroneous rape convictions of African American men like Worthy James, John Underwood, and Samuel Taylor. These efforts were difficult, because there were no black attorneys in Montgomery, and white attorneys who defended black clients faced alienation, ridicule, and violence from white Montgomerians. Parks and Nixon pressed on despite the difficulties, and Parks worked on affidavits and kept track of branch membership (Theoharis 2013, 25).

Rosa's life was not filled with hopelessness and despair, and she received encouragement from other women in the movement. Ella Baker had a particularly profound impact on Rosa Parks's life and activism. A civil rights stalwart, Baker was part of the national NAACP leadership team. She was director of branches, and she held conferences designed to strengthen local leadership. Rosa Parks attended two of these conferences: in Atlanta, Georgia, in 1945 and in Jacksonville, Florida, in 1946. She learned a great deal about organizing and activism at the workshops, and, more importantly, she began a strong friendship with Ella Baker. Theoharis reflected, "Baker made a powerful impression on Parks. . . . From then on 'whenever she came to Montgomery, [Ella Baker] stayed with me. She was a true friend—a mentor'" (Theoharis 2013, 25). Rosa Parks looked up to the older, more experienced Baker, and the two shared a passion for empowering youth in the movement.

The Baker-led conferences energized Rosa Parks—energy that sustained her through tumultuous times in the local NAACP branch. By fall 1946, challenges arose to E. D. Nixon's leadership. Some of the leaders of the branch were successful members of the local elite—what Nixon called "insurance men"—who did not support Nixon's efforts to engage working class Montgomerians. They levied accusations with the national office of dictatorial rule, and they further objected to what they saw as militant tactic on his part. The national NAACP had long embraced more conservative approaches than many of their branches, so these accusations struck a chord. Rosa's old classmate, Johnnie Carr, characterized Nixon's rivals as people who wanted to "use the organization for a nice place to sit for one hour, and preside over a meeting, after which no special effort is made to put the organization to work of the masses," according to Jeanne Theoharis (Theoharis 2013, 26). Rosa Parks escaped much of this ridicule, but at least one of Nixon's detractors offered a gender critique of Parks, calling for "a man secretary to handle things with a firm hand" (Theoharis 2013, 26). Even with mounting opposition, both Nixon and Parks won reelection in 1946.

The following year, Parks served on a three-person executive committee that recommended E. D. Nixon assume the role of head of the Alabama state conference, a position he won in 1947 and held for two years. In 1948, after delivering a "powerful address" and receiving "thunderous applause," conference members elected Rosa the first secretary of the Alabama state conference (Theoharis 2013, 27). Together, Nixon and Parks continued to agitate for change in their new roles. Lynching became another pressing issue for them, and they lobbied for federal antilynching legislation. Her work challenging lynching, rape of black women, false imprisonment of black men, and police brutality, among other causes, took a toll on Parks, eating up her nights and weekends in the struggle for civil rights. However, she persevered, buoyed by her faith and her determination to see racial justice.

This fighting spirit and constant vigilance drew her to a new protest when the Freedom Train came to Montgomery in 1947. The Freedom Train was a traveling exhibit scheduled to visit all forty-eight existing states, bringing original copies of the Declaration of Independence, Bill of Rights, and U.S. Constitution, among other documents. In Montgomery, the committee convened to plan for the train's visit consisted of only white members, and Parks led efforts to integrate the group. At a national level, the Freedom Train's creation, coordination, and planning included several groups, including the Justice Department, the National Archives, the Office of the President, and the American Heritage Foundation. Responding to growing pressures from black activists and those sympathetic to black uplift, the American Heritage Foundation executives made a private decision: "No segregation of any individual or groups of any kind on the basis of race or religion [will] be allowed at and exhibition of the Freedom Train held anywhere" (Green 2007, 118). They made that decision public two weeks after the train began touring, even bypassing planned stops in the South where the citizens refused to adhere to that rule (Green 2007, 118). Thanks to agitation on the part of Rosa Parks and her colleagues, Montgomery officials agreed to appoint blacks to the committee and to bar segregation at the Freedom Train exhibition (Theoharis 2013, 29).

Rosa took a group of youths to the exhibition when it arrived in December 1947, and the group did not experience segregation while there. Her visit, however, brought the ire of white Montgomerians, and Rosa received threatening calls following this trip. Ku Klux Klan (KKK) activity also rose toward the end of the 1940s, due in part to backlash over black advancements and increased agitation on the part of African Americans. In Alabama, that activism came in response to leaders like Rosa Parks and E. D. Nixon. Increased KKK backlash proved detrimental to the NAACP, and Theoharis noted that membership in Montgomery fell from 1,600 to 148 in 1949.

Compounding the external bullying of groups like the KKK, internal strife abounded. Rosa Parks pulled back from much of the NAACP work in 1949 when her mother grew ill, and it seemed the local and state NAACP suffered without her steadfast efforts to bring people together across socio-economic class lines. E. D. Nixon lost the branch presidency in 1950 to insurance man Robert Matthews, and the state conference replaced him with insurance agent W. C. Patton in 1949 (Theoharis 2013, 30). Still, Parks continued to work with Nixon through his endeavors with the Montgomery chapter of the Brotherhood of Sleeping Car Porters, and she reclaimed her role of NAACP branch secretary in 1952 after her mother's health improved. Rosa Parks maintained hope for the future despite all of the hardships she faced, and she increasingly saw work with youth as her calling in these dark days.

6

Youth Movements

"I have this message for you and all young people: Complete your education, maintain high moral standards, and demonstrate that you are worthy of the consideration of an employer or the opportunity that come to you. When I was a young person . . . I knew I wanted to reach out to young people and help them shape their lives, but I did not know how this would come about. . . . We knew the challenges facing young people who we wanted to help develop. I have been preparing myself for more than 30 years, since working with the Youth Council of the NAACP. I just had to wait for the proper time" (Parks 1996, 75).

Rosa Parks knew from an early age that she wanted to work on youth empowerment. She reaped the benefit of family members who strengthened and encouraged her through her childhood and adolescence. Her above advice, recorded in the 1996 book *Dear Mrs. Rosa Parks: A Dialogue with Today's Youth*, mirrors the lessons she learned from her mother and maternal grandparents. As an educator, Rosa's mother Leona McCauley pushed her children to learn as much as they could. Even before Rosa started school, her mother encouraged her husband, James McCauley, to take a job in Tuskegee, Alabama, so that their children could have access to the superior education offered in connection with Booker T. Washington's Tuskegee Institute. When Rosa was eleven, her mother enrolled her in Miss White's Montgomery Industrial School for Girls, even though tuition payments proved extremely difficult. Jeanne Theoharis noted that "Miss White's school embodied Leona McCauley's advice to her daughter to 'take advantage of the opportunities, no matter how few they were'" (Theoharis 2013, 8). At times, Leona McCauley endured financial hardship in order to pay for the best education for Rosa and Sylvester McCauley. When it became impossible to pay for additional education for her kids, Leona McCauley still ensured that there were plenty of books in the house and that her children cultivated their love of reading and knowledge. Not only did Rosa learn valuable lessons at Miss White's school—lessons that reinforced her mother's training—but she also connected with future activists, like Johnnie Carr, who worked alongside her in the fight for black equality.

From her maternal grandmother, Rose Edwards, Rosa learned dignity, morality, and self-determination. She described her grandmother as "the calm one," and Rose wanted "to teach her . . . about the cost and terms of survival" (Parks 1992, 16; Theoharis 2013, 7). Rosa's grandparents complemented each other well. Whereas her grandmother focused on dignity, morality and survival, her husband, Sylvester Edwards "was very emotional and excitable" (Parks 1992, 16). Sylvester had looked white, and he "took every bit of advantage of being white-looking" (Parks 1992, 16). Rosa recalled that he would call white people by their first name, a social taboo, and he maintained firearms to ward off any violence perpetrated against him or his family. Theoharis accurately surmised, "Rosa would constantly have to balance . . . militancy [that] could get a person killed" with "resistance [that] pushed back on the oppression and at times made it diminish" (Theoharis 2013, 7).

Rosa found that balance throughout her life, and the balance was situational. She had to determine the correct response in each case of oppression. Moreover, she took it upon herself to train young people in these decision-making processes and tactics of resistance. Her passion for working with youth led her in 1949 to found the NAACP Youth Council (YC) alongside her friend Johnnie Carr. By her own admission, 1949 was a tumultuous year for Rosa and for black Montgomerians. She reflected, "For some reason there were a lot of cases [of white supremacist violence against black people] in 1949" (Parks 1992, 93) One case that stood out to her was the arrest of Edwina and Marshall Johnson. The two siblings, sixteen and fifteen years old respectively, hailed from Newark, New Jersey. This case likely struck a nerve with Parks because of their age. Visiting Montgomery, they were unfamiliar with the city's segregation laws, a common theme among Northern black children visiting the South, like the 1955 case of Emmett Louis Till. The Johnson children boarded a Montgomery bus and sat down in the white section. Outraged, the white bus driver, S. T. Lock, drew his pistol and forced the teens off the bus. At that time, bus drivers carried firearms and wielded enforcement powers similar to those granted the police. Lock also contacted the police, who arrested Edwina and Marshall Johnson and held them in jail for two days. At their trial, according to Parks, the judge, Wiley C. Hill, threatened to put them in reform school, but in the end, the two had to pay a fine.

Rosa also recalled incidents of racial violence and intimidation outside of Montgomery. She wrote in her biography of Isaac Woodard, the black World War II veteran blinded by police officers in Batesburg, South Carolina, after an altercation with a town bus driver. Although Rosa remembered the event occurring in 1949, the attack on Woodard happened in 1946. Isaac Woodard was riding a bus home after his discharge from the army at the time of the attack. Still wearing his uniform, he asked the driver if he minded stopping so Woodard could use the restroom. The two argued, and the bus driver notified the Batesburg police. The officers, including police chief Lynwood Shull, arrested Woodard and brutally beat him before throwing him in jail. The attack was so egregious that it left Woodard blind in one eye. Police charged Woodard with drunk and disorderly conduct. He was convicted and fined for this alleged offense. Meanwhile, the police officers who savaged Woodard faced charges of violating his civil rights; however, the officers were acquitted of all charges (CNN 2019).

Cases like this had profound impacts on Rosa Parks, and they grated on her sense of morality, cultivated in her by her grandmother. Isaac Woodard must have reminded Rosa of her brother Sylvester, who also served in the army during World War II. She reflected, "In the armed forces, which were controlled by white racists," second class citizenship for blacks was "business as usual" (Parks 1992, 90). Conversely, "people in England and France received the African-American soldiers warmly. Many of these soldiers had white girlfriends, and some even married English, or French or Italian women" (Parks 1992, 90). The level of disrespect and oppression proved too much for Rosa's brother, and, having returned home to a segregated Montgomery, he decided to move north to Detroit, Michigan. Black war veterans like Sylvester "found that they were treated with even more disrespect, especially if they were in uniform," because "Whites felt that thing should remain as they had always been and that black veterans were getting too sassy" (Parks 1992, 92).

Black people, however, took heart when they saw members of their race in uniform. They were mindful of African American efforts to secure freedom abroad, and they increasingly demanded those freedoms at home. In fact, during World War II, African Americans adopted slogans and movements, like the Double V Campaign, aimed at uncovering the rampant racism in the United States. Made popular by the *Pittsburgh Courier* in 1942, the Double V Campaign demanded victory against racial oppression in the United States while the nation fought for victory against fascism abroad. To blacks, and to many others in the United States, it was antithetical to demand black soldiers go overseas to fight for freedom from oppression for

---

Northern Racism in America

Racism, although less overt, existed in every major city in the North. The 1950s was a decade of tremendous prosperity in the United States. In the North, tracts of housing were springing up in numerous suburbs. The most popular of these, Levittown, began in what was a Long Island, New York, potato field. The GI Bill and new financing options made these new homes an affordable method of building equity. Many Americans were also using GI Bill money to fund undergraduate and graduate educations. Frequently, industries that were based in urban areas began moving to cheaper suburban and rural plants. This new model of American life systematically excluded black America. Suburban developers refused to sell to black families; some colleges and universities refused to accept black applicants; and black people, who could not find housing outside of the city, were excluded from jobs developing outside urban areas.

---

foreign people only to return home to segregated or oppressive conditions prescribed because of their racial identity.

Rosa and the NAACP YC took active roles in protest efforts, challenging existing segregation laws and practices in Montgomery. Lamenting the fact that black people could not check books out of the main public library in the city, YC members repeatedly traveled to the building and attempted to borrow books. This was a major issue because the black library branch, the one blacks had to use, did not have a good selection of books. If the black library branch did not have a book, which was frequently the case, the staff there would have to request it from the main library. There were no guarantees that the main library would honor those requests, and black people had to make a second trip to the black branch, which was inconveniently located across town, to get the book if the main library granted the request. Traveling across town meant riding the segregated and oppressive buses for many black Montgomerians, a task that further enforced their second-class citizenship status. Despite continued agitation, the black youth could not obtain access to the main library, but their efforts signaled to the white establishment that they were not content with business as usual in Montgomery.

White backlash against black agitation and advancement grew steadily at the end of the 1940s and into the 1950s. White Southern politicians delivered scathing indictments against black people, and some even called for outright violence reminiscent of the "redeemer" culture following the Civil War. Emblematic of these race baiters was Mississippian Theodore Bilbo. During his 1946 senatorial reelection campaign, Bilbo challenged "every 'red-blooded white man to use any means to keep the niggers away

---

SEGREGATION

Despite several victories, black life in the 1940s and the 1950s remained circumscribed by the racist state laws and city ordinances. These laws mandated the racial segregation of citizens in all realms of society, including amusement, recreation, prisons, training schools, employment, restaurants, tax records, police forces, libraries, hospitals, travel, and housing. Segregation manifested itself in the signs first seen during the Jim Crow era—signs that read "Colored" and "White." Any attempt by black people to challenge the system of Jim Crow would bring bodily harm or even death.

Numerous Southern politicians, including James Davis (GA), Carl Vinson (GA), Orval Faubus (AK), Herman Talmadge (GA), and Olin Johnston (SC), to name a few, banded together to maintain white domination by disfranchising large numbers of black voters. These politicians became the backbone for the Dixiecrat party, a Southern branch of the Democratic Party established for the purposes of maintaining segregation and white rule in the South. These politicians found increasing support when, in the mid-1950s, White Citizens Councils, organizations made up of the "better" people of Southern towns, were developed in direct response to the *Brown* decision. These organizations claimed defense of Southern tradition as their main goal, but they succeeded in inflaming the general public and inciting riot or near-riot conditions in the South.

---

from the polls. You know and I know what's the best way to keep the nigger from voting. You do it the night before the election. I don't have to tell you any more than that. Red-blooded men know what I mean'" (Mace 2014, 13). As Bilbo urged, much of that backlash involved violence, and parents of the children in the NAACP YC became increasingly afraid of white retaliation. For this reason, Montgomery NAACP membership dropped at the tail end of the 1940s, and Rosa Parks eventually had to disband the YC due to lack of participation.

Rosa Parks kept busy, however. In addition to advising the YC, she was secretary of the senior branch of the NAACP (Parks 1992, 94). She also continued to assist E. D. Nixon with his activism even after he lost his posts as state conference president and Montgomery branch president of the NAACP. Nixon remained active in the Brotherhood of Sleeping Car Porters, and he was a constant agitator for racial justice. For his part, Nixon continued to encourage and support Rosa even though the two had a slight rift when she returned to the role of branch secretary after Nixon lost his presidency (Theoharis 2013, 30). In truth, E. D. Nixon had little support from the national office of the NAACP. Nationally, the NAACP maintained a careful approach, choosing to avoid sensational cases and distance themselves from militant leaders like Nixon. For this reason, the national NAACP offered little support for the Scottsboro Boys, whose rape trials made the national leadership nervous. The result of this reticence was that "activists like Parks and Nixon labored in relative loneliness" (Theoharis 2013, 30).

Still, the national NAACP did put their full weight behind causes they felt were safe enough to pursue, and school desegregation was one of these issues. Across the nation, cases challenging segregation emerged on court dockets. In Topeka, Kansas, thirteen parents joined a class-action suit claiming the 1879 law segregating Kansas schools was unconstitutional. Oliver Brown, a World War II veteran and father of Linda Brown, head-lined the suit. Similar conditions existed in South Carolina, where twenty parents challenged segregation in a class action suit *Briggs v. Elliott*, wherein Harry Briggs sued the president of the Clarendon County, South Carolina, school board, R. W. Elliott. In the state of Delaware, African Americans rallied for school desegregation under the auspices of *Bulah v. Gebhart* and *Belton v. Gebhart*. African Americans in the nation's capital, Washington, D.C., shared in the fight through *Bolling v. Sharpe*. Beginning in 1947, the Consolidated Parents Group Inc. formed to fight for integration of D.C. schools. The efforts took added shape when organization founder Gardner Bishop attempted to force the integration of eleven students into the newly built John Philip Sousa Junior High School. Denied admission, the parents filed suit. Students led the charge in Prince Edward County, Virginia. Sixteen-year-old Barbara Johns led a student strike pro-testing the deplorable conditions at the all-black Robert Russa Moton High School. Refused satisfactory responses from school officials, black people in Prince Edward County filed a class-action suit that included over 160 plaintiffs (National Park Service n.d.).

All of these cases, and many more protests across the country, marked a tipping point in American education and American race relations. African Americans screamed, "Enough," and they demanded equal educational opportunities for their youth. Most of these complaints did not begin with cries for integration; rather, most of the plaintiffs wanted facilities and experiences—educational, busing, and otherwise—that mirrored what white students received. This fight resonated with Rosa Parks, for she had limited access to education as a youth, and her mother had to sacrifice so much to give her and her brother the education they did receive. In fact, she did not complete her high school education until 1933 at the age of twenty-one, because the state did not provide high school education for black students. Rosa noted that in 1940, only 7 percent of African Americans in Alabama had a high school diploma (Parks 1992, 64–65).

The cases, collectively known as *Brown v. Board of Education of Topeka, KS* (*Brown*), appeared on the U.S. Supreme Court docket in December 1952. The Court decided to combine the cases because the issues involved therein were so similar, and the questions raised by the cases warranted a collective decision. Variations did exist, however. In the Delaware integration case, the lower courts ruled in favor of the plaintiffs and ordered that these students gain access to the all-white school, a ruling the defendants appealed. The U.S. District Court had ruled previously that the Virginia students attended inferior schools, thus violating their constitutional rights, and that the school board needed to provide equal facilities for the plaintiffs. A three-judge U.S. District Court panel offered a similar decision in the South Carolina case, but they declined to force integration. Regardless of variations in previous individual decisions, the U.S. Supreme Court ruled on May 17, 1954, that segregation in public education is inherently unequal. The *Brown* decision dealt a striking blow to the 1896 Supreme Court ruling in *Plessy v. Ferguson* that established separate-but-equal policies at the heart of public school segregation, Jim Crow laws, and white supremacist culture in America.

Written by Chief Justice Earl Warren, who took that seat in 1953 after then chief justice Fred M. Vinson died, the majority opinion brought an extreme white backlash. Warren understood how monumental this ruling was, and he worked vigorously to have it be a unanimous decision. In the end, all of the justices agreed. The following year, the justices returned to the school segregation question, issuing the *Brown II* ruling that dictated the terms of integration: a very vague "with all deliberate speed." White supremacists and others who detested the idea of integration dubbed the ruling a Communist plot, and, beginning in Mississippi, White Citizens Councils emerged as white supremacists united across lines of socioeconomic class to defy any form of integration.

Brown "led to a potent and violent conservative backlash, which centered on the fear that integration would lead to young white women engaging unwillingly or willingly in sexual relationships with black men" (Mace 2014, 18). Perhaps, Grace Elizabeth Hale best explained the white backlash when she noted that "rape of white women signaled metaphorically white men's fear of the loss of ability to provide for white women and physically their fear, given their treatment of black women, of the loss of white racial purity" (Hale 1999, 232–233). Southerners had a "blatant disregard for— and in fact open defiance of—*Brown* [and] Pete Daniels argued that in response to the call for racial equality in the twentieth century, Southerners resurrected the post-Civil War Lost Cause argument" (Mace 2014, 19). Most often they "claimed outsiders were interfering in their state and disrupting Southern race relations" (Mace 2014, 19).

The NAACP, whose legal defense team sponsored and argued the *Brown* cases and many others, became even more of a target for white supremacists following this landmark decision. Amid an "intensified politics of race . . . most white southern tolerance for the NAACP disappeared [replaced by] 'a counter-movement . . . to deny the legitimacy of the new definition of values that the integration movement espouse[d] and to prevent the followers of this movement from gaining any greater measure of control'" (Parks 1992, 99–100). These attacks occurred at the local and national level; still, activists like Rosa Parks weathered the storm, buoyed by their own self-determination and the fact that school segregation was finally outlawed. Rosa reflected, "You can't imagine the rejoicing among black people, and some white people, when the Supreme Court decision came down in May 1954. . . . It was a very hopeful time. African Americans believed that at last there was a real chance to change the segregation laws" (Parks 1992, 99–100).

The decision spurred at least one black attorney to return to the South in hopes of improving the conditions for African Americans. Fred Gray opened a law office in Montgomery in the wake of *Brown*, thus doubling the city's cadre of black attorneys, joining Charles Langford. As the only black lawyers in the city, the two assisted black Montgomerians in legal matters. Parks recalled another black counselor, Mahalia Ashley Dickerson, who practiced for a time before Gray returned to the South, but she had to leave because, as a single mother, she did not find enough business to support her and her family (Parks 1992, 100). Thus, with the addition of Gray to the legal compliment, black Montgomerians again had a choice when it came to legal representation in all matters, including school integration cases.

In the end, white supremacists succeeded in thwarting much of the promise felt because of the *Brown* decision. It would take decades before the integration ruling would take root in schools across the nation. By that time, white segregationist had devised other ways to keep integration from happening. When black students finally entered many formerly all-white schools, they found that much of the white student body had already found other avenues for education, and many schools remained largely unintegrated even with the desegregation ruling.

Rosa Parks did find encouragement in the *Brown* ruling. She remembered her mother struggling to find work as a teacher, in part because the state did not provide secondary education for black youth. Parks also recalled NAACP efforts to help black teachers fight for equal pay during the 1920s and 1930s. Her mother left a job in the Montgomery school district because the pay for black teachers was so deplorable (Parks 1992, 97–98). Parks noted that the fight for better pay for teachers in Birmingham lasted seven years, and she cited fear of retaliation as a reason why many black teachers there refused to sign on to the NAACP-sponsored suit. In her memoirs, Rosa Parks also reflected on the many school integration law suits filed before the 1954 *Brown* decision. She recalled that "about a dozen other suits against unequal elementary and high schools had been filed in Arkansas, Texas, North Carolina, Virginia, and Missouri by various organizations, including the NAACP" (Parks 1992, 99). Rosa kept close watch over civil rights cases such as these because she, like her ancestors, was predisposed to justice fights and because her love of knowledge led her to read the newspapers voraciously.

E. D. Nixon went on the offensive after *Brown*, and Rosa was a constant collaborator. Nixon assisted twenty-three black students in their attempt to register at the all-white William Harrison School, but the school denied them admittance. The Montgomery branch of the NAACP "decided to approach the school board directly to press for a desegregation plan . . . [and] . . . began soliciting signatures from parents to push for the implementation of *Brown* in Montgomery" (Parks 1992, 34). Some of the parents did sign the petition, and, in response, the Board of Education printed their names and addresses in the local newspaper so that white Montgomerians could conduct a campaign of fear and intimidation against them. White voter registration officials took similar actions when a critical mass of black people attempted to register for the franchise (Theoharis 2013, 34). The intimidation efforts found success, and most black parents refused to fight for school integration. Rosa "grew discouraged in the wake of *Brown* by the 'apathy on the part of our people,'" and she "thought the situation was 'hopeless'" (Theoharis 2013, 35). Increasingly disillusioned, Rosa Parks needed to get away and recharge herself for the fight ahead. Myles Horton's Highlander Folk School offered just such an opportunity.

That same year, Rosa first met Virginia Durr, a white native of Birmingham, Alabama, who became a stalwart confidant and friend for Parks in the coming years. Durr had embraced segregation until she went to college at Wellesley in Massachusetts. There she first dined as equals with an African American, and only because she was assigned that seating. She married attorney Clifford Durr, whom she met after returning home from college. Virginia was one of the founding members of the Southern Conference for Human Welfare, a group of prominent Southern liberals, including her brother-in-law, Supreme Court Justice Hugo Black (Woodham n.d.). The Durrs lived in Washington, D.C., for a time, and Virginia became an activist and social reformer. In 1948, she chaired Progressive Party presidential candidate Henry Wallace's Virginia campaign, and she ran for the U.S. Senate as a Progressive Party candidate. Durr even testified before Congress, having been called before Senator James O. Eastland's (MS) Senate Internal Security Subcommittee because she was accused of having ties to Communists (Theoharis 2013, 35). Eastland, a rabidly racist politician and ardent segregationist, "resurrected the 'Lost Cause' rhetoric employed in the wake of the Civil War—an argument that lauded valiant Southern efforts to maintain regional status quo in the wake of the insurmountable forces of outside aggression—as a justification for white supremacy, racial oppression, and lynching" (Gallagher and Nolan 2010, 1, 3). "This Neo-Lost Cause exacerbated already tense race relations and created a climate of hatred that bred extralegal violence and murder" (Mace 2014, 14).

In 1951 the Durrs moved back to Alabama, and they were among the most progressive whites in the state. Their stance on race relations alienated them from the white community of Montgomery, and Clifford Durr's law practice struggled in light of it. Still, the Durrs maintained an integrationist stance, and they both gravitated to Rosa Parks, E. D. Nixon, and other black activists in the city. Rosa Parks recalled, "When they talked about returning to Alabama, she [Virginia Durr] had to decide if she wanted to, because she knew she and her husband didn't have the same attitude about segregation as most white people in Alabama did." However, Virginia Durr eventually decided that "in coming back to Alabama . . . she wanted to be part of our efforts to end segregation, even though that meant being ostracized and made to suffer" (Parks 1992, 96–97). Undeterred by white supremacist culture in Alabama, Virginia Durr hosted an interracial women's prayer group to which Rosa Parks belonged. The group lasted for a time until white men, largely fathers and husbands of the white participants, protested and forced the prayer group to disband (Parks 1992, 96).

The Durrs took heart, though, in what they were doing alongside the black community. Virginia Durr and Rosa Parks had a particularly strong bond. Though it started as a working relationship—Rosa sewed for Durr—the two encouraged and supported each other through the struggle for racial justice. At the urging of Virginia Durr and E. D. Nixon, Rosa Parks decided to attend a workshop at the Highlander Folk School (Highlander). Located in Monteagle, Tennessee, Highlander organized and educated activists to effect social change. Myles Horton founded the school in 1932 alongside Don West, James Dombrowski, and other progressive-minded individuals (Highlander Center n.d.). In 1955, Horton contacted Virginia Durr, who was a member of the board, and notified her that he had a scholarship for a member of the Montgomery community. Durr contacted Rosa about the opportunity, and she secured transportation funds from fellow white liberal Aubrey Williams (Theoharis 2013, 35–37). The workshop, "Racial Desegregation: Implementing the Supreme Court Decision," spoke directly to Rosa's passion for the uplift and education of black youth. At a time where she was feeling so much disappointment with Montgomery blacks' lack of participation in the integration fight, Highlander came as a welcome respite. Parks knew Durr presented this opportunity to encourage her because she was getting "obscene phone calls" for leading the youth (Theoharis 2013, 36). E. D. Nixon, who "felt the branch hadn't done enough and continued to press the chapter-along with the national organization-to do more about implementing the decision," also urged Parks to attend the workshop and bring back ideas to motivate blacks in the city (Theoharis 2013, 34).

Originally, Highlander organized labor activists, but by the 1950s, the school included civil rights activism as a focus of their workshops. Parks attended one of these workshops in 1955, a ten-day event with an eye to school integration. Rosa feared retaliation if people found out about her trip, so Durr accompanied her part of the way to Tennessee (Theoharis 2013, 37). She recalled she was struck by the fact that it was a "white school" once she arrived, and she wondered why Virginia Durr didn't disclose that fact when she suggested Rosa attend a workshop (Parks, 1992, 102). To her recollection, Durr did not mention race, and Rosa was shocked when she arrived by bus in Chattanooga, Tennessee, and a white man drove her the fifty miles to the school. Grundy County, Tennessee, the county where the school resided, was all white, and Parks recalled, "I didn't have any contact to speak of with the white people outside the school, but I knew they weren't at all happy about the school, because they had burned the building at the first opportunity they had (Parks 1992, 102). Still, the Highlander staff continued their efforts, determined to persist despite white supremacist objections to their racial uplift efforts. Rosa remembered how beautiful it was at Highlander, a school "on a plateau in the mountains that was surrounded by gardens and herds of cattle" (Parks 1992, 103). It took a little time, but Rosa did relax and enjoy herself. She knew a couple of the presenters, Charles Gomillion and Ruby Hurley, and that helped eased her tensions (Theoharis 2013, 37).

Black activists were part of the staff at Highlander, and prominent civil rights activist Septima Clark taught classes and led the citizenship school. Clark, a former teacher in Charleston, South Carolina, lost her job because of her agitation for equal pay for black teachers. Rosa remembered well her mother's anger over the low pay offered to black teachers, and Parks felt a kindred link to the elder Clark. Rosa was so comfortable with Septima that she asked her to ride part of the way back to Montgomery with her. As was the case on her way to Highlander, where she had Virginia Durr escort her for a portion of the trip, Rosa feared white backlash as she returned from Highlander. Such was the nature of black lives in white supremacist America: black people never knew when violence would strike them, and they took precautions to ensure their safety. Clark rode with Parks to Atlanta, Georgia, before Rosa rode the rest of the way back to Montgomery (Rouse 2001, 103).

Septima Clark, like Rosa Parks, worked through her local NAACP branch. She was also active with the Charleston, South Carolina Young Women's Christian Association (YWCA), a group that was on the forefront of civil rights efforts and empowerment of black youth in that city.

Friends in the YWCA introduced her to the Highlander Folk School, and Clark gravitated to their message and their work. Her activism put her in contact with many prominent progressives, and Clark was a friend to South Carolina judge Julius Waites Waring. Waring was a fixture in South Carolina race cases in the 1940s and early 1950s before retiring to New York with his second wife in 1952. Waring handed down decisions "equalizing the salaries of black and white teachers and ordering the state to desegregate its law school or create an equal facility for blacks" (Yarborough n.d.). These rulings put Waring in direct contact with Clark, and the two shared a belief in racial justice.

Waring also challenged South Carolina's efforts to salvage its all-white Democratic primary during his time on the bench. This was necessary because when resilient African Americans found ways around all of the traditional disfranchisement methods, the Southern wing of the Democratic Party created white primaries. Essentially, black people were excluded from voting in primary elections, because the state Democratic Party was designated a private organization that could grant membership to whomever it pleased. Naturally, no African Americans were eligible for membership. This was the most difficult fight for Southern blacks; however, in the 1944 Supreme Court ruling *Smith v. Allwright*, a legal effort led by NAACP attorney Thurgood Marshall, the Court deemed white primaries unconstitutional.

Together with his second wife, whom he married in 1945 amid scandal because the new nuptial came on the heels of his divorce from his first wife of more than thirty years, Waring made a complete break from white supremacist racial traditions. The couple hosted prominent black guests at their home and attended integrated meetings in Charleston and across the country. He had a particular disdain for many Southern liberals and argued that, "such 'gradualists' were even worse than avowed segregationists" (Yarborough n.d.). Waring was one of three judges empaneled to hear arguments in *Briggs v. Elliott* (1951), one of the suits folded into the class action *Brown* case. Although the panel ruled against desegregation two votes to one, Waring wrote the dissent, a vicious attack on segregation or, as he called it, fundamentally inequality (Yarborough n.d.).

Doubtlessly, Septima Clark appreciated Judge Waring's stance on race. As director of the citizenship school at Highlander, Clark "taught adults to read and write and learn about basic citizenship so they could become teachers of others, so they could register to vote" (Parks 1992, 104–105). She wanted to empower black people, and Waring had similar leanings. Rosa looked up to Clark, who was more than a decade older, and she noted that Clark "was very much at home at Highlander" (Parks 1992, 104–105). Parks too began to feel at home in this Tennessee locale, and she found it difficult to leave (Parks 1992, 107). She valued her time at Highlander—ten days where she attended workshops and learned tactics for fighting school segregation. The experience fed her and fueled her passion to work with black youth. Parks also noted, "It was quite enjoyable to be with the people at Highlander. We forgot about what color anybody was. I was forty-two years old, and it was one of the few times in my life up to that point when I did not feel any hostility from white people" (Parks 1992, 105–106). Highlander was a welcome reprieve from the oppressive racism of her hometown. The school was a place where she "experienced people of different races and backgrounds meeting together in workshops and living together in peace and harmony." Parks felt free to share "without any repercussions or antagonistic attitudes from other people" (Parks 1992, 106–107).

In all, forty-eight people attended the workshop intended "for men and women in positions to provide community leadership for an orderly transition from a segregated to a non-segregated school system in the South" (Theoharis 2013, 38). Parks found the atmosphere to be exactly what she needed. She bonded with Septima Clark, and the two continued to exchange correspondences after the workshop. She also admired Myles Horton. In particular, she appreciated his humor. Rosa reflected, "I found myself laughing when I hadn't been able to laugh in a long time" (Theoharis 2013, 38; Parks 1992, 105). Parks further appreciated that Highlander had a deep Christian foundation. Horton was inspired by Jesus's life and work, and Rosa Parks carried a similar sensibility that drove her activism (Theoharis 2013, 39). Rosa did not speak much during the workshop; Horton remembered her as the quietest attendee, but she documented everything (Theoharis 2013, 40).

Rosa Parks's time at Highlander was very different from her typical life in Montgomery. When it came time to leave the school, she wanted to see her family, but she lamented going back to her assistant tailor job at Montgomery Fair. Every day at work, Parks had to "be smiling and polite no matter how rudely you were treated." What's more, her trips to and from work often entailed riding the city buses, where she had to endure untenable segregation rules. Rosa Parks maintained hope that race relations would change in Montgomery, but she could not foresee that this change would begin soon and that her rebellion would be the catalyst for this transformation.

7

Battle on the Bus

"There were rules regarding racial segregation. The white passengers would occupy the front of the bus and Negro in the back. There actually was no violation of the city ordinance in my arrest[.] [B]ut . . . I refused to obey the bus drivers who had police power to rearrange seating to have you stand to prevent the inconvenience of a white passenger[.] I want to make it very clear, however, I was not sitting in the white section or the very front of the bus, but the first seat right back of where we were supposed to be occupying. But many people did say that I had taken the front seat of the bus which was a . . . misunderstanding" (Parks, Horton, and Nixon 1973).

"[W]hen I refused to obey him when he asked that I stand, and when the, all of the front seats in the bus were occupied by white passengers, the driver wanted four people, a man in the seat with me and two women across the aisle, to stand in order for this white man to be accommodated with a seat. The other three people did stand up and I when I refused to stand up, the policemen were called, two came, placed me under arrest and had me taken to jail" (Parks, Horton, and Nixon 1973).

For Rosa Louise Parks, the time spent at the Highlander Folk School in the summer of 1955 sharpened her focus and strengthened her resolved. At Highlander, a school in Monteagle, Tennessee, that focused on training people to battle civil rights violations, Parks experienced firsthand what it could be like to live, work, and learn side by side with whites. The workshop she attended, "Racial Desegregation: Implementing the Supreme Court

Decision," focused on desegregation efforts across the South. In all, twenty cities or communities sent representatives to this workshop—forty-eight people in all. Rosa Parks represented the city of Montgomery, Alabama, and more specifically the NAACP Youth Council of Montgomery. She returned to her home city, ready to force desegregation there, and Rosa had a particular eye toward ways to empower and support local youth.

Earlier that year, Montgomery police had arrested fifteen-year-old Claudette Colvin for refusing to relinquish her seat on a Montgomery bus. Like Rosa Parks months later, Colvin was sitting in the black section of the bus when police took her into custody on the afternoon of March 2, 1955. Colvin, an "A" student at Booker T. Washington High School, sat "left . . . of the rear door" of a crowded bus that Friday (City of Montgomery Police Department 1955). Jo Ann Gibson Robinson, former Women's Political Council (WPC) president and prominent civil rights activist, remembered Colvin as "quiet, well-mannered, neat, clean, intelligent, pretty and deeply religious" in her memoirs on the Montgomery Bus Boycott (Robinson 1987, 37). Though gendered in tone, the references to Colvin's appearance and manners corresponding to prevailing views of how women should look and act in 1950s America, Robinson's recollections show the fifteen-year-old in a favorable light.

That day, the bus was so crowded that some of the passengers, white and black, had to stand, and the aisles filled with bodies with each stop. Colvin sat with a pregnant African American woman, but two white women sat across the aisle in the same row. Montgomery's unwritten segregation laws prohibited blacks from sitting in the same row as whites on the buses, and the bus driver, Robert Cleere, demanded that the two African American women relinquish their seats in compliance with the de facto practice. After some threats and bullying from Cleere, the pregnant woman vacated her seat, leaving Colvin the primary target of the driver's anger. There were no empty seats on the bus at this time, and the actual law in Montgomery required black people to relinquish their seats only if there were another seat available. This rarely remembered caveat to the segregation laws meant Colvin was adhering to the law when she refused to give up her seat.

Black Montgomerians secured this amendment to the segregation law shortly after city officials instituted the law in 1900. At that time, blacks staged a boycott that won from officials the amendment that "no rider had to surrender a seat unless another was available" (Theoharis 2013, 47). Cleere, like many other drivers, ignored this part of the law, and countless black Montgomerians experienced abuse, verbal or otherwise, on the bus lines. Some of these abuses led to physical altercations. Glenda Gilmore recounted one incident where a "local black GI, home on leave, sat down in a front seat, [and] the bus driver threw him off the bus and shot him in the leg" (Gilmore 2009, 376). The physical and psychological toll of these injustices were real and immeasurable. The WPC worked to determine these outcomes, and found that "all the pent-up emotions resulting from bitter experiences on local transportation lines often were released upon husbands, wives, or children, resulting in injuries that necessitated hospital care" (Robinson 1987, 36) It is no wonder when black women endured constant verbal assault, called "'black nigger,' 'heifers,' 'whores' and so on" when they rode the buses (Robinson 1987, 36). Black men faced similar ridicule and derision, so much so that Raymond Parks determined to stop riding the buses even before Rosa Parks's arrest.

Further complicating the Colvin situation, when the driver made his initial demand, the aisles were so crowded that Colvin would have some difficulty vacating her space (Robinson 1987, 38). Sensing the impending conflict, however, some African Americans chose to vacate the bus rather than experience or even bear witness to such unpleasantness. As the bus emptied of blacks unwilling to risk white backlash, and as seated African Americans vacated their seats for standing whites to occupy, Claudette Colvin sat resolute. Fully enraged now, the white bus driver notified the police, and they came to deal with Colvin. The arrest report described that Colvin "struggled off the bus and all the way to the police car. Aft we got her in the police car she kicked and scratched me on the hand, also kicked me in the stomach" (City of Montgomery Police Department 1955). Police charged her with "misconduct, resisting arrest, and violating the city segregation laws" (Robinson 1987, 38–39). What the police report did not include, and what Colvin remembered, is that the driver said, "I've had trouble with that 'thing' before" (Hoose 2009, 31). The dehumanization of Claudette Colvin exhibited by this statement was sadly commonplace in Montgomery society. White supremacy ruled the day, and blacks, feeling the constant effects of white brutality, wanted to fight back.

Jo Ann Robinson recounted the effects of the Colvin arrest: "The news traveled fast. In a few hours every Negro youngster on the streets discussed Claudette's arrest. Telephones rang. Clubs called special meetings and discussed the event with some degree of alarm. Mothers expressed concern about permitting their children on the buses. Men instructed their wives to walk or to share rides in neighbors' autos" (Robinson 1987, 39).

Clearly, the Colvin arrest shook the black community, and black Montgomerians took action. Some Montgomerians felt the Colvin case could be the break they needed in order to break down white supremacy on the buses, and a group petitioned bus and city officials for comprehensive reform in transportation laws and practices. Boycott was on the minds of many as local black organizations met to discuss Colvin. The Robinson-led WPC was poised for a boycott. Robinson recalled that "the question of boycotting came up again and loomed in the minds of thousands of black people. . . . The women felt not that their cup of tolerance was overflowing, but that it had overflowed; they simply could not take anymore" (Robinson 1987, 39). In fact, Robinson had threatened a boycott the year before in a letter to the mayor, Tacky Gayle (Theoharis 2013, 52). She realized that the buses "could not possibly operate" without black ridership because blacks made up three-quarters of the bus patrons (Theoharis 2013, 52). Yet, some black Montgomerians doubted that a bus boycott would change the state of race relations in the city, and those who were ready to boycott knew it would take the entirety of the black population to make this successful.

Some also doubted whether Claudette Colvin was the right symbol for a movement. Many worried that she was too young and that she would fall victim to violence if her arrest were the source of the boycott. People were wary of battling with the city government, and none of the sixty-eight-odd black organizations in the city issued a unifying call to boycott after the Colvin arrest. That did not mean that groups of black Montgomerians did not mobilize around Colvin, however. Although there was no collective boycott, black leaders did come together because "a period of unrest began that permeated the thoughts of blacks" (Robinson 1987, 40). Robinson remembered that the leaders of the black organizations decided to form a sort of steering committee, with two representatives from each organiza-tion. That body elected Rufus Lewis as their president. Lewis, a former teacher and football coach at Alabama State, joined his in-laws' family funeral home business, Ross and Clayton Funeral Home. Self-employment allowed Lewis to agitate without fear of losing his job—something rare for black Montgomerians—and he was an ideal candidate to lead this com-mittee of black organizations.

Rosa Parks did not speak about Colvin much in her autobiography, *Rosa Parks: My Story*, but the case had a profound impact on her. She told Studs Terkel, "When this news came to me I felt that much of what we had done in committees, meetings and other means drawing up petitions and plac-ing them in the hands of officials without any results was just a brush-off. I felt that a lot of time and effort had been wasted and that it was time to demonstrate and act in whatever way we could to make known that we would no longer accept the way that we had been treated as a people" (Parks, Horton, and Nixon 1973).

She recalled, in the wake of Colvin's arrest, "I worked very diligently with the Youth Council of the NAACP and of the few young people that I could get to pay attention to what I was trying to get them to see about desegregating the schools and other public facilities. I wanted our leaders there to organize and be strong enough to back up or support any young person who would be a litigant if they should take some action in protest to segregation and mistreatment" (Parks, Horton and Nixon 1973).

Black leaders, buoyed by the formation of the steering committee and emboldened by the formation of the Interdenominational Ministerial

Alliance, formed by Montgomery's black ministers to push for racial justice, developed a special committee to consult with Commissioner David Birmingham about bus segregation issues. Birmingham oversaw the police, so he was a logical person to lobby for reform. Jo Ann Robinson remembered the commissioner as a "gentleman, and honest man, and a Christian" (Robinson 1987, 40–41). Birmingham responded to the lobbying by calling a meeting between activists, police, and the bus company. Cleere requested to be at the meeting, but he never showed up. J. H. Bagley, bus company manager, represented the transportation group. Attending this meeting, Jo Ann Robinson recalled, "The police officers admitted that, in arresting the girl, they had acted under the command of the driver . . . [and] . . . Bagley stated that the driver had admitted to him that the girl had been sitting in the back and that here were no other seats available at the time" (Robinson 1987, 41). Blacks left this meeting feeling confident that Claudette Colvin acted within her rights and that she would be absolved of any wrongdoing resulting from the bus incident. Moreover, attorneys for the represented parties planned to redefine the law "so that all would know what the law meant for everyone" (Robinson 1987, 41).

Despite the feeling of goodwill that existed after the meeting, when the Colvin case came to court, black Montgomerians learned she was being tried under state rather than city law. The state law did not have a provision allowing her to remain in her seat if there were no other seats available. Robinson recollected, "Instead of being exonerated as we anticipated, Claudette Colvin was found guilty" (Robinson 1987, 42). Once again, white supremacist officials thwarted any efforts toward black civil rights. Claudette Colvin, who entered the court feeling calm, issued "agonizing sobs [that] penetrated the atmosphere of the courthouse" at the verdict, and many others "brushed away their own tears," according to Robinson (Robinson 1987, 42).

The Colvin verdict further mobilized black Montgomery. Support, financial and otherwise, also poured in from across the country. Many blacks in Montgomery determined not to ride the buses in the wake of the verdict. While this agitation soon waned, it lay important groundwork for the eventual 381-day boycott ushered in by Rosa Parks's December 1, 1955, arrest. Meanwhile, black activists planned Colvin's appeal and continued to consider mounting a massive protest. Rosa Parks kept some distance from all of these actions even though, as leader of the NAACP Youth Council, a group to which Colvin belonged, she was keenly aware of them. She recounted, "I didn't feel anything could be accomplished. I had decided that I would not go anywhere with a piece of paper in my hand asking white folks for any favors" (Parks 1992, 112). Rosa Parks saw petitions to grant reprieve from the current racial hierarchy as counterproductive because they did not force the question of the constitutionality of racial segregation and the fundamentality of black equality. Black self-determination did not require white approval or favors from white people. If the laws were going to change, it was going to occur because of a full acknowledgment of and an unwavering commitment to equal citizenship regardless of race.

Rosa Parks was tired of racial injustice, and she refused to settle for half measures. She, alongside other activists like Jo Ann Robinson and E. D. Nixon, considered taking Colvin's case to federal court. Rosa remembered sitting up with her grandfather as he wielded his shotgun ready to take out any Ku Klux Klan member foolish enough to threaten his family. She heard how Claudette Colvin's father "stayed up all night long with his shotgun. We all stayed up. The neighbors facing the highway kept watch" (Theoharis 2013, 54). For Rosa Parks, the Colvin case hit close to home, and it is likely that experiences from her own childhood resurfaced in stark relief.

Much debate revolved around taking Colvin's case to the federal level. Increasingly, activists felt she was not the right model case. As Jeanne Theoharis noted, some saw Colvin as "'feisty,' 'uncontrollable,' 'profane,' and 'emotional'" (Theoharis 2013, 57). These adjectives likely were euphemisms for her socioeconomic class. E. D. Nixon and Jo Ann Robinson, in particular, disagreed about Colvin. Nixon saw it as a poor test case, whereas Robinson wanted to carry Colvin to the federal courts. Eventually, Nixon's arguments won out, and local activists began to distance themselves from Colvin. When Nixon and others learned she was pregnant and soon to be an unwed teenage mother, there was no longer any question about Colvin as test case. Parks recounted that black activists ended their work with Colvin because "if the white press got hold of that information, they would have a field day. They'd call her a bad girl, and her case wouldn't have a chance. So the decision was made to wait until we had a plaintiff who was more upstanding before we went ahead and invested any more time and effort and money" (Parks 1992, 112). Theoharis argued that leaders already determined Colvin was out even before learning of her pregnancy, and the impregnation served as an excuse for the previous decision (Theoharis 2013, 58). The sad reality of assumed black immorality and the equally troubling idealizing of female chastity made Claudette Colvin a difficult case to stomach in light of 1950s gender and racial norms. Colvin later reflected on this situation, "I'm not disappointed. Let the people know Rosa Parks was the right person for the boycott. But also let them know that the attorneys took four other women to the Supreme Court to challenge the law that led to the end of segregation" (*Chicago Tribune* 2005). Rosa Parks kept tabs on Colvin even after black leaders abandoned the case. She also continued to pressed NAACP Youth Council members to challenge segregation at every turn, because white supremacist rule meant that white people could attack black bodies with abandon anytime they saw fit to do so.

Rosa Parks and the nation bore witness to the horrid effect of white supremacy on black bodies in September of 1955 when news broke of the lynching of Chicago youth Emmett Louis Till. Fourteen-year-old Emmett Till left his mother's Chicago home on August 20, 1955, to vacation with his great-uncle Mose Wright and his family in Mississippi. Till spent several uneventful days playing with his cousins and learning to pick cotton. At the end of the week, he and some relatives traveled to the nearby whistle-stop town of Money, Mississippi, to shop. Reports about what happened differ, but it is commonly agreed upon that Till bought bubble gum and then whistled at Carolyn Bryant, a white woman who was tending the Bryant family store while her husband was out of town making deliveries. In the predawn hours of Sunday morning, August 28, 1955, half-brothers Roy Bryant and J. W. Milam, along with others, traveled to Mose Wright's house and kidnapped Emmett Till. They took him to the plantation managed by another brother, Leslie Milam, and proceeded to beat him without mercy. During the relentless beating, Milam shot Emmett Till in the head. Later, the perpetrators took the body to the Tallahatchie River and dumped him into the water, weighed down by a cotton gin fan tied to his body with barbed wire. On August 31, 1955, a fisherman saw Emmett Till's feet sticking up out of the water and contacted the county sheriff's office. The sheriff, in turn, retrieved the body and attempted to bury the bloated and waterlogged remains in an unmarked grave at a local black cemetery. Till's relatives stopped the burial and ensured that the body was returned to Chicago, where his mother insisted that the pine box containing her son's remains be opened. She viewed the body, and, after hours of meticulous inspection, confirmed that it was that of Emmett Till.

Subsequently, Mamie Till-Mobley held a public open-casket wake and funeral. Her efforts memorialized the lynching and turned the public's critical eyes toward the state of Mississippi. Bryant and Milam, who had been questioned and arrested on August 29, 1955, were indicted by a grand jury and stood trial on the charge of murder. The murder trial began with jury selection on September 19, 1955. During the five-day trial, the jury heard testimony from black Mississippians Mose Wright, Add Reed, and Willie Reed and black Chicagoan Mamie Till-Mobley for the prosecution. The defense presented testimony from Tallahatchie County Sheriff H. C. Strider and an expert witness who both claimed there was too much decomposition for a body that was only in the river for three days. Moreover, Strider argued the body was too large to be that of a fourteen-year-old boy. The defense also called Carolyn Bryant to the witness stand, but the presiding judge, Curtis Swango, dismissed the jury during her testimony and later ruled that the jury would not hear her account. Based on the testimony and closing arguments, the jury retired to discuss the case. After roughly an hour of deliberation, the jury returned a verdict of not guilty, but Bryant and Milam still faced kidnapping charges in nearby Leflore County. In November 1955, Roy Bryant and J. W. Milam appeared before a grand jury in Leflore County on the charge of kidnapping, but the panel did not indict.

Like countless other Americans, and particularly African Americans, Rosa Parks closely followed the developments in the lynching of Emmett Till through the black press. She had recently returned from Highlander Folk School, refreshed and energized to continue her fight for racial justice through her work with the youth, and the brutal murder of young Emmett Till had a profound effect on her. She would later tell her good friend, Reverend Jesse Jackson Sr., "When I thought about Emmett Till, I could not go to the back of the bus" (Jackson 2005, 20). The mid-1950s was the high-point of per-capita newspaper circulation, and magazine circulation was high. The Johnson Company publications *Ebony* and *Jet* boasted a particularly strong readership. With television news only broadcasting for fifteen minutes, the television networks could not cover the Till lynching in as much detail as newspapers and magazines. By all accounts, there were more print media employees at the trial than radio and television employees, so the print had an advantage of sheer numbers when covering Till.

Rosa Parks understood the power of the print media to shape the news. Upon her return from Highlander the *Montgomery Advertiser* and *Alabama Journal* published a press release about the workshop Parks attended. Historian Jeanne Theoharis believes Parks possibly wrote the press release, and she points to the fact that the piece mentioned "Mrs. Rosa L. Parks attended the workshop from Montgomery as a representative of the NAACP Youth Council" (Theoharis 2013, 41). So, Rosa Parks was well-versed in the power of the media, and she read the papers voraciously, having grown up in a household that valued the written work. When she saw the photo of Emmett Till's brutalized body on the pages of *Jet* magazine, Parks wept with outrage and grief (Theoharis 2013, 43).

John H. Johnson, founder of *Jet* and *Ebony* magazines, envisioned publications that would keep the black community informed. To that end, he started *Ebony* in 1945 and *Jet* six years later. The magazines were instant hits, and Johnson served as the publisher of both magazines in 1955. Born in Arkansas in 1918, Johnson's father died in a work accident when Johnson was young, leaving his mother in charge of the family. She worked tirelessly to save money so that the family could move from the blatant white supremacy in the South to the growing Northern Black neighborhood in Chicago's South Side. After two years of saving, the family made the trek to Chicago, Illinois. Johnson remained in the Windy City, and he based his publication empire there. Chicago-based, Johnson Publication was at the center of the events surrounding the Emmett Till lynching, and they chose *Jet* magazine as the vehicle for the coverage.

Although a handful of newspapers and magazines printed pictures of Emmett Till's mutilated body, when people recall the photo, they almost exclusively attribute it to *Jet* magazine. Johnson Publication's staff writer Simeon Booker, a former Neiman Fellowship winner who joined the staff of *Jet* in 1953, covered the story for *Jet*. As he reported on the lynching and aftermath, Booker also served as an important liaison between the black press and the NAACP national office. Booker told NAACP Executive Secretary Roy Wilkins that black reporters could help the NAACP "raise more money and also could inform more people of the intimate details of the trial." Additionally, Booker offered to make photos from the Till lynching available for publication by the NAACP. This gesture came in large part because of the request by Mamie Till-Mobley that the photos "be given wide publication" (Booker 1955). It was this sharing of information and combining of efforts that made the Till case such a media firestorm and kept Emmett Till in the national spotlight long after his body was pulled from the Tallahatchie River.

Like the Scottsboro Boys, Recy Taylor, Jeremiah Reeves, Claudette Colvin, and countless other African Americans abused by white supremacy, Emmett Till presented the NAACP national headquarters with a difficult decision. Some leaders wanted to foreground the Till lynching as a model of the evils of white supremacy, but others worried that the alleged sexual undertones of the event—in her trial testimony, Carolyn Bryant accused Till of accosting her and making sexual advances—evoked images the organization wanted to avoid. Still, the NAACP chose to use the Till lynching, and they hurled scathing attacks against the Southern white establishment, including a pointed expose, "M is for Mississippi and Murder." The national office also funded speaking tours to raise awareness about the Till lynching. Emmett Till's mother, Mamie Till-Mobley, was a frequent presenter until disagreements over finances that arose in November of 1955 created a rift in their partnership. This schism left the NAACP searching for a new violation to spotlight, and Rosa Parks's arrest on Thursday afternoon December 1, 1955, was the solution.

Many in Montgomery were ready for action. The arrest of Claudette Colvin in March of 1955 raise the ire of black Montgomerians. Compounding the situation, white Montgomery's response to the Colvin case, the *Brown* decisions, and increased agitation on the part of the African American community was to step up the oppression. White Citizens Councils begun in Mississippi in 1954 as a white supremacist backlash to the *Brown* decision fanned the flames of racial tension. Civil rights activist Medgar Evers said of the Citizens Councils that they "may not be the old Klan in a bedsheet. It looks more like a new one in a tuxedo" (Muller 1955, A:49). In 1955 alone, Claudette Colvin (March 2), Aurelia S. Browder (April 29), Mary Louise Smith (October 16), and Susie McDonald (October 21) were arrested for perceived infractions on Montgomery buses (Montgomery Bus Boycott: Biographical Sketch n.d.). Perception was one of the most oppressive aspects of Southern culture. Many of the rules and norms were unwritten, subjective, leaving African Americans constantly guessing what white people wanted, and whites would frequently cry foul or accuse them of a crime. The bus laws were case in point. African Americans did not have to vacate their seats if there were no other seats available, but many white bus drivers were either ignorant of or overlook that part of the law. Power was at stake, and white people lorded that power over black people by constantly shifting and reinterpreting the written law. Rosa Parks recounted, "'Whites would accuse you of causing trouble when all you were doing was acting like a normal human being instead of cringing" (Theoharis 2013, 46). Jo Ann Robinson estimated that "about three out of five [black riders] had suffered some unhappy experience on the public transportation lines" (Robinson 1987, 43).

Visiting Montgomery in November of 1955, New York congressman Adam Clayton Powell encouraged blacks there that they could counter white supremacy with their own economic pressures (Theoharis 2013, 44). A guest of E. D. Nixon, Powell met with Nixon, Parks, and other Montgomery activist during his stay. Later that month, Dr. T. R. M. Howard, a Mississippi activist, delivered a keynote address at a rally decrying the lynching of Emmett Till and two others, George Lee and Lamar Smith (Theoharis 2013, 45). For her part, Rosa Parks was busy organizing a youth workshop to be held on December 3 at Alabama State under the auspices of the NAACP Youth Council.

With this workshop on her mind, Rosa Parks boarded the Cleveland Avenue city bus at Court Square, headed home after work. The workshop

SOUTHERN WHITE POLITICS

For over a century, Southern Congressmen had used filibusters, or making speeches on the floor of Congress ad infinitum, to prevent civil rights legislation from coming to a vote in the Senate and House of Representatives. In 1828, South Carolina Democrat John C. Calhoun wrote anonymously in the *South Carolina Exposition and Protest* that states had the right to nullify federal law if the citizens felt the law was not in keeping with the tradition of the state. Certainly, white Southerners did not feel the *Brown* decision was in line with Southern ideology, so in 1956, eighty-three Congressmen from Mississippi, Louisiana, Georgia, South Carolina, Florida, Tennessee, Alabama, North Carolina, and Arkansas signed the *Southern Manifesto*, in which they vowed not to abide by the *Brown* decision.

preoccupied her mind, for Parks was trying to secure permission from college president H. Councill Trenholm, to use a building at Alabama State for this Saturday workshop. Additionally, Parks was thinking about the NAACP Senior Branch elections coming the following week. For these reasons, she was not paying attention to the driver of the bus when she boarded and paid her fare. Such vigilance was common among African Americans. The wrong bus and the wrong driver could mean misery, for each driver had their own rules and the blanket authority to administer those rules at will.

Jeanne Theoharis described how Parks, "deciding to wait for a less crowded bus, . . . picked up a few things at Lee's Cut-Rate Drug" (Theoharis 2013, 61). Around 5:30 p.m., she finally boarded a bus driven by James Blake. Blake was the same driver who, in 1943, had another altercation with Parks and threw her off the bus. Rosa remembered usually avoiding Blake-driven buses, choosing rather to wait for the next transport than to open herself up to further torture from this man. As she had already paid her toll by the time she paid any attention to the driver, Rosa decided to chance it and ride on this bus. Rosa Parks recalled Blake as "tall and heavy, with red, rough-looking skin. And he was still mean-looking" (Parks 1992, 113). During the 1943 incident, Parks feared Blake was going to hit her, so hot was the anger in his face. On this December 1955 day, Blake was equally heated, and he hurled thinly veiled threats against black passengers, including Rosa Parks.

Parks found a vacant seat in the middle of the bus when she boarded, even though there were already black people standing in the aisle. Later, she speculated that maybe the standing patrons noticed her and left the seat open for her. After all, Parks was "respected in all black circles," according to Jo Ann Robinson (Robinson 1987, 43; Parks 1992, 115). She sat in the aisle seat next to a black male, and there were two black females across the aisle. Contrary to some popular narratives of the incident, Parks was not sitting in the front of the bus, the area reserved for white passengers. She was squarely in the black section, back from the first ten seats that made up the white section of every bus. Court exhibit C in the case of *Browder v. Gayle* identified Parks as sitting in the first row behind the reserved section.

Traveling one stop to the Empire Theater, the bus began to fill with white riders, and one white man remained standing after the whites-only seats became occupied. Blake noticed this fact and immediately asked the black people in Rosa's row to stand and make room for the white passenger. Parks remembered, "The driver looked back and noticed the man standing. Then he looked back at us. He said, 'Let me have those front seats'" (Parks 1992, 115). Blake's reference to "front seats" likely meant the front seats in the black section, but his wording also spoke to the conditionality of seating on buses. If the reserved ten seats filled, then row by row, the black sections of the bus became effectively part of the white section. This is why, even though Blake only needed one seat to accommodate the standing white man, he asked for passengers in Rosa's row to relinquish the entire row of seating. De-facto Montgomery law prohibited blacks and whites from sitting in the same row of a bus. That would be too much like equality for the white establishment. No one in Parks's row moved upon first request, and Blake became more assertive. Rosa Parks remembered the driver threatening, "'Y'all better make it light on yourselves and let me have those seats'" (Parks 1992, 115). At this second exclamation, the other three people in Parks's row stood and relinquished their seats. Still, Rosa Parks sat because she could not see how standing up was going to 'make it light' for me" (Parks 1992, 115). At least one witness remembered Blake being much more confrontational and demeaning, yelling, "'Niggers, move back,'" to Parks and her row mates (Hendrickson 1989).

Armed and imbued with police powers James Blake had a history of abusing black passengers. When Blake asked the second time that black passengers in Rosa's row relocate, three of the four relinquished their seats. Rosa, who was seated in the aisle seat, moved her legs so that the man seated next to her could exit the row. Rosa refused to get up, choosing rather to slide over to the window seat once the male passenger vacated that seat. Parks recalled in her memoirs, "The more we gave in and complied, the worse they treated us" (Parks 1992, 115). Many thoughts ran through her head as she took her stand. She thought of her grandfather wielding his shotgun to ward off the Ku Klux Klan. Rosa thought of the brutalized body of fourteen-year-old Emmett Louis Till. Claudette Colvin and the other women arrested that year also influenced Rosa Parks. Her time at Highlander, where she workshopped with others about how to break down white supremacist segregation undergirded her choice. So many things drove Rosa Parks to stay seated amid threats from the bus driver and the police.

Following the arrest, a popular narrative developed that Rosa Parks, a quiet, unassuming seamstress, was just too tired to get out of her seat. Scholars, activists, and cultural analysts framed this December day as "one solitary act on the bus" by a "simple seamstress" who was "'quiet,' 'humble,' 'dignified,' 'soft-spoken,' and 'not angry'" (Theoharis 2013, xxii–xxiii). This presentation of Parks blots out her life of activism ahead of her bus stand, and that activism motivated her to stay in her seat. Parks remained resolute in her decision even though other African Americans chose to exit the bus amid the brewing controversy. Parks recalled, "Not everyone got off the bus, but everybody was very quiet" (Parks 1992, 116–117).

When Rosa Parks refused a third command to get out of her seat, James Blake told her, "Well, I'm going to have you arrested," to which Rosa responded, "You may do that" (Parks 1992, 116). As Jeanne Theoharis further highlighted, Rosa told Blake, "I got on first and paid the same fare, and I didn't think it was right for me to have to stand so someone else who got on later could sit down" (Theoharis 2013, 63). She recalled, "My convictions meant much to me. . . . Over the years, I have been rebelling against second-class citizenship. It didn't begin when I was arrested" (Theoharis 2013, 68).

James Blake responded to Rosa Parks's resistance by leaving the bus to call his supervisor from a pay phone. The supervisor instructed Blake to exercise his powers and throw her off the bus. Blake then called the police. Officers Day and Mixon responded to the call. One of the officers asked her why she would not relinquish her seat, and the resolute Parks turned to the officer, asking in response, "Why do you all push us around?" (Theoharis 2013, 65). When the officers replied, "I don't know, but the law is the law, and you're under arrest," Parks remembered thinking, "Let us look at Jim Crow for the criminal he is and what he had done to one life multiplied millions of times over these United States" (Theoharis 2013, 66).

Ushering Parks off the bus and to the squad car, one officer grabbed her purse and the other her shopping bag. They asked James Blake if he really wanted to press charges against Rosa, and Blake told them he would come down to the station after his next bus run. James Blake would not let this presumed offense go unpunished, and E. D. Nixon later said that "that was the worst thing ever happened" to Blake. Surely, his response to *Washington Post* reporter Paul Hendrickson's impromptu 1989 interview showed that the altercation with Rosa Parks haunted his life. When Hendrickson, who traveled to Blake's home to interview the former driver, asked about the December day, Blake "seemed to crack open. 'No! No! It's over, get away,'" Blake said as he "bolted backward, as if stung by yellow jackets." Initially trying to bolt the door shut, Blake eventually did speak briefly with Hendrickson. James Blake lamented, "Okay, I'm going to tell you one thing about it, no, I'm going to tell you two things about it. The first is that niggers all up and around here were calling up my house for weeks after it happened, just any hour of the day or night, making the vilest threats to me and my wife and family you ever heard. You ever seen that in your history books? . . . The second thing . . . I wasn't trying to do anything to that Parks woman except do my job. She was in violation of the city codes. What was I supposed to do? That damn bus was full and she wouldn't move back. I had my orders. I had police powers—any driver for the city did" (Hendrickson 1989). Thirty-four years after Rosa Parks's historic arrest, James Blake continued to blame others for his choices, and he continued the racist practice of referring to Rosa Parks in the vilest of terms.

It is possible the arresting officers thought it a bad idea for Blake to press charges. Parks recalled one of the officers mentioned the NAACP when he asked if Blake wanted to press charges. Still, the officers had to take Rosa Parks to the station. Officers again asked her why she did not relinquish her seat during the drive to the station, but Parks remained silent. She did not speak until she arrived at City Hall to fill out paperwork ahead of her trip to the city jail on North Ripley Street. When she did speak, Parks asked for a drink of water, which was denied her. Having filed the necessary paperwork, the officers transported Parks to jail. She remembered being resigned when she arrived at jail, and she asked to make a telephone call. Rosa Parks already had a plan of action, even before she arrived at the city jail. Jeanne Theoharis wrote, "I told myself I wouldn't put up no fuss against them arresting me. . . . As soon as they arrested me, I knew, I'd call Mr. Nixon and let him know what had happened" (Theoharis 2013, 67).

E. D. Nixon already knew of the arrest. Bertha Butler learned of the arrest and notified Arlet, Nixon's wife, who subsequently told her husband. Primed for action, E. D. Nixon immediately phoned the jail to inquire about the charges. Denied any information, Nixon turned to legal counsel to get answers. He first called African American attorney Fred Gray, but he was unable to reach him. Nixon then turned to Clifford Durr, husband of Virginia Durr. A white couple, the Durrs were very active in civil rights issues. Clifford Durr called and learned that Parks was arrested for violating segregation laws, and he also got information about the bail.

Meanwhile, Rosa, who was finally able to make a phone call, reached her husband and mother on the line. Her mother peppered her with questions about her health and safety, and Rosa was able to assure her mother that she was in good health. Rosa Parks then spoke with Raymond, and he told her he would be right down to get her. She knew that it might take a little time, as Raymond did not own a car and would have to get a ride to the jail. Bail was also an issue, and Raymond called an acquaintance to secure bail money. Raymond Parks arrived at the jail just as his wife was exiting the building. E. D. Nixon and the Durrs beat him to the building, and Nixon had already posted the one-hundred-dollar bail necessary to release Rosa Parks.

Bail money was often hard to secure for underpaid African Americans, and while in jail, Rosa struck up a conversation with a widow who had been incarcerated for over two months. The woman, who fought back against her boyfriend who was abusing her, did not have anyone to post bail for her, and Parks agreed to contact the woman's brothers and notify them that their sister was in jail. Parks fulfilled her promise, and she saw the woman on the street a few days after (Theoharis 2013, 71; Parks 1992, 121–122).

Leaving the jail cell after posting bail, Rosa Parks first encountered Virginia Durr, who, crying, hugged Parks like a sister (Parks 1992, 123). Rosa Parks exited the building and walked down the steps, where she came across her husband who had just arrived. She rode home with Raymond in his friend's car, and Nixon and the Durrs followed to the Parks residence in a separate car. The group, along with Rosa's mother, spent the rest of the night discussing what the arrest could mean for challenging Montgomery's segregation laws. E. D. Nixon believed that "Jim Crow dropped in our lap just what we are looking for," and he worked to convince the others that the Parks case was the ideal test case to bring down racial segregation (Theoharis 2013, 72). Everyone in the Parks home that evening hated segregation, and they soon agreed that this was the moment and the case that would bring down Jim Crow. They did not yet know how the protest would take shape, but the group was committed to the fight. Black Montgomery was also ready to take on the battle. Discussions of boycotting and active resistance had consumed the thoughts of many local blacks since the arrest of Claudette Colvin, and the public was ready to take a stand behind the woman who remained in her seat.

8

The Montgomery Bus Boycott

"I did not want to be mistreated, I did not want to be deprived of a seat that I had paid for. It was just time . . . there was opportunity for me to take a stand to express the way I felt about being treated in that manner. I had not planned to get arrested. I had plenty to do without having to end up in jail. But when I had to face that decision, I didn't hesitate to do so because I felt that we had endured that too long. The more we gave in, the more we complied with that kind of treatment, the more oppressive it became" (Parks and Neary 1992).

When E. D. Nixon learned that police had arrested Rosa Parks, he immediately reached out to African American attorney Fred Gray, but Gray was out and did not answer the call. Later that evening, the attorney contacted Jo Ann Robinson, president of the Women's Political Council (WPC). Their conversation was precise, and by the end, Robinson had determined that it was time for the WPC to act, even if no one else was onboard. Gray asked if Robinson was ready, and she responded affirmatively. Robinson remembered she began sketching notes on the back of an envelope, prepared to make good on a boycott action her organization had been planning for months. "The Women's Political Council will not wait for Mrs. Parks's consent to call for a boycott of city buses. On Friday December 2, 1955, the women of Montgomery will call for a boycott to take place on Monday, December 5," the notes read. Meanwhile, at the Parks residence, Rosa, surrounded by her husband, her mother, Charles and Virginia Durr, and E. D. Nixon, came to a similar decision.

Robinson, who was in full action mode, contacted John Cannon, the chair of the business department at Alabama State, because he had access to the mimeograph machine used to make copies. Together with two of her students, Robinson spent the early morning hours of Friday, December 2, copying leaflets announcing a one-day bus boycott. Printed three to a page, the process of copying, cutting, and bundling the leaflets took until four o'clock Friday morning. Having produced thirty-five thousand copies of the announcement, Robinson and her two students dropped stacks of leaflets off at schools as well as "business places, storefronts, beauty parlors, beer halls, factories, barber shops, and every other available place" (Robinson 1987, 46–47). Remarkably, in the midst of all of this activity, Robinson was still able to contact WPC members and teach her 8:00 a.m. class. She recalled, "We weren't even tired or hungry" (Robinson 1987, 46). The prospect of breaking down Jim Crow energized Robinson and her students for the work ahead. This enthusiasm spread throughout black Montgomery. Robinson remembered, "Practically every black man, woman, and child in Montgomery knew the plan and was passing the word along. No one knew where the notices had come from or who had arranged for their circulation, and no one cared. Those who passed them on did so efficiently, quietly, and without comment. But, deep within the heart of every black person was a joy he or she dared not reveal" (Robinson 1987, 47).

Rosa Parks also felt the energy permeating Montgomery, and she believe her case could be the turning point: "I had no police record, I'd worked all my life, I wasn't pregnant with an illegitimate child. The white people couldn't point to me and say that there was anything I had done to deserve such treatment except to be born black" (Parks 1992, 125). The leaflet produced by Jo Ann Robinson and her two students captured this mood and this moment:

This is for Monday, December 5, 1955
   Another Negro woman had been arrested and thrown into jail because she refused to get up out of her seat on the bus and give it to a white person.

It is the second time since the Claudette Colvin case that a Negro woman has been arrested for the same thing. This has to be stopped.

Negroes have rights, too, for if Negroes did not ride the buses, they could not operate. Three-fourths of the riders are Negroes, yet we are arrested, or have to stand over empty seats. If we do not do something to stop these arrests, they will continue. The next time it may be you, or your daughter, or mother.

This woman's case will come up on Monday. We are therefore, asking every Negro to stay off the buses Monday in protest of the arrest and trial. Don't ride the buses to work, to town, to school, or anywhere on Monday.

You can afford to stay out of school for one day. If you work, take a cab, or walk. Please stay off all buses Monday. (Parks 1992, 127)

Rosa Parks went about her normal routine on Friday, December 2, except she took a taxicab to work rather than ride the bus. John Ball, who was head of men's alteration at Montgomery Fair, where she worked, showed surprise when she arrived at work for the day. He expected Rosa to be "a nervous wreck" and stay home that day. Rosa shocked Ball when she responded, "Why should going to jail make a nervous wreck out of me?" (Parks 1992, 128–129). The arrest and jailing did affect Rosa, however; she recalled, "I didn't realize how much being in jail had upset me until I got out," as she reflected on the day's experience after returning home. However, she was not shaken or cowed. She was determined that this event would not cause her to live in fear. Her faith in God and her belief that she was doing what was right sustained her, as did the support of her family and friends. Following her routine, she took her lunch break at the law office of Fred Gray. Rosa frequently assisted Gray during her lunch, minding the office and answering the phones so that the attorney could run errands. The day after her arrest, the office "was like a beehive," described Parks. "People were calling and dropping by to ask about the boycott and the meeting the ministers had called for that night" (Parks 1992, 129).

Montgomery was changing, and Rosa could feel it. Friday evening, she went to Dexter Avenue Baptist Church, pastored by Dr. Martin Luther King Jr., for a meeting about the impending boycott. She recalled some in attendance had reservations about the collective protest, even after she recounted her arrest story. Parks recalled that many of the clergy left the meeting in the midst of the discussion, but those who stayed largely determined to preach about the arrest and boycott in their Sunday sermons. The group also decided to meet again on Monday, December 5, to discuss the effectiveness of the daylong boycott and plan next steps. A group at the meeting also created a shorter version of the leaflet developed under the leadership of Jo Ann Robinson. The condensed version read:

> Don't ride the bus to work, to town, to school, or any place on Monday, December 5.
>
> Another Negro woman has been arrested and put in jail because she refused to give up her bus seat.
>
> Don't ride the bus to work, to town, to school, or anywhere on Monday. If you work, take a cab, or share a ride, or walk.
>
> Come to a mass meeting, Monday at 7:00 P.M., at the Holt Street Baptist Church for further information. (Parks 1992, 130)

After a very busy Friday, Rosa Parks made final preparations for the NAACP Youth Council workshop planned for the following day. Having secured the use of a building at Alabama State, she looked forward to a successful, well-attended event. Much to her dismay, as the workshop began, Parks saw that only five youths had attended. She put a great deal of effort and planning into this workshop, and Rosa began to think that the lack of interest was a harbinger of things to come on Monday during her trial and the one-day bus boycott. She had previously witnessed black Montgomerians choosing to stay home or otherwise out of the line of fire out of fear of white supremacist backlash. For her, the failure to draw a crowd to her workshop signaled business as usual in the city. Rosa saw Monday, however, that African Americans would take to the street in response to her arrest. Students took the day off school in support of their beloved mentor. One member of the Youth Council, Mary Frances, exclaimed, "They've messed with the wrong one now," and it became a chant echoing through the hundreds of Parks supporters. After her trial, Rosa came across another Youth Council member and asked why she had not attended the Saturday workshop. Her response riveted Rosa; the young girl said, "I had to be passing out those leaflets" (Parks, Horton, and Nixon 1973). In that moment, Rosa Parks understood two things. First, Montgomery, from the youth to the aged, were going to support this protest. Second, she had done her job well, for her Youth Council advisees "were wise enough to see that it was more important to stand on the street corners and pass these papers out to everyone who passed than to sit in a meeting and listen to someone speak" (Parks, Horton, and Nixon 1973). Rosa took joy in seeing that "we had to learn a great deal from the youth [because of the fact] that they themselves would not be riding the bus" (Parks, Horton, and Nixon 1973).

Monday was a watershed day for Rosa Parks, one when she saw a realization of much that she hoped and dreamed possible for Montgomery's black youth, and much of their response was due to her tireless mentoring and support. Montgomery's clergy also offered energizing and encouraging messages from pulpits across the city on Sunday, December 4. Jo Ann Robinson firmly believed that "the black ministers and their churches made the Montgomery Bus Boycott of 1955–1956 the success that it was." She recalled, "The ministers gave themselves, their time, their contributions, their minds, their prayers, and their leadership." Most of all, "They gave . . . confidence, faith in ourselves, faith in them and their leadership [and] that helped the congregations to support the movement" (Robinson 1987, 54). For a people so steeped in faith, "they would need moral support and Christian leadership" to pull off the boycott (Robinson 1987, 53). If the congregants did not feel they had the support of their clergy and their God, they might not have had the resolve to persevere. With clergy onboard, "the churches could serve as channels of communication, as well as altars where people could come for prayer and spiritual guidance," Robinson believed (Robinson 1987, 53).

Still, ministers would not automatically sign up for such a potentially dangerous mass uprising. Boycott organizers like Jo Ann Robinson needed to win the support of Montgomery ministers, and she knew where to go to announce the protest. Friday morning, December 2, a large group of clergy were meeting on Highland Avenue at Hilliard Chapel AME Zion Church. WPC officers learned of this meeting, and Robinson made sure there was an ample supply of leaflets waiting at the church, ensuring that "many of the ministers received their notices of the boycott at the same time, in the same place. They all felt equal, included, appreciated, [and] needed" (Robinson 1987, 53). Robinson's reflections on this strategic move showed that some jealousy and competition existed among Montgomery's "disciples of God," and she knew that those feelings, when channeled properly, could create peer pressure positively steering the ministers to support the boycott. For Robinson and others on the WPC executive board, the Friday morning meeting seemed like divine intervention (Robinson 1987, 53). E. D. Nixon had similar plans, and he phoned Reverend Ralph Abernathy and other clergy ahead of this Friday evening meeting (Parks 1992, 127). Dr. Martin Luther King Jr. was on that call list, and King was hesitant to commit when Nixon first called because he was relatively new to town and had a young family to protect. When Nixon phoned King a second time, the young minister assented, in part because Abernathy was onboard. Abernathy and King spent the rest of the day getting other clergy to consent to a meeting that evening.

Not all members of the black establishment were as eager to support the boycott, however. Robinson remembered, "When I returned to campus that Friday for my two o'clock class, after delivering the notices, I found a message from Dr. Trenholm, asking me to come to his office immediately" (Robinson 1992, 48). The president was angry that college resources went into publicizing the boycott, and he confronted Robinson on the subject. Trenholm worried about the reputation of the school he had dedicated his life to support, and he did not want negative publicity to endanger the institution or his role as its head. Robinson recalled being scared the he would fire her for entangling Alabama State in the bus boycott, but, to Trenholm's credit, he sat her down and asked her to recount the entire story. He even found a substitute teacher to conduct Robinson's class while she explained the bus boycott to him. As she recounted the events of Thursday, December 1, Trenholm softened his reaction. He did ask pointed questions, including if there were any available seats on the bus when Rosa Parks refused to move, and Robinson assured him that Parks was acting within the law because there were no other seats available. Satisfied that Robinson had not recklessly endangered the reputation of Alabama State, and feeling confident that Parks acted within her rights, Trenholm ended the meeting by telling the English professor, "Your group must continue to press for civil rights" (Robinson 1987, 50). He cautioned her, however, "to be careful, to work behind the scenes, not to involve the college, and not to neglect [her] responsibilities as a member of the faculty of Alabama State College" (Robinson 1987, 50).

Robinson had tremendous respect for Trenholm, and she understood how the boycott put him in a difficult position. She noted in her memoir that Trenholm gave his life for Alabama State, and he was dedicated to protecting the school and his legacy with the institution. Trenholm took over the college in 1925 while it was still a two-year junior college. Through his leadership, fundraising efforts, and personal financial sacrifices, the institution grew enrollment and began granting four-year degrees. Rosa Parks's own mother took continuing education classes there as part of the renewal process for her teaching certificate, and Rosa attended the laboratory school in her youth (Robinson 1987, 48–49). Trenholm maintained an air of indifference to the boycott, but at least he stayed "mentally and spiritually involved" (Robinson 1987, 50). Jo Ann Robinson provided nightly updates to the president at his request. In a rather strange tradition among black academics at the time, the WPC president would phone Trenholm's wife, Portia, and have her relay the news to Trenholm instead of calling him directly (Robinson 1987, 51).

In later years, Trenholm's reluctance to show vocal support for black uplift demonstrations would put him at odds with civil rights leaders like Martin Luther King, but he avoided ridicule in the early days of the bus boycott. In fact, city officials asked him to consult during the process of negotiations between the boycotters, the city, and the bus company, and Robinson noted, "Many times I went to him for advice for the WPC, and he never sent me away without submitting workable solutions to almost insoluble problems" (Robinson 1987, 50–52).

Clearly, Robinson's strategies worked, and the Friday evening meeting, attended by clergy and community leaders, was a direct result of the morning leaflet deposit. In all, Robinson estimated that over one hundred ministers and community leaders attended the Friday evening meeting. After a period of heated debate, meeting attendees began to mobilize the boycott. Many opposed to the bus boycott left the meeting early, and those left behind moved to organize and plan for the protest. Alfonso Campbell took leadership of the transportation committee charged with establishing alternatives for bus travel. This was one of the most important steps, for some black Montgomerians had too far to travel or were otherwise unable to get where they needed to go on Monday without using the buses. The group also planned the next meeting, an open assembly Monday evening at Holt Street Baptist Church, pastored by Reverend A. W. Wilson. They chose that location because of the church's capacity: "It had a large basement that accommodated hundreds, an even larger main auditorium, and an upstairs area as well. In addition, various smaller rooms were equipped with loudspeakers. Thus, thousands could fit within this one building. And around the building was a huge outdoor space. . . . Outside loudspeakers would be able to carry the message to those who could not squeeze into the church" (Robinson 1987, 56). It was unclear how much space would be needed, but the organizers planned for an enormous crowd. Robinson recalled that the Monday meeting would offer time to reflect on the one-day boycott and offer space for black Montgomerians to channel their anger into focused collective action. She believed, "It was a good thing . . . that the ministers had agreed to take over the boycott's leadership, to direct an emotional appeal for passive resistance" (Robinson 1987, 56).

Charged with shepherding black congregations in a segregated South, many clergy subscribed, at least in part, to what James H. Cone called *A Black Theology of Liberation*. Chiefly, "in a society where persons are oppressed because they are *black*, Christian theology must be *black theology*, a theology that is unreservedly identified with the goals of the oppressed and seeks to interpret the divine character of their struggle for liberation" (Cone 1970, ix). Cone extolled, "The function of theology is that of analyzing the meaning of that liberation for the oppressed so they can know that their struggle for political, social, and economic justice is consistent with the gospel of Jesus" (Cone 1970, ix). For Cone, and doubtlessly for many black Montgomerians, "any message that is not related to the liberation of the poor in society is not Christ's message [just as,] any message that is indifferent to the theme of liberation is not Christian theology" (Cone 1970, ix). Sunday, December 4, 1955, was a test for these clergy. Would they proceed with business as usual, or would they embolden their flock to stand up against racial injustice?

At Dexter Avenue Baptist Church, Reverend Martin Luther King Jr. asked his congregants to "challenge 'the iron feet of oppression'" (Theoharis 2013, 86). Reverend Ralph Abernathy too preached a message of economic self-determination via the boycott. Rosa Parks's friend, Pastor Robert Graetz, a white minister who shepherded the black congregation at Trinity Lutheran Church where Rosa Parks held Youth Council meetings, also preached a black liberation message. As Jeanne Theoharis recounted, Graetz "told his black congregation of his plans to participate in the boycott and to make his own car available to help shuttle people around town, and urged his congregation to do the same" (Theoharis 2013, 86–87).

Publicity also came from an unlikely source: Montgomery's mainstream press. Before leaving town for a trip, E. D. Nixon, who worked on the train line as a Pullman porter, met with a local white reporter for the *Montgomery Advertiser* (Parks 1992, 127; Theoharis 2013, 82). The reporter, Joe Azbell, secured front-page space to print the entire boycott announcement produced by Jo Ann Robinson and her team. Jeanne Theoharis noted that Azbell was an opportunist rather than a race progressive, and his efforts to publicize the boycott were about getting an exclusive story rather than trying to uplift the black race (Theoharis 2013, 82, 270). Azbell's story, which ran on Sunday, was not exclusive, for the *Alabama Journal* had run an article the previous afternoon. According to Jo Ann Robinson, the paper learned of the boycott after an African American woman showed the leaflet to the white women who employed her. Robinson noted that "in spite of her concern over the plight of her black peers and without any sense of obligation to her people," this woman disclosed the heretofore secret bus boycott, and it "was only a matter of minutes before the bus company, the City Commission, the chief of police, and the press knew its contents" (Robinson 1987, 54–55). Local television and radio stations also carried the story, and E. D. Nixon reflected, "We couldn't have paid for the free publicity the white folks gave our boycott" (Theoharis 2013, 82; Robinson 1987, 55). Rather than dissuading the black populace as white people anticipated, this coverage served to inform all African Americans about the one-day boycott and embolden them to join in the fight. Robinson reflected, "The news that circulated through the newspapers, radio, television, and other channels of communication covered every possible isolated place not reached by the leaflets" (Robinson 1987, 55). Black Montgomery was poised for a revolution, and everyone was onboard with staying off the buses.

Rosa Parks remembered the dark sky as she readied herself on Monday morning, December 5, 1955. She faced her trial on charges of violating Montgomery's segregation laws. Others also woke with a sense of anticipation of what the date would bring. Jeanne Theoharis recounted that Martin Luther King Jr. and his wife, Coretta, rose early that morning as well; the young minister "believed if 60 percent of the black community stayed off the bus, the protest would be a success" (Theoharis 2013, 87). Jo Ann Robinson was elated to see nearly empty buses. Black Montgomery heeded the call, and some black domestic workers notified their white employers earlier in the weekend that they would not work on Monday. Aware of this intended work stoppage, Montgomery's white officials mobilized the police force to escort the buses, assuming that the black domestic workers chose to call out because they feared violence from other black people if they crossed the boycott line and rode the bus to work. That morning, two motorcycled officers followed every Montgomery bus servicing black communities under orders to "protect Negro riders" (Robinson 1987, 57). What the white leaders in Montgomery did not realize was that black Montgomery had reached a tipping point, and the community was united in their support of the one-day bus boycott. An article entitled "Extra Police Set for Patrol Work in Trolley Boycott" in the *Montgomery Adviser* Monday morning offered that "Negro goon squads" reportedly had been organized to intimidate other Negroes who rode buses on Monday. The articled reassured its readers, "The threat was being met by city authorities with the promise to 'call out every city policeman and every reserve policeman, if necessary, to maintain law and order'" (Robinson 1987, 57). White Montgomerians did not get it. This was a massive uprising orchestrated by a unified black community, and the foreseen threat came from white supremacy, not any alleged "Negro goon squad." In fact, the police escort had the opposite effect of what was intended. Rosa recalled that "some of the people who didn't know what was going on thought the police were there to arrest them for riding the buses, not to protect them" (Parks 1992, 131).

The one-day boycott was a resounding success. Black leaders stood in awe at the courage and resolve of the black community. E. D. Nixon commented, "We surprised ourselves" (Parks 1992, 132). For her part, Rosa Parks found the day, "'gratifying' and unbelievable' [seeing how] people 'were willing to make the sacrifice to let it be known that they would be free from this oppression'" (Theoharis 2013, 87). She reflected, "As I look back on those days, it's just like a dream. The only thing that bothered me was that we waited so long to make this protest" (Theoharis 2013, 87). Jo Ann Robinson said of the protest that "nary a colored soul [paid] a single fare. Instead, hundreds of people were walking or boarding taxis or private cars" (Robinson 1987, 58). The public was energized by events, and the *Montgomery Advertiser* later ran an article describing how a "seventy-two-year-old man who had ridden the bus for thirty or forty years sat on his front porch and laughed heartily every time a bus drove by." Another woman covered in the article was "gleeful that the buses were driving by her house 'as naked as can be'" (Robinson 1987, 60). Perhaps the most poignant reflection came from a black Montgomery woman who caught a ride from one of the ministers as she walked across town. When the minister asked the woman if she were tired, she responded, "Well my body may be a bit tired, but for many years now my soul has been tired. Now my soul is resting. So I don't mind if my body is tired, because my soul is free" (Robinson 1987, 60). Many popular accounts of the Montgomery Bus Boycott attribute some or all of these words to Rosa Parks, and a narrative of a tired seamstress who made one uncharacteristically courageous act that set off a movement gained momentum. As the one-day boycott proved successful, and energy grew toward a sustained movement, others, predominately black men, stepped into the limelight. Such was the culture of gender roles within the black liberation movement. Leaders moved to frame the boycott, and that framing did not include foregrounding Rosa Parks's life of agitation and activism.

Leaders of the boycott felt it was imperative to frame the uprising as both unified and peaceful. They knew anything that could corroborate reports in the local mainstream press of "Negro goon squads" could sway popular opinion of the movement. White hegemony meant that white people had the power to dominate and control national narrative, particularly the narrative of race, and black organizations and individuals knew they had to be better than perfect to appear above reproach in the eyes of the white public. Black Montgomerians learned hard lessons from organizations like the NAACP, both at the local and national levels, throughout the century. From the Scottsboro Boys to Recy Taylor, Jeremiah Reeves, and Claudette Colvin, the NAACP either failed to secure justice or distanced themselves from the cases. Active in all of these cases, Rosa Parks knew the importance of image, and that is why she noted in her autobiography, "I had no police record, I'd worked all my life, I wasn't pregnant with an illegitimate child. The white people couldn't point to me and say that there was anything I had done to deserve such treatment except to be born black" (Parks 1992, 125).

Focusing on the peaceful nature of the one-day boycott, WPC President Jo Ann Robinson reflected that only one black person was arrested in connection to the protest. Fred Daniel, a nineteen-year-old young man, was joking with a group of African Americans at a bus stop, the group pretending they were going to board an oncoming bus. When the bus stopped to receive the passengers, the group demurred, and Daniel grabbed the arm of one of his friends to help her across the street. Motorcycle police, who were trailing every bus, pounced on Daniel and arrested him for allegedly preventing the woman from boarding the bus. The woman, by the name of Percival, rebuked the officers and explained that she had no intention of riding the city bus, so the police dropped the disorderly conduct charges and released Fred Daniel (Robinson 1987, 59).

Robinson reflected tongue-in-cheek that "that day was rough on the bus drivers. They complained to the police department that they were being "'persecuted and molested' in various places by colored children who ridiculed them and stuck out their tongues at them as they passed by" (Robinson 1987, 59). How ironic it must have seemed for black Montgomery that the same men who had abused, attacked, and derided them for decades on the city buses now claimed abuse as a result of the one-day bus boycott. White claims of black violence always met ready ears, and Montgomery officials ordered black school principals to "stop the children from gathering on corners and poking out their tongues at the embarrassed motormen" (Robinson 1987, 59). School officials heeded the order, but there is no evidence the requests changed the feeling of joviality the youth felt seeing black people stand up for their rights.

Whites would use any excuse to fire blacks, and open support of black resistance efforts was an unforgivable crime in the eyes of many white people. Jo Ann Robinson confronted these issues head-on when Alabama State president H. Councill Trenholm called the English professor into his office the day after she copied all of the leaflets. As unremarkable as this exchange between city officials and black educators may seem, it underscores the level of power whites had over blacks in Montgomery. As public employees, the black teachers and principals had to toe an uneasy line between supporting the black community uprising and maintaining their employment.

Even with this atmosphere of fear and intimidation, hundreds of supporters surrounded the courthouse and filled the halls of the building as Rosa Parks approached the doors. She was the star of the show at this moment, but a narrative of quietude and passivity would soon subsume her role in the boycott and the legacy of her decades of activism. Rosa and Raymond Parks met that morning with Attorney Fred Gray and E. D. Nixon in Gray's office before the group walked to the courthouse. Rosa recalled, "I was not nervous . . . I knew what I had to do" (Parks 1992, 132). She prepared well for the occasion, selecting an outfit "to reflect a dignified and proud citizenship [that was] an in-your-face challenge to the degradation that segregation had long proffered" (Theoharis 2013, 88). Her attire included "a straight, long-sleeved black dress with a white collar and cuffs, a small black velvet hat with pearls across the top, and a charcoal-gray coat" (Parks 1992, 132).

The trial did not last long, and Parks did not testify, but a white woman took the stand for the plaintiffs and claimed there were open seats on the bus that day. Appalled by that testimony, NAACP defense committee member Andy Wright told E. D. Nixon, "You can always find some damn white woman to lie." One need only look at the Scottsboro case or the trial of Jeremiah Reeves to find some justification for Wright's generalization. Rosa's attorneys entered a "not guilty" plea, but they knew she would be convicted. The whole point was to hear a guilty verdict so that appeals could be drawn up and the community could continue to rally around Rosa Parks. Fred Gray and Charles Langford both counseled Parks, although Gray was the attorney of record for the defense. Rosa's case came before Judge John Scott in the segregated City Recorder's Court (Theoharis 2013, 88; Parks 1992, 134). Despite testimony from a prosecutorial witness that there were empty seats on the Cleveland Avenue bus, the prosecuting attorney moved to have the charges against Parks changed to violating state rather than city laws. At the city level, Rosa did not violate any ordinances because that law allowed black people to remain in their seats if there were no other seats available. State law, however, enforced strict segregation regardless of availability of other accommodations. Over Gray's objections, Judge Scott allowed for the change in charges. James Blake testified at the trial, and his testimony contradicted that of the white woman who claimed there were empty seats on the bus. Still, with Rosa on trial for violating state rather than city ordinances, the contradictions in testimony did not matter. The fact was, Rosa sat while a white man stood, and that was enough to secure a conviction in the eyes of the court (Parks 1992, 134–135; Theoharis 2013, 88–89).

The court fined Rosa Parks ten dollars for violating segregation laws, and she had to pay an additional four dollars in court fees. Though the crowd decried the verdict, no violence ensued. After the verdict, Rosa Parks and her attorney Fred Gray stayed behind to complete paperwork, and

E. D. Nixon went outside to address the crowd. Jeanne Theoharis recounted his speech, "See this man out here with this sawed-off shotgun? Don't give him a chance to use it. . . . I'm gonna ask you all to quietly move from around this police station now; Mrs. Parks has been convicted and we have appealed it, and I've put her in the car. . . . As you move, don't even throw a cigarette butt, or don't spit on the sidewalk or nothing" (Theoharis 2013, 89). Nixon, like Jo Ann Robinson, realized the importance of framing the protest as orderly and peaceful. They didn't need an altercation between police and African Americans distracting the public from the monumental nature of the one-day boycott. The protestors complied, and the crowd dispersed, knowing that they would have the opportunity to speak openly once the evening's planned rally at Holt Street Baptist Church began.

The black church has long been a source of inspiration and a refuge where African Americans retreated to speak openly about their feelings regarding the oppressive hand of white supremacy. That is at the heart of black liberation theology, the church as incubation chamber for edification, uprising, and mass resistance. James Cone outlined, "Participation in divine liberation places the church squarely in the context of the world. . . . The church cannot be the church in isolation from the concrete realities of human suffering" (Cone 1970, 140). The black liberation movement in Montgomery, and across the globe, relied in part on the safety and sanctity of the black church, and much of the organizing around the Montgomery Bus Boycott occurred in black churches and through the work of religious black women and men.

Rosa Parks knew the Monday evening meeting could be monumental in terms of coordinating the black community and redoubling efforts to break down white supremacy in Montgomery. After her trial, she went to Fred Gray's law office because she knew that was where she could help the movement. Over the course of the afternoon, she answered calls and took messages. Phone calls poured in as black Montgomerians reacted to her conviction. Parks did not identify herself to any of the callers, and most had no idea they were speaking to the woman whose trial precipitated their call (Parks 1992, 134). At the end of the day, Nixon drove Rosa home, and she prepared herself to attend the mass meeting that evening.

While Parks tended the phone at Gray's office, the attorney went to a meeting of clergy and other local leaders. The group, predominately male, formed the Montgomery Improvement Association (MIA) to coordinate the protest efforts. The group debated allowing an existing organization to drive the uprising, but the consensus was that a new group, free of any entanglements from national headquarters, would be more powerful and nimble. Rosa Parks also noted that the NAACP in Montgomery, one of the debated options, was too weak. Attendees also felt a local organization would counter any claims that this movement was driven by outside agitators. They selected a leader: Dr. Martin Luther King Jr. King was a popular choice because of his youth and oratory skills. The more seasoned clergy in the city also hesitated to take charge of a group and a movement that could potentially fail. King did not share these reservations, or he did not let such reservations dissuade him from taking the leadership post. Rufus Lewis nominated King in part because he did not like E. D. Nixon's militant politics, and he did not want MIA to take on a militant stance. The son of prominent Atlanta minister Martin Luther King Sr. and Alberta Williams King, the younger King boasted a bachelor of arts degree from Morehouse University, a bachelor of divinity from Crozer Theological Seminary, and a doctorate from Boston University. MIA founders saw the need for a centralizing leader to push the movement forward. Jeanne Theoharis postulated that others, like Rosa Parks, who did not attend this meeting, would have preferred "broad-based structures of decision making and leadership as a way to sustain a mass movement," but meeting attendees held leadership positions and favored centralized power structures (Theoharis 2013, 91). Historian Joseph Fitzgerald analyzed this paradigm and argued that organizations like the Student Nonviolent Coordinating Committee (SNCC) which formed in 1960, benefited from a decentralize non-hierarchical philosophy. "Participatory democracy" or local people "lead[ing] their own movements and determin[ing] their own goals and how to achieve them" was a more effective and sustainable program, according to Fitzgerald (Fitzgerald 2018, 72).

MIA had nine officers, only one being a woman. King served as founding president, and the other officers were as follows:

First Vice President—Reverend L. Roy Bennett

Second Vice President—Moses W. Jones, MD

Financial Secretary—Erma Dungee

Recording Secretary—Reverend Uriah J. Fields

Corresponding Secretary—Reverend E. N. French

Treasurer—E. D. Nixon

Assistant Treasurer—C. W. Lee

Parliamentarian—Reverend A. W. Wilson

The group pledged themselves to "protect, defend, encourage, enlighten, and assist the members of the black community against unfair treatment, prejudice, and unacceptable subordination" (Robinson 1987, 64). MIA also employed an executive board of some thirty-five men and women to coordinate the masses (Robinson 1987, 64).

The stage was set for the Monday evening rally. Fifteen thousand people crowded in and around Holt Street Baptist Church for the event. They spilled into the streets and blocked traffic for three blocks due to the sheer volume of people. The loudspeakers set up outside the church building broadcast the proceedings up to two blocks away. Martin Luther King Jr. had to park his car and walk several blocks, Virginia Durr failed to gain entry into the building, and Rosa Parks had to fight through the crowd to make it to the platform. Parks felt the jubilation in the crowd, and she soaked in the spectacular nature of it all. Rosa did ask if she should say a few words, but she was told she had said enough. That sentiment characterized the rest of the bus boycott and her legacy in civil rights lore. She became a symbol of, rather than a major actor in, the narrative of the Montgomery Bus Boycott and the modern civil rights movement.

Plenty of people did speak that evening however. E. D. Nixon kicked off the event imploring people to stay the course, for, "this is going to be a long-drawn-out affair. For years and years I've been talking about how I didn't want the children who came along behind me to have to suffer the indignities that I've suffered all these years. Well, I've changed my mind—I want to enjoy some of that freedom myself" (Parks 1992, 137–138). Martin Luther King Jr. also took the podium, and he delivered the first of many captivating speeches. The people were so stunned by his oratory that they "were quiet for a moment and then rose to their feet, cheering and clapping. . . . Outside the crowd erupted in thunderous applause" (Theoharis 2013, 92). King opened his speech by cautioning the audience that this business was serious. He continued:

> There comes a time when people get tired. We are here this evening to say to those who have mistreated us so long that we are tired—tired of being segregated and humiliated; tired of being kicked about by the brutal feet of oppression.
>
> There comes a time my friends when people get tired of being plunged across the abyss of humiliation, when they experience the bleakness of nagging despair. There comes a time when people get tired of being pushed out of the glimmering sunlight of last July and left standing amid the piercing chill of an Alpine November.
>
> We had no alternative but to protest. For many years, we have shown amazing patience. We have sometimes given our white brothers the feeling that we liked the way we were being treated. But we come here tonight to be saved from that patience that makes us patient with anything less than freedom and justice.
>
> One of the great glories of democracy is the right to protest for right.
>
> These organizations [White Citizens' Councils and the Ku Klux Klan] are protesting for the perpetuation of injustice in the community, we are protesting for the birth of justice in the community. Their methods lead to violence and lawlessness. But in our protest there will be no cross burnings. No white person will be taken from his home by a hooded Negro mob and brutally murdered. There will be no threats and intimidation. We will be guided by the highest principles of law and order.

Our method will be that of persuasion, not coercion. We will only say to the people, "Let your conscience be your guide." Our actions must be guided by the deepest principles of our Christian faith. Love must be our regulating ideal. Once again we must hear the words of Jesus echoing across the centuries ("Love your enemies, bless them that curse you, and pray for them that despitefully use you"). If we fail to do this our protest will end up as a meaningless drama on the stage of history, and its memory will be shrouded with the ugly garments of shame. In spite of the mistreatment that we have confronted we must not become bitter, and end up by hating our white brothers. As Booker T. Washington said, "Let no man pull you so low as to make you hate him."

We are not wrong in what we are doing. If we are wrong, the Supreme Court of this nation is wrong. If we are wrong, the Constitution of the United States is wrong. If we are wrong, God Almighty is wrong. If we are wrong, Jesus of Nazareth was merely a Utopian dreamer who never came down to earth.

If you will protest courageously, and yet with dignity and Christian love, when the history books are written in future generations, the historians will have to pause and say, "There lived a great people—a black people—who injected new meaning and dignity into the veins of civilization." This is our challenge and our overwhelming responsibility. (King 1955)

The question at hand was whether to continue boycotting the city buses, and the speakers that evening helped inspired people already boiling over with a desire to liberate themselves from oppression. Fifteen thousand strong decided Monday evening December 5, 1955, that the boycott would continue. They lauded their leaders, praised Rosa Parks for her steel will, encouraged each other to persevere, and founded a movement centered on three demands:

1. Courteous treatment on the buses;

2. First-come, first-served seating with whites in front and blacks in back;

3. Hiring of black drivers for the black bus routes.

Reverend Ralph Abernathy read these demands to the crowd and asked them to stand if they agree to sustain the bus boycott. Rosa Parks recalled, "People started getting up, one or two at a time at first, and then more and more, until every single person in that church was standing, and outside the crowd was cheering, 'Yes'" (Parks 1992, 140). The Montgomery Bus Boycott was born even as leaders of the movement who told her she had said enough quieted Rosa Parks's public voice.

9

"Tired of Giving In"

"People always say that I didn't give up my seat because I was tired, but that isn't true. I was not tired physically, or no more tired than I usually was at the end of a working day. I was not old, although some people have an image of me as being old then. I was forty-two. No, the only tired I was, was tired of giving in." (Parks 1992, 116)

Rosa Louise Parks took a stand on December 1, 1955, by refusing to give up her seat on the Montgomery Bus Line. Fully within her rights based on city ordinances, she still faced arrest, trial, and conviction because she challenged the unwritten customs and the culture of white supremacy that pervaded Montgomery, Alabama. This heroic act was but one of countless instances wherein black people stood up to their oppressors, and the stand was part of Rosa Parks's long history of activism. On her seventy-seventh birthday, she reportedly reflected, "I would like to be known as a person who is concerned about freedom and equality and justice and prosperity for all people" (National Women's Hall of Fame n.d.). Although the public remembers "the mother of the civil rights movement" as just such a person, the predominating narrative of Rosa Parks focuses on that one December day.

Much of this narrative of Rosa Parks emerged through deliberate framing on the part of the Montgomery Improvement Association (MIA) because they wanted to protect the organization from "a vicious Cold War climate and longstanding Southern fears of outside influence" (Theoharis

2013, 94). Portraying an accurate picture of Parks as an NAACP leader who agitated for the rights of black people like Recy Taylor and Jeremiah Reeves opened the movement up to scrutiny. The white public would see her act of defiance as part of larger protest efforts, and Rosa would become antagonistic, emasculating, and anti-American in their eyes. MIA leaders felt it was important that Parks fit the mold of what Laura McEnaney called "militarized maternalism," a patriotic champion of middle-class American values who, in fulfillment of her Cold War "maternal" duty, passed these traits on to the youth (McEnaney 1999, 448). Gender norms led to her election as Montgomery NAACP secretary in 1943, and those same norms dictated the actions of the MIA (Theoharis 2013, 94).

The MIA leadership was overwhelmingly male, and women held largely clerical and advisory roles. This did not mean that women were not at the heart of the bus boycott, however. Women did much of the work of initiating, coordinating, and advertising, as well as bringing the lawsuits that led to the eventual success of the boycott. MIA, the organization created to lead the bus boycott, would not have worked if not for the efforts of women. Maude Ballou served as personal secretary to MIA president Martin Luther King Jr. Martha Johnson was secretary-clerk and managed the affairs of the rest of the leadership team. Hazel Gregory served as general overseer, managing the MIA office and handling all of MIA's needs. Erna Dungee served as the financial secretary who accounted for all of MIA's finances. These were MIA's only compensated employees, and they were the engine that drove the movement. Of course, all of this was possible because Rosa Parks refused to be cowed in the face of a white supremacist bus driver. Still, men served as the mouthpiece and gained much of the public acclaim (Robinson 1987, 66).

Despite clear evidence to the contrary, the bus company executives denied that their drivers abused black riders. When MIA leaders met with the city commissioners and bus company representatives on December 8, the white leaders rejected their demands. Undeterred and poised for a protracted fight, Montgomery blacks continued to stay off the buses. Meanwhile, the MIA continued to build the infrastructure for success, including renting "a very large building, with some five rooms" (Robinson 1987, 66). Key to the boycott's success was the coordination of a massive carpooling network. Movement organizers solicited drivers and cars for this undertaking. Mindful that white officials would look for any way to disrupt the efforts, the MIA accepted only licensed drivers and insured automobiles. This solicitation was largely clandestine, for anyone speaking openly about transportation in front of white people risked repercussions. As Jeanne Theoharis recounted, "The MIA established forty stations across the city. Drivers charged ten cents, like the bus" (Theoharis 2013, 95). Harkening back to the famous Double V campaign initiated by Pittsburgh's black press, the *Pittsburgh Courier*, "people would use the 'V for victory' sign to identify themselves to riders and drivers." Twice-weekly rallies helped keep black Montgomerians fortified and energized for the boycott, and these meetings brought the black public together in solidarity and strength. These meetings also allowed the MIA to update the public on the boycott and discuss finances.

This movement required sustained contributions of time and energy as well as money. Georgia Gilmore established a group, the Club from Nowhere, to collect monetary donations for the cause. At every Monday night protest rally, Gilmore's group would present their figures to the crowd. Encouraged by these fundraising efforts, Inez Ricks founded another group, the Friendly Club, to raise funds as well. Mondays became a source of friendly competition between the two groups as each informed the masses how much their group raised the previous week. Robinson noted, "The two teams . . . enjoyed competing to raise the money needed for the movement. They also represented a vital element of each Monday night's entertainment, giving people another way to rid themselves of their frustrations and pent-up emotions" (Robinson 1987, 72). Attendees "began to look forward to seeing which group would win each week's competition" (Robinson 1987, 72). Not everyone in Montgomery was able to attend the twice-weekly meetings, but it was imperative to keep everyone informed of the developments in the bus boycott. Here again was a place where the women of the movement took the lead. WPC president and MIA executive member Jo Ann Robinson began an MIA newsletter that went out weekly to thousands of black people in the city. Robinson was perfectly equipped for this leadership role as an English professor at Alabama State. Despite her busy schedule of teaching and organizing, each week she committed a couple of hours to compiling information and creating the newsletter. MIA staff members Erna Dungee and Hazel Gregory handled copying and distribution efforts. With donations coming in to MIA from across the country, the two women made sure to mail interested parties outside the city of Montgomery as well (Robinson 1987, 74–75).

With money coming in from Montgomerians and, as the media coverage increased, from sources around the globe, it was imperative for the MIA to keep careful track of their finances. For decades, the Internal Revenue Service (IRS) and Federal Bureau of Investigation (FBI) kept watch over the finances of black organizations like the NAACP in hopes of finding irregularities that would open the door to prosecution (Mace 2014, 102). The Cold War era brought heightened attention to civil rights agitation, and "Americans readily labeled Communist anything they saw as subversive or contrary to national principles of democracy" (Mace 2014, 102). Surely, through McCarthyism and entities like the House Un-American Activities Committee (HUAC), "the government took steps to silence alternative voices . . . when they challenged the official narrative of race and American democracy" (Mace 2014, 22). The MIA distributed funds across two major banks, the Alabama National Bank and the Citizens Trust Company in Atlanta, Georgia. Both were highly reputable financial institutions, and the MIA used two banks to avoid having too much money in one location. Additionally, the Alabama-based bank account allowed for easy access for emergent needs, while the Georgia-based bank held larger reserves of funds for big expenditures (Robinson 1987, 73). With the funds, the MIA handled typical expenses like gas and vehicle maintenance. They also made big purchases like additional vehicles. Jeanne Theoharis noted the MIA purchased station wagons to carry even more passengers. In the midst of oppressive scrutiny, the MIA needed to ensure that carpool vehicles would not draw suspicion for carrying too many occupants. The boycotters called these cars "rolling churches" because each had the name of one of the local churches sprawled across the front (Theoharis 2013, 97). Affiliating these vehicles with black churches rather than the MIA was another strategic move. As many of Montgomery's white churches already had vehicles to carry worshippers, "it was difficult to complain about black churches doing the same" (Theoharis 2013, 97).

As the boycott waged on, the MIA was spending nearly $3,000 per week on transportation (Theoharis 2013, 96). With fifteen dispatchers and twenty full-time drivers, the MIA "arranged fifteen to twenty thousand rides per day" (Theoharis 2013, 96). Each time a vehicle went on a run, the occupants risked police harassment and worse. Officers patrolled constantly looking for any excuse to stop the car and invent a violation. Still, black Montgomery pressed on with their collective eyes on the prize. Rosa Parks was integral to this effort. She worked as a dispatcher from the early days of the Montgomery Bus Boycott. She maintained full confidence in the movement and a stalwart belief in her convictions that bus discrimination needed to end. When asked if she felt the movement would fail, Rosa responded, "The very fact that people demonstrated their unity on the first

---

RACE AND THE COLD WAR

Scholarship provides a clear analysis of the fusion of U.S. domestic policy and Cold War diplomacy. In the Cold War era, Americans were increasingly concerned with how the world viewed them. Additionally, this country was battling with the Soviet Union for the trust, respect, and resources of nonwhite nations in Latin America, the Middle East, Asia, and Africa. In this tenuous environment, diplomats increasingly spoke of culture rather than race as the identifier of difference. However, race still dominated U.S. domestic policy.

day was very significant and to me that was a success" (Theoharis 2013, 97). She did not worry about the movement, because black Montgomery had united.

MIA leaders continued to voice their demands publicly and at meetings with city and bus officials; however, there was no progress. City officials in particular refused to treat the boycott seriously, even though the bus company was losing a good deal of money each day. The Montgomery Bus Boycott was, at its heart, an economic boycott of segregated facilities, and the bus company suffered the most under this economic action. In this way, the movement resembled other financial power plays like the "Don't Buy Where You Can't Work" movement of the 1930s and beyond. During the 1930s African Americans in northern cities boycotted and picketed businesses that refused to hire black people or that would only hire them for menial, low-paying jobs. In the midst of the Great Depression, black people felt the tremendous weight of unemployment and poverty at a much higher rate than white Americans, and the "Don't Buy Where You Can't Work" campaign aimed to punish potential employers for blatant discriminatory activities. The companies, already struggling because of the global economic hardships and decreases in customer base, were ready targets for this type of economic boycotting, and many soon relented and adapted, if only slightly, their hiring processes to be less discriminatory (*In Motion* n.d.).

The lessons learned in the "Don't Buy Where You Can't Work" campaign, in terms of black organizing efforts, African American economic power, and white people seeing the power of black collective action, had a major impact on race relations in the nation. Whites, individually and collectively, felt the power of a united black offensive, and black people felt the strength of their unity. When Brotherhood of Sleeping Car Porters founder Asa Philip Randolph joined Bayard Rustin and others to form the March on Washington Movement of 1941 to end segregation in the defense industry, white federal government officials, all the way up to President Franklin Delano Roosevelt, took notice. Blacks had proven in the previous decade that their collective protest could effect change, and Roosevelt did not want to see another uprising like those in the 1930s. In response to the threat of a march, the president issued Executive Order 8802 desegregating the defense industry (Gavins 2016, 193). Employing similar tactics, black people in the Mississippi Delta caused the economic ruin of Emmett Till's murderers after the two men, Roy Bryant and J. W. Milam, sold their confession to reporter William Bradford Huie. Huie wrote a follow-up article to this confession, entitled, "What Happened to the Emmett Till Killers?" In the article, "Milam told Huie that Till's death had haunted the families." Specifically, "they [the Bryant-Milam family] have been disappointed. They have suffered disillusionment, ingratitude, resentment, misfortune. For years before the slaying, the numerous Milam-Bryant clan had operated a chain of small stores in the Delta, stores dependent on Negro trade. . . . Now, all these stores have been closed or sold. The Negroes boycotted them and ruined them" (Mace 2014, 140–141).

The Montgomery Bus Boycott also built on these historic collective actions from the twentieth century, and black Montgomerians knew well that the bus company could not exist without the patronage of black riders. White Montgomery however, seemed blind to that fact, particularly in the leadership circles. Instead of taking the boycotters seriously, in late December 1955, the city commissioners invited Montgomery White Citizens Council president Luther Ingalls to one of the meetings with MIA leaders. For black leaders, this was a clear sign that city officials did not understand the heart of the protest. Black Montgomery banded together to decry the immorality and inhumanity inherent in segregation. As Jeanne Theoharis highlighted, the inclusion of Ingalls signaled that officials saw the MIA as a special interest group equivalent on moral and ethical grounds to the segregationist and white supremacist White Citizens Council. They envisioned this as solely an economic disagreement devoid of moral factors. Even the mainstream newspapers characterized the boycott in terms that ignored the moral foundation of the boycott and the intrinsic immorality of segregation. One article in the *Montgomery Advertiser* offered that "the white man's artillery is far superior . . . and commanded by more experienced gunners [plus] the white man holds all the offices of the government machinery" (Theoharis 2013, 98). Slightly more than a decade removed from World War II and embroiled in a pseudo-cold war against Communism, these white Americans saw the bus boycott in militarized terms, and they touted their arsenal of power. What they did not factor in was the fact that the Montgomery Bus Boycott was a moral battle over the consciousness and soul of America's culture of race relations. In that battle, blacks had a superior argument.

Although black people waged their protest on moral grounds rooted in nonviolent, direct action, it is inaccurate to portray African Americans as unwilling to fight to defend their freedoms. Black people had always been willing to take up arms, or maintain arms, to defend themselves against the oppression of white supremacy. In Rosa Parks's own life, she experienced the importance of armed self-defense. She remembered her grandfather sitting up with his shotgun poised to mow down any Ku Klux Klan members who threatened his family. However uneasy the presence of firearms might have made Rosa, her grandmother, or her mother, there is no indication that they made any moves to dissuade Rosa's grandfather from readying his gun. During the Scottsboro case, Rosa sat at meetings where firearms covered the table. Black people, including Martin Luther King Jr., owned firearms, and, contrary to popular narratives of the civil rights Movement, nonviolent, direct action did not preclude armed self-defense.

They were two sides of the same coin, so to speak. Both were necessary tactics in the battle for black equality, and black people employed these strategies as appropriate to any given situation. For the Montgomery Bus Boycott, Rosa Parks concluded nonviolence "was more successful . . . than it would have been if violence had been used" (Theoharis 2013, 100).

Still, white Montgomerians used every tactic at their disposal to quell the movement. Police waged an intimidation war against black citizens, "getting after the groups of blacks who were waiting at the bus stop for the black-owned cabs to pick them up. They threatened to arrest the cab drivers if they did not charge their regular fare, which I think was forty-five cents, to go downtown instead of ten cents like the buses charged" (Parks 1992, 142). Rosa lost her job in January of 1956. Montgomery Fair did not say openly that they fired her, and the company did not cite the bus boycott as the reason for the termination of her position. Rather, when the young tailor decided to open his own shop, the company determined that without a head tailor, they no longer needed Rosa's services. Without a head tailor to do clothes fitting for the men, there was not enough sewing work for Rosa, the company maintained. Montgomery Fair did pay her through the end of the pay period and included her bonus money in the severance process. Raymond also found himself unemployed that year. When the owner of the private barbershop where he worked made a rule that employees could not talk about the bus boycott or Rosa, Raymond left the workplace. He refused to work at a place where he could not talk about his wife. Interestingly, the owner of the shop coupled Rosa and the Montgomery Bus Boycott. Unlike the leadership of the MIA, who framed Rosa as the impetus for but not the core of the bus boycott, for this white man, any conversation about Rosa Parks was a conversation about the bus boycott (Parks 1992, 142–143).

For Rosa Parks, the loss of her job was a blessing in disguise. She could spend more of her time and efforts working on the bus boycott. Rosa noted in her autobiography, "I was on the executive board of the MIA and I did whatever was needed" (Parks 1992, 143). Some of what was needed was positive publicity, and she "started traveling quite a bit, making appearances because of my arrest and the boycott" (Parks 1992, 143). Rosa also continued as a transportation dispatcher and helped distribute clothes to the black community. The latter was a pressing need—so many black people lost their jobs because of their participation in this black uprising (Parks 1992, 143).

Death threats were a constant drain on black families, including Rosa and Raymond Parks. Rosa would hang up as soon as she recognized a call was threatening, and the situation reached such a level and frequency that her mother and husband began answering the phone most of the time (Theoharis 2013, 101). Again, whites made Rosa Parks synonymous with the bus boycott, and most of the calls were directing threats toward her. Although her actions did rally the black community in support of a bus boycott, Rosa's two decades of previous agitation did not generate these types of threatening calls. Her arrest thrust her into the spotlight, but the beam of light was narrow and focused solely on the afternoon in December when she refused to give up her seat.

Even with all of the animosity directed toward her, friends reported that Rosa had a peace about her life and her role in ushering in the boycott. Citing a conversation Rosa had with Mary Hays Carter, Jeanne Theoharis offered, "Well you have to die sometime. I never set out to plan to hurt anyone and if this boycott happened to be attributed to me and my activity, then if they could kill me, I would just be dead" (Theoharis 2013, 102). Theoharis also noted that Rosa gained a sense of peace from her faith, and she had "a wash of religious conviction" about the boycott, feeling it "was God's plan" during a period of prayer. Her experience mirrors that of Mamie Till-Mobley, mother of slain youth Emmett Till. Till-Mobley "was having difficulty resolving her son's murder in her mind until a 'divine' presence told her: Mamie, it was ordained from the beginning of time that Emmett Louis Till would die a violent death. You should be grateful to be the mother of a boy who died blameless like Christ. . . . Have courage and faith that in the end there will be redemption for the suffering of your people and you are the instrument of this purpose. Work unceasingly to tell the story so that the truth will arouse men's conscience and right can at last prevail" (Mace 2014, 11). For Till-Mobley, Rosa Parks, and countless other African Americans, faith was the vehicle for encouragement and strength in the face of white terrorism.

Segregationists also threatened other white people they felt were helping sustain the Montgomery Bus Boycott. Many white women in the city chose to drive their black domestic workers to work every day rather than lose the assistance these women provided. Some of these white women received threatening phone calls and letters. Other communications offered names of people violating the white code by driving their laborers. Parks recalled one such letter that read:

Dear Friend,
   Listed below are a few of the white people who are hauling their Negro maids. This must be stopped. These people would appreciate a call from you, day or night. Let's let them know how we feel about them hauling Negroes. (Parks 1992, 146)

Mayor Gayle issued a public appeal to these white women to stop offering transportation to their staff, and the women replied, "Well, if the mayor wants to come and do my washing and ironing and look after my children and clean my house and cook my meals, he can do it. But I'm not getting rid of my maid" (Parks 1992, 145). Although this statement showed that at least some white women were not willing to bend fully to the will of white men, it also speaks to the levels of servitude black women found themselves in and the overwhelming privilege experienced by well-to-do white women in Montgomery. Many of these white women refused to do these listed tasks on their own and they were wholly dependent on black women for domestic work in their homes.

Ardent segregationists employed other avenues of intimidation as well. Membership in both the Ku Klux Klan and White Citizens Council rose steadily, and even Mayor W. A. Gayle boldly announced his membership in the Montgomery White Citizens Council (Parks 1992, 146). Strategic deception also played a role in boycott resistance. Rosa remembered, "In late January the three city commissioners met with three black ministers who were not part of the MIA. These ministers agreed to a plan for bus seating. . . . Then the commission told the *Montgomery Advertiser* that Sunday the paper ran big headlines announcing the end of the boycott" (Parks 1992, 146). Having learned of this unsanctioned meeting ahead of the Sunday publication, MIA leaders took to the streets in black communities, warning the people that the paper was about to publish lies. The boycott was not ending, and people should continue to stay off the buses. The public responded as such, remaining off the buses the coming Monday and beyond.

White supremacists accosted black walkers and carpool drivers throwing all manner of things at them whenever they could do so. Jeanne Theoharis noted the boycotters "were often pelted with food, stones, urine, and other things. . . . According to [Jo Ann] Robinson, police officers (or men dressed as police officers) were responsible for a great deal of violence—paint and manure thrown on homes, bricks thrown through their windows, yards and automobiles destroyed, nails scattered on streets to puncture tires" (Theoharis 2013, 105). Yet, the boycott continued against all of the odds, because the black community's resolve and moral conviction grew with each progressive act of violence and each failed attempt at negotiation. Black Montgomerians kept going because they agreed with Rosa Parks's sentiment: "If you are mistreated when you ride and intimidated when you walk . . . why not do what hurt them most—walk and let them find $3000 per day to pay for it" (Theoharis 2013, 105).

In truth, the bus company could not afford to let the bus boycott continue, but they were at the will of the city government and the people of Montgomery. The bus company could not acquiesce to boycotters because they needed the blessing of white city officials, but they could not abide the city's intransigence toward the boycott because of their own financial strain. J. H. Bagley, the bus company official, wanted to find a solution to this standoff. He traveled to Mobile, Alabama, where buses were already integrated, to study a model of what Montgomery's bus system could look like (Robinson 1987, 79). City officials rejected the Mobile model outright, and the boycott dragged on through the winter of 1956.

Feeling the full weight of the boycott, the bus line had to raise fares and lay off bus drivers (Theoharis 2013, 105). Bagley also made some moves to distance the bus company from the unbending city commission, proclaiming the bus company did not "have anything to do with making the laws— you see we operate under the city commission and they regulate the seating and what they (the MIA) asked for is against the law. We do what the law says and if they change the law, we will change—this is between them and the city commission and the laws of Ala, the bus company has nothing to do with it" (Theoharis 2013, 106). In truth, black people, at least openly, were not asking for full integration of the buses. The MIA platform called for:

1. Courteous treatment on the buses;
2. First-come, first-served seating, with whites in front and blacks in back;
3. Hiring of black bus drivers for the black bus routes.

These demands stemmed from the predominant practices of current and former white bus drivers. The drivers' disrespect of and open hostility toward black people was the issue, and it was a moral issue. White people's treatment of African Americans was immoral, and these awful practices germinated because the laws dictated white supremacy over black people. Jo Ann Robinson painted Bagley in a favorable light, claiming he "was a kindly person caught in the throes of a segregated transportation system not of his making. He was a warm, intelligent person, concerned with his own job but also concerned with the riders who kept those wheels moving" (Robinson 1987, 79). Personality aside, the fact remained that the bus company hired and continued to employ white bus drivers who behaved vilely toward black riders, and Bagley was complicit in this culture of abuse.

The abuses before and during the boycott strengthened black resolve. Rosa Parks told a friend, "We do not know what else is to follow these previous events. . . . [We are] praying for courage and determination to withstand all attempts of intimidation" (Theoharis 2013, 107). Courage and determination were necessary to withstand the white backlash toward the bus boycott leaders and supporters. On January 30, 1956, white zealots bombed Martin Luther King Jr.'s house, with his wife and daughter inside. Vigilantes later bombed E. D. Nixon's house. Both incidents raised extreme anger in the black community. This was a moment where the movement could have flipped to more aggressive and violent tactics, but MIA leaders managed to refocus black outrage into further determination to see the boycott to fruition (Theoharis 2013, 107). The MIA posted armed guards at key homes, including the house where Rosa lived with her husband and her mother. Again, the Montgomery Bus Boycott proved that a movement could employ nonviolent, direct actions as a guiding principle without neglecting armed self-defense. With each tactic and each escalating threat wielded by white supremacists, the black community responded with appropriate and effective counters. Not only that, but black Montgomery employed their own strategies proactively in order to control the movement.

One of these strategies of course was the transportation system that Jo Ann Robinson called, "one of the most effectively planned mass transportation systems in American history" (Robinson 1987, 91). At its height, they carried about thirty thousand people to and from work each day on top of all of the nonwork-related transport of African Americans (Parks 1992, 145). Beginning as early as 5:00 a.m., cars rolled out collecting passengers. The system included some 325 private cars and forty-three "dispatch stations" (Robinson 1987, 91). These stations were located strategically at black churches, funeral homes, popular stores, service stations, and clubhouses, to name a few. Dispatch stations operated, at their peak, cars every ten minutes from 5:00 a.m. to 10:00 a.m., the time most African Americans began their travel to work. After 10:00 a.m., dispatch stations offered hourly pickups. At 1:00 p.m., the forty-two "pickup stations" went into peak operation operating on a pickup schedule of every ten minutes until 8:00 p.m. (Robinson 1987, 92). The pickup stations were in areas where white people lived and operated stores, because the majority of Montgomery blacks worked for white people and needed transportation from those locales to their homes as the end of their workday. Central hubs, effectively transportation junctions, existed downtown at the black-owned McDonough street parking lot and Dean's Drugstore. Jo Ann Robinson reflected, "The parking lot belonged to a black woman whose family had owned property for years . . . [and] Dean's was the business place of pharmacist Dr. Richard Harris, an ardent race man" (Robinson 1987, 92). She continued, "The two places were the central exchange point for transfers. All cars worked specific areas and returned to these two stations. If one person was going across town and the remaining 'load' was going to town, all of the passengers were taken to Dean's or to the parking lot, where cars going in all directions would pick people up and take them where they were going." Furthermore, "because the sites were private property, authorities did not have authority to molest passengers or to question them there" (Robinson 1987, 92–93). In the early days of the boycott, drivers paid for gas on their own, but as the MIA funds grew, the Transportation Committee began collecting receipts and reimbursing drivers. Robinson admitted the driving took a toll, and "exhausted, we were going to sleep at the dinner table with a spoon of food halfway between the plate and the mouth" (Robinson 1987, 94).

The bus boycott had an unintended economic effect on downtown business, overwhelmingly white-owned. Black Montgomerians focused their efforts on the boycott, and many chose to scale down their Christmas gift-giving and celebrations in December 1955. Local merchants felt this pinch as black patrons spent the holidays "in meditation and prayer" instead of shopping and entertaining (Robinson 1987, 97). Many also chose to give money they would have spent on presents to the MIA, thus helping to sustain the movement. Robinson reflected that the bus company decided to suspend bus service starting December 22, 1955, and lasting through the Christmas holiday. As such, whites who did not own cars could not get to downtown stores to shop, and businesses suffered even greater losses. The bus company announced the transportation holiday under the guise of giving drivers time off for Christmas, but it was economic pressure, brought on by blacks boycotting city buses, that forced the suspension of bus services. One merchant announced, "Montgomery stores took in $2 million less during December 1955 than during previous Christmas seasons" (Robinson 1987, 97).

The MIA took out an advertisement that ran in the newspaper on Christmas day. The piece "explained the purpose of the organization, the position it had taken in connection with the boycott, [and] the fairness of black citizens' request for improved seating condition. . . . The ad ended with a prayer for peace on earth and good will to all mankind" (Robinson 1987, 99). It was hard to argue with the moral stance adopted in this advertisement, and newspapers around the world began to take more notice of the MIA and the Montgomery Bus Boycott, Robinson recalled, "There seemed hardly a spot on the globe . . . that did not carry the news" (Robinson 1987, 100).

With the bus boycott in full swing, many white Montgomerians began to take notice and to voice their opinions about the protest movement. Whites looked to their local newspapers as a venue through which they could state their case. The *Montgomery Advertiser* began printing letters to the editor that spoke to the bus boycott. Taken in concert, these letters expressed a general anger at the protest, but some letters did also take issues with the way bus drivers treated black people on Montgomery buses. In much the same ways as for Mississippians with the lynching of Emmett Louis Till, for Alabamians, the bus boycott "became the battleground upon which many waged a rhetorical war over the merits and the morality of racial segregation and racial equality" (Mace 2014, 98). Some readers touted race relations in Montgomery as the best in the country and blamed outside agitation from the NAACP for inciting black Montgomerians to boycott (Robinson 1987, 104–105). While still critical of the collective protest, some other letters showed a bit of sympathy for blacks in Montgomery. One reader lamented that the treatment of black people on the buses should have Montgomerians "bow our heads in shame," and another reader said that "much improvement can be made" (Robinson 1987, 101–102). White backlash to the bus boycott extended to white citizens who supported the protest or questioned the merits of current bus policies. Letter authors received constant threats against their homes, their families, and their lives. Police did nothing to quell these threats, and they increased as the calendar moved into 1956. Intimidation tactics grew as the membership rolls of the White Citizens Council swelled. Among the new recruits to the white supremacist organization was City Commissioner Clyde Sellers, who was also the police commissioner. He joined the WCC in January, and his dramatic entry aired on television and received coverage in newspapers (Robinson 1987, 111–112).

White backlash only strengthened black resolve to see the boycott to a successful conclusion. Meanwhile, the bus company was losing a great deal of money, terminating bus routes, and laying off workers to cut costs. On January 18, Commissioner Sellers presented a "Get Tough" policy intended to get black people back on the buses. Police engaged in a fear campaign, ramping up aggression against black people waiting for rides and harassing those walking along the streets. As with other efforts, this "Get Tough" policy failed to break the boycott. In response, Montgomery Mayor W. A. Gayle terminated negotiations with black leaders on January 23, 1956, claiming that "we have pussyfooted around with this boycott long enough" (Robinson 1987, 119). In the absence of any measures of good will on the part of city officials, black people readied themselves for a protracted protest, and they plowed forward with planned legal actions intended to test the constitutionality of Montgomery's segregation laws and practices.

The city's intransigence paved the way for the destruction of legal segregation in Montgomery and across the nation. Until January 1956, black Montgomery asked collectively for better treatment on segregated buses. By the end of January, with violence on the rise and no movement from city and bus officials, black people pushed the call for the abolition of segregation. It is important to note however that this move was not a reactive response to the stubbornness of the city. Rather, black people had proactively planned for legal actions to destroy segregation even before the bus boycott began. Black Montgomery was ready for a court challenge, and when city officials refused to compromise, they struck with full legal force.

The success of the Montgomery Bus Boycott was due in part to the fact that black people waged the justice campaign on many fronts, one of them a legal front. After white terrorists bombed King's house on Monday, January 30, 1956, the time for negotiations had ended. Attorney Fred Gray gained permission from his five clients to press a lawsuit against segregation laws on Montgomery buses. All of the plaintiffs were women, and each suffered indignity and harassment from bus drivers and the city police officers who arrested them. Interestingly, Rosa Parks was not among the plaintiffs in the case. Even though her arrest sparked the bus boycott, she was not part of the legal challenge that ensued.

Fred Gray filed suit on behalf of Claudette Colvin, Mary Louise Smith, Jeanatta Reese, Aurelia Browder, and Susie McDonald on February 1, 1956, four years before the Greensboro Four (Greensboro, North Carolina) ushered in a period of nonviolent collective protest known as the sit-in movement. Just as young activists created the Greensboro protests, this court case featured two teenagers, Colvin and Smith. Gray named as defendants, Mayor W. A. Gayle, city commissioners Clyde Sellers and Frank Parks, Police Chief Goodwyn J. Ruppenthal, the Montgomery City Bus Line, and bus drivers James F. Blake and Robert Cleere. Just hours after the suit was filed, white supremacist bombed E. D. Nixon's home in retaliation. Violent retaliation was on the rise, and the intimidation only got worse for black Montgomery.

City officials decided to take their own legal action in an effort to destroy the bus boycott. According to Alabama State Code, Title 14, Section 54, it was illegal for a group of people to conduct activities that would endanger any "person, firm, corporation or association of persons doing a lawful business" (Robinson 1987, 142). Originally designed to prevent labor strikes, the city used this statute to challenge the legality of the bus boycott. Montgomery Circuit Court Judge Eugene Carter empaneled a grand jury to investigate the boycott under this code. Suddenly, the MIA its MIA leaders had their documents seized and their effort scrutinized by a group of eighteen people. E. T. Sinclair was the only African American on this panel, and he was only there because Carter feared a higher court might overturn any grand jury ruling because of there not being any black voices on the panel. Even so, it only took agreement among twelve of the eighteen members of the grand jury for the body to issue a ruling. Sinclair's voice and vote could not swing the outcome of the case (Robinson 1987, 141–143).

The grand jury move sent ripples of concern through the black community, and Jeanatta Reese decided to back out of the lawsuit against Montgomery segregation. She declared publicly that she did not know what she was doing when she signed on to the case and that she only agreed after facing significant pressure to file suit. Robinson recalled, "Later [Reese] said privately that she had known what she as signing, but wanted to withdraw her name because she could not stand the pressure" (Robinson 1987, 142). Seizing this opportunity, the predominantly white grand jury indicted Fred Gray for "representing clients without authority" (Robinson 1987, 143). The Montgomery Bus Boycott and subsequent social and legal actions drew attention from across the country and around the globe. Ardent segregationist Senator James O. Eastland (Mississippi) traveled to

Montgomery and spoke before a crowd of fifteen thousand white suprema-cists on February 10 (Robinson 1987, 143–144). Although Eastland did not mention the bus boycott in his speech, his presence and his record on race underscored white resistance to desegregation efforts. Eastland was "sent to Washington in 1941 to fill the Senate seat vacated after the death of Pat Harrison. Over the course of thirty-six years, Eastland fought to maintain white rule in his home state. Eastland labeled the 1954 *Brown v. Board of Education of Topeka, KS (Brown)* decision that outlawed segregation in public education a communist plot. During the 1955 Emmett Till saga, Eastland's office disclosed to Mississippi's rabidly racist *Jackson News* Emmett Till's father, Louis Till's, questionable military record, and East-land led the effort to make events like Till's open casket funeral illegal" (Mace 2014, 14).

Still, some white Montgomerians continued to work for compromise. The Men of Montgomery (MOM) was a coalition of nearly forty white busi-nessmen who met at least three times with MIA leadership in hopes of set-tling the bus segregation question without legal action. Once again, whites undersold the power of black Montgomery, and the compromises MOM offered underestimated the depth of anger and conviction held by blacks in the city. Coming out of one of these meetings, Jo Ann Robinson knew that "it was evident . . . that blacks would never return to public carriers except on an integrated basis. . . . They felt that eventually the City would have to give in and integrate those buses" (Robinson 1987, 145). Still, MIA leaders did carry the MOM proposal to the MIA meeting. Five thousand Montgo-merians attended the subsequent MIA meeting on Monday, February 20, to hear the proposed compromise. With the grand jury decision due out the following day, blacks voted down the MOM compromise and chose to risk further harassment, arrest, and even violent repercussions rather than to settle for anything less than full desegregation (Robinson 1987, 146–147).

As scheduled, the grand jury issued its decision on Tuesday, February 21. They deemed the bus boycott illegal, and the city prepared to arrest 115 protest leaders, all of them black. Anticipating the unfavorable ruling, the MIA had already prepared to bail out anyone arrested because of the boy-cott. Moreover, as Robinson wrote, "the boycotters had been expecting the announcement, and it seemed to allay the fears of those blacks who tended to be nervous, for 115 people could not possibly get lonely or afraid in jail together" (Robinson 1987, 149). The grand jury and Montgomery officials thought a mass arrest would intimidate blacks into breaking the protest, but the sheer number of arrest warrants issued assured black leaders that they would not be alone in their incarceration, and there was power, strength, and protection in numbers.

Rosa Parks was among those arrested and indicted for her role in the bus boycott. In the end, police arrested 89 of the 115 people on the list, and the MIA was prepared to bail everyone out of jail. Indictments followed on Friday, February 24, and the crowds supporting those arrested gave city officials pause. Robinson remembered, "The indicted persons, along with some 200 sympathizers, filed through the courthouse doors" (Robinson 1987, 155–156). The event intended to break the back of the movement further energized the black community for the protest efforts. Blacks came out in full force to support their protest leaders, and white officials and facilities were overwhelmed.

It was nearly a month before trials began, and Martin Luther King Jr. was the first to stand. Judge Eugene Carter, the man who empaneled the grand jury, presided over King's trial. Again, blacks came out in force to the legal proceedings, around five hundred strong (Robinson 1987, 159). The trial began on March 19 and lasted for several days. Over that time, the court heard numerous testimonies and examined page after page of MIA records. In the end, the court convicted King of breaking the law and fined him $500. The other eighty-eight protestors arrested waited to know if they were the next to stand trial, but King was the only person tried by the city. Their efforts at intimidation through legal means failed miserably. The MIA was stronger than ever, and the transportation system flourished despite every effort to destroy it. In fact, every plot to break the boycott had the opposite effect. Press coverage of the mass arrests and Dr. King's trial generated more support for the Montgomery Bus Boycott, and even more money poured in from outside sources. For her part, Rosa Parks increased her speaking engagements, raising additional funds for the NAACP and the MIA.

From New York to San Francisco, Rosa traveled through the spring of 1956, recounting her ordeal in December 1955 and the subsequent bus boycott. Much of her experience was positive, and she met many in solidarity with her and the movement. There were, however, some negative experiences. One such occasion came when a white reporter in San Francisco tried to intimidate and bully her during a scheduled interview. Rosa remembered breaking down, screaming, and crying at the offense. This loss of composure was very rare for Parks, and she attributed it to her grueling travel and speaking schedule. Roy Wilkins, executive secretary of the NAACP national office, helped to comfort her on this occasion. Emmett Till's mother, Mamie Till-Mobley, also broke down during her speaking engagements. Till-Mobley spent time in the hospital diagnosed with exhaustion due to the intensity of the schedule thrust on her by the NAACP national office. Both women learned to pace themselves, for they were much more useful to the movement when they were well (Parks 1992, 152–153; Mace 2014, 101–102).

Although she was not part of the lawsuit, Rosa Parks's work was invaluable for the legal battle. Her efforts at raising awareness helped turn the tide of public opinion toward desegregation, and she was the symbolic mother of the movement. Along with the nation, Rosa watched closely as the legal battle over segregation raged on. In June, a panel of three federal judges ruled that Montgomery's segregation laws violated the Constitution. Specifically, the court determined that segregation on the bus lines did not guarantee black citizens equal protection under the law as dictated in the Fourteenth Amendment. The first section of the Amendment read, "All persons born or naturalized in the United States, and subject to the jurisdiction thereof, are citizens of the United States and of the state wherein they reside. No state shall make or enforce any law which shall abridge the privileges or immunities of citizens of the United States; nor shall any state deprive any person of life, liberty, or property, without due process of law; nor deny to any person within its jurisdiction the equal protection of the laws." As citizens, black Americans were entitled to every right and privilege available to white citizens, and fair and equal treatment on Montgomery buses was one of those rights. States could not pass laws that infringed upon those rights, and Alabama segregation laws, as well as the laws and practices on buses in the city of Montgomery, ignored these Constitutional rights. It was clear to two of the federal judges that black Montgomerians experienced second-class citizenship on these buses, and the harassment, abuse, arrests, ridicule, and worse that black citizens encountered on these transports violated their civil rights. Having begun proceeding on May 11, the court, in a two-to-one decision, used *Brown v. Board of Education of Topeka, KS* as a precedent in this ruling. While Though knew Rosa Parks's arrest precipitated civil unrest and this monumental legal decision, Parks herself was not part of the suit, because she still had other legal actions pending. Fred Gray, who filed the suit known as *Browder v. Gayle*, did not want Rosa Parks's other legal actions, actions directly related to her leadership in the MIA, to cloud the segregation case. Aurelia Browder thus was the lead defendant against Montgomery mayor W. A. Gayle et al. Susie McDonald, Mary Louise Smith, and Claudette Colvin joined Browder on the suit, and future Supreme Court Justice Thurgood Marshall and the NAACP legal defense team joined the prosecutorial group as legal counsel.

Richard T. Rives wrote the majority opinion in the case, with Frank M. Johnson concurring. Seybourn Lynne dissented, but the majority opinion stood, meaning bus segregation was unconstitutional. *Browder* struck the final blow to separate but equal laws enacted after the 1896 Supreme Court decision *Plessy v. Ferguson* that set the legal precedent for segregation, Jim Crow, and the proliferation of white supremacy. The Montgomery case, like *Plessy* before it, dealt directly with segregation on public transportation, so *Browder*, not *Brown*, struck down the precedents of the 1896 Supreme Court ruling (Bernstein 1963, 193–204).

Despite the federal district court ruling, Montgomery officials continued segregation practices on public transportation. For five more months, segregation ruled the day on Montgomery buses, and over that time, black people remained steadfast in their resolve not to ride under those conditions. The city appealed the decision to the U.S. Supreme Court, still hoping to win a victory that would mean the justification of segregation. Hoping to distract attention from the district court defeat, city commissioners pursued an enjoinder—in other words, a cessation—of the MIA transportation program while they awaited an appeal decision in *Browder v. Gayle*. By changing the conversation to the legality of bus boycott activities rather than the legality of segregation laws, the commissioners hoped to generate some goodwill toward white Montgomery and criminalize black Montgomery. In the midst of this legal action at the state court level, the Supreme Court, on November 13, issued their *Browder* decision upholding the opinion of the district court that segregation violated the equal protection clause of the Fourteenth Amendment. The city tried one more tactic, requesting that the Supreme Court reconsider their ruling, but, on December 17, the Court rejected any further deliberation on this case. The Court sent a formal order to integrate the buses on December 20, and that day, the MIA voted to end the Montgomery Bus Boycott. The protest that began on December 5, 1955, was finally over, and black Montgomery basked in the glow of their triumph and resolve in the face of oppression. As Jo Ann Robinson remembered, that day, "it was terrible to watch women and children weep, hearing the news, and even more awful to see grown men stand and cry until their whole bodies shook with bitter memories of the past" (Robinson 1987, 163). Black Montgomerians put their lives on the line and threw their whole weight behind this push for their civil rights. The seemingly endless battles and the final victory left them wracked with tears of joy and, at the same time, persistent scars from the long days of enduring white supremacy. Of course, the ruling changed little in terms of race relations in Montgomery or in the nation as a whole, but black people rejoiced on this day because they won another battle in the long war for black liberation.

10

A Symbol Frozen in Time

"I would like to express the significance of the fact that in 1955 this protest movement against racial segregation began in Montgomery, Alabama the cradle of the Confederacy[.] . . . [I]t spread across the country in many forms in many ways, including the student sit-ins and all kinds of protests[.] . . . [C]oming back to Montgomery for the Selma to Montgomery march, was a just rounding-off of that era and in the movement[.] . . . The people witnessed many significant changes and unbelievable changes in the hearts and minds of Black people. And I learned much myself. I learned that no matter how much you try and how hard you work, to give people an incentive, it's something that you cannot yourself give another person[.] . . . [I]t has to be within the person to make the step and to have the belief and faith that they should be free people, and the complacency and the fear and the oppression that people have suffered so long after the emancipation of chattel slavery and the replacement of the mental slavery of people who believe, actually believe that they were inferior to others because of the position that they had to hold and the oppression they had to endure, when that was thrown off and they began to stand up and be vocal, be heard and make known their dissatisfaction against being treated as inferior beings[.] . . . [I]t is my belief now, especially with the young people as well as some few older ones who are left in spite of all the assassination, that we will never go back to that time again in our lives. And even with much of what has happened to our dismay, and to our unhappiness and our feeling

135

FREEDOM RIDES

The Freedom Rides of 1961, organized by the Congress of Racial Equality (CORE), were a series of bus trips from Washington, D.C., to destinations in the South. The revolutionary aspect of the rides was the fact that the black and white people who rode on these buses refused to obey laws segregating public transportation and bus terminals. Current Congressman John Lewis, one of the initial seven black riders, was attacked and brutally beaten when he attempted to enter the Greyhound bus terminal's white waiting room in Rock Hill, North Carolina. However, he continued on the rides. Additionally, these riders had their bus firebombed in Anniston, Alabama; and once they arrived in Montgomery, Alabama, an angry mob beat the riders so badly that they had to be hospitalized. Images of this brutality hit the print and television media, and Attorney General Robert Kennedy sent federal marshals to restore order. When the riders eventually made it to Jackson, Mississippi, they were arrested. That summer, over three hundred Freedom Riders served time in Mississippi prisons. However, their efforts were successful, for African American activism increased, and the media presented America and the world with more images of white brutality and racial hatred against innocent African Americans.

that we wish things could have been another way, it is much better to make changes than to remain or go back to the old way of life[.] . . . I continue to be hopeful that there will be a way for us to eventually know [sic] freedom with all its meaning and what it should be here in this country" (Parks, Horton, and Nixon 1973).

After the Montgomery Bus Boycott, Rosa Louise Parks continued her tireless efforts for racial uplift. However, the mother of the civil rights movement paid a high price for her activism. Though she described losing her job at Montgomery Fair in early 1956 as a blessing of sorts, the termination left her in a desperate financial situation. Her husband, Raymond Parks, also found himself unemployed that year, and the couple struggled to make ends meet. As Jeanne Theoharis noted in her biography, "Understanding the fullness of Parks's political life requires looking at the economic insecurity, health issues, fear, and harassment she endured the year of the bus boycott and for the ensuing decade" (Theoharis 2013, 117). For sure, "being a heroine was difficult" (Theoharis 2013, 117).

In recounting her story, Rosa Parks herself did not go into much detail about her hardships, and some of that is due to her willingness to put the movement for racial uplift above her own personal narrative. Theoharis pointed out, "The erasure of Parks's hardships stem partly from the ways she was publically cast as a tired seamstress. . . . Montgomery activists, including Parks herself, had realized the importance of a symbol to coalesce around. . . . But the danger of symbols is that they get fixed in time. They require honor but not necessarily assistance, so the fact that the figure was a real woman with a real family who was suffering became difficult to see" (Theoharis 2013, 117). Mamie Till-Mobley, the mother of Emmett Till, also suffered great financial distress while she fought for justice in her son's lynching. Till-Mobley agreed to conduct a West Coast speaking tour during the month of November 1955, but after consulting with her financial advisor, she realized the allotted funds would not cover her expenses. Her financial advisor informed her that she would not be able to pay her bills with the current arrangement. Rosa Parks also conducted a good number of speaking engagements under the auspices of the NAACP and other organizations, and those public engagements interfered with her availability to work. Moreover, her public image as a civil rights agitator meant many white employers refused to hire her (Mace 2014).

For both Rosa Parks and Mamie Till-Mobley, a life dedicated to racial uplift meant constant sacrifice, economic alienation, and, very often, living life as a symbol rather than as a person. During the bus boycott, this meant that Rosa Parks lost her job at the white department store and that the black community did not rally behind her to secure full-time employment for her or her husband. Granted, Montgomery blacks did not have independently wealthy benefactors in their ranks who could afford to support the Parks family, but the Montgomery Improvement Association (MIA) did employ some full-time staff members. Rosa Parks did not demand a job at MIA—that was not her style—but she "recognized the possibility of a job for her within the organization." Jeanne Theoharis speculated that "social position" played a role in MIA hiring practices, as the four paid female employees in MIA were "sophisticated, socially prominent, well-trained 'young ladies' who were members of the [Women's Political Council] WPC with professional husbands. Rosa Parks, who was decidedly working class, was a seamstress and she was married to a barber" (Theoharis 2013, 119).

Still, some close friends, like Virginia Durr, recognized the Parks family economic woes and endeavored to assist the family. Durr and her husband, despite being white, did not have the finances to assist Rosa Parks on their own, but Virginia did write to her close friends asking for assistance. One letter recipient was Myles Horton, founder of the civil rights–oriented Highlander Folk School. Rosa Parks attended a workshop at this Tennessee-based school in the summer of 1955, shortly before she refused to give up her seat on the Montgomery bus. Highlander had a powerful effect on Parks, and she had tremendous respect for Horton. Myles Horton, for his part, did invite Parks to speak at Highlander, and he offered her some financial support, but it was not enough to stall the financial distress. Martin Luther King Jr. also noted Rosa Parks's financial woes, and he asked that MIA donate some funds to the family. In his letter, addressed to Reverend Ralph Abernathy, King noted that "'because of her tremendous self respect she had not already revealed this [her financial distress] to the organization." This letter led to the release of $300 from the MIA account to the Parks family (Theoharis 2013, 121).

Even with her numerous speaking engagements on behalf of the MIA and the NAACP, Rosa Parks could not clear enough money to support her family. This is because she turned over to the sponsoring organizations money raised at her engagements. Jeanne Theoharis noted that this was not always the case. Some boycott speakers kept a portion of the funds raised at these events as payment for their time and effort (Theoharis 2013, 122–124).

Rosa Parks's strain was not limited to financial issues. Following her bus stand, she and her family endured constant threats through the mail and over the phone. She recalled that the threats continued even after the *Browder v. Gayle* Supreme Court decision that ruled Montgomery's bus segregation laws unconstitutional. The intimidation campaign got so intense that Raymond Parks "slept with a gun nearby at all times." Hoping to deter would be callers, Rosa's mother, Leona McCauley, would phone her friends like Bertha Butler and stay on the phone for long stretches of time. In this way, Leona ensured that the intimidators encountered a busy signal when they called the Parks home with their threats (Parks 1992, 161).

The entire Parks family felt the effects of the violence and fear campaign waged against the black boycotter in Montgomery. Raymond Parks, longtime civil rights strategist and organizer, suffered health issues connected to the stress of the bus boycott. He began drinking after his wife's arrest, and, having succeeded in shielding Rosa from some of the major threats against their family during the Scottsboro trials and other events, he felt a sense of powerlessness during and after the bus boycott. Being forced to resign his position in the wake of Rosa's arrest did not help matters. Jeanne Theoharis surmised, "This period may have been harder on Raymond Parks and Leona McCauley than on Rosa Parks because it was they who were home answering more of the incessant hate calls and death threats. Rosa was away from home making appearances for the MIA around the country, so she escaped some of the daily vitriol that her husband and mother endured" (Theoharis 2013, 102).

Raymond Parks suffered a nervous breakdown during the Montgomery Bus Boycott, and he reportedly visited a psychiatrist. Still, Raymond's support of Rosa and her work was unwavering. He faced his own personal demons, drinking more and chain-smoking during the boycott, but he never backed away from supporting Rosa through the ordeal. Rosa always acknowledged the tremendous support she received from her husband, and family friend and poet Nikki Giovanni corroborated this based on her experiences with the family. Jeanne Theoharis quoted Giovanni saying, "Nobody would say that Coretta wasn't courageous because she worried about Martin. So why say it about Raymond?" (Theoharis 2013, 123). For her part, Rosa likened Raymond struggles to those of a person in a war zone effected by the "trauma of battle" (Theoharis 2013, 124).

Theoharis further noted that Rosa Parks also felt the physical and psychological effects of this war zone. Rosa was sick a lot as a child, and some of these ailments came back following her arrest. Parks "developed painful stomach ulcers and a heart condition that would plague her for many years" (Theoharis 2013, 124). Her insomnia first manifested in her youth as she sat up with her grandfather ready to ward off Ku Klux Klan attacks came back during the bus boycott. Some three decades removed from the experiences of her youth, Rosa Parks again spent sleepless nights beside the most important man in her life as he armed himself against would-be attackers.

Rosa was able to escape some of the awfulness due to her speaking schedule. In March of 1956, she returned to Highlander Folk School, this time to speak at a workshop about the bus boycott. That same month, Parks took her first flight, traveling to Detroit, Michigan, to speak about and raise money for the boycott. There she spent time with her brother Sylvester, who had moved to Detroit after his service in the army during World War II. Sylvester McCauley also felt the weight of the bus boycott, even from Detroit. He worried about blacks in his native Montgomery, particularly his sister, brother-in-law, and mother, and he consistently urged Rosa to move away from Alabama and settle in the North (Theoharis 2013, 127).

During her travels, Rosa Parks met many prominent activists and celebrities. In New York, in 1956, she met stars like Sammy Davis Jr., Cab Calloway, and Pearl Bailey as well as political figures Ralph Bunch and Eleanor Roosevelt. In the late summer of 1956, Parks returned to Highlander in a ceremony commemorating the one-year anniversary of her initial visit. Parks continued to travel throughout the rest of 1956, even as black Montgomery continued to wage the boycott. Rosa was a star outside of Montgomery, but the black community in the city continued to offer her little to no financial support. Yet, she persisted, convinced of the importance of her work and of the work of the boycott. Despite multiple court rulings against bus segregation, Montgomery officials persisted with existing segregation policies. However, it was clear the public opinion was on the side of black protestors. This massive public support outside of Montgomery helped sustain the boycott financially and increased the necessity for yet more public appearances from Rosa Parks. At one point in 1956, she embarked on a ten-day tour with at least ten speaking engagements. The pace was exhausting, yet Rosa Parks met each demand with determination and resolve, knowing how her efforts would help to further racial justice (Theoharis 2013, 128–129).

The end of the bus boycott did not bring relief for Rosa and her family. Neither she nor Raymond could find employment after the boycott. They were pariahs, and white business owners refused to offer them work. There existed within white Montgomery a full-frontal economic boycott of the Parks family that rivaled the boycott levied by the black community against city officials and the bus company. The Parks family, however, did not have the resources of the city or the bus company necessary to weather the storm of this boycott. Increasingly, the notion of escaping Montgomery's hardships appealed to Rosa and Raymond Parks, and Sylvester McCauley's suggestions to move to Detroit began to resonate with them.

As the Parks family weighed their options, Rosa and E. D. Nixon teamed up again for a renewed push for black voter registration. The two estimated that with a small budget, they could set up a voter registration office that would employ Rosa full time in registration efforts. Many MIA leaders, however, saw a different pathway for black uplift following the successful bus boycott. Martin Luther King Jr. and the ministers of the MIA formed the Southern Christian Leadership Conference (SCLC) in January 1957 to lead black uplift efforts. King and the ministers had a vision that conflicted with that of Parks and Nixon. In part, the conflict fell on socioeconomic class lines as the black working class in Montgomery suffered the most disenfranchisement. Nixon and King clashed over competing visions, and in the middle was Rosa Parks and her increasingly dire financial situation. Nixon and Parks had a plan for uplift that would empower the black masses and employ Parks in the process. King and the well-to-do ministers wanted a more high-profile initiative, and their plan did not include provisions for Rosa Parks. Quoting Virginia Durr's assessment of the situation, Jeanne Theoharis offered, "Parks 'has been a heroine everywhere else, [but] they have not given her a job here although she has needed on desperately. . . . They know she cannot get a job, they know she has suffered and is suffering and they blandly do nothing about it as all and this drives me nearly nuts and makes me distrust them very much indeed'" (Theoharis 2013, 138).

For her part, Rosa Parks contemplated the lack of support she received during and after the bus boycott. In an early draft of her autobiography, she outlined a chapter entitled "In the Shadow" (Theoharis 2013, 139). In that chapter, Rosa Parks planned to discuss conflicts in the MIA, her displeasure with Martin Luther King, and the lack of financial support after she lost her job. Specifically, the chapter notes read, "Jealousy and dissension within the Montgomery Improvement Association—Rosa Parks has lost her job at Montgomery Fair department store over the incident that sparked the boycott and feels that she should be given a job with the Montgomery Improvement Association—but King refuses, and Rosa feels angry—she goes through extreme financial difficulties—by the time Rosa is offered a job in the voter registration drive that King decides to start, she has accepted a job at Hampton" (Theoharis 2013, 139).

Hampton University in Hampton, Virginia offered Rosa Parks a chance for economic renewal, but that relief did not come until 1957. Throughout 1956 the Parks family struggled to make ends meet while Rosa persisted with her grueling speaking schedule. Death threats abounded during that time, and Rosa, Raymond, and Leona all suffered health setbacks. Raymond's drinking continued to increase, and Rosa's heart condition grew worse. Jeanne Theoharis recounted, "Leona McCauley grew worried about her daughter's safety," and she "became 'very suspicious because of the very underhanded things that have happened to her and her family since Rosa sat on that bus and refused to move'" (Theoharis 2013, 140). Dealing with her own physical ailments and suffering the financial hardships and constant intimidation alongside her daughter and son-in-law, Leona began to push the family to join her son Sylvester in Detroit.

Without sustained support from the Montgomery Improvement Association, and with minimal provisions coming from places like Highlander Folk School, the Parks family suffered greatly. The only foreseeable recourse was to leave Montgomery and settle somewhere that offered more economic opportunities. Rosa and Raymond agreed with Leona, and the family moved to Detroit in the summer of 1957. This came as welcome news to Sylvester, who had long pushed to have Rosa, Raymond, and Leona resettle in his new hometown. Rosa recalled that she had long wanted to leave Montgomery, but Raymond felt a draw to stay and work for social uplift there. After all, he had spent so much of his young adult life working on social justice issues like the Scottsboro case, and he wanted to improve conditions in Alabama more than he wanted to leave the troubles behind. The bus boycott, and the lack of support the Parks family received in the years after Rosa's arrest, changed Raymond's mind. Jeanne Theoharis noted, "The decision also came partly from the unfriendly reception Rosa was receiving from certain members within Montgomery's civil rights community" (Theoharis 2013, 140–141). On this point, Rosa told a *Pittsburgh Courier* reporter, "I can't exactly say that the reaction from what happened in the boycott made me leave. I really had been thinking about leaving for a long time. But I guess something did have a part in our deciding to go, or rather my husband's deciding for us." Douglas Brinkley noted, "Much of the resentment sprang from male chauvinism" (Brinkley 2000, 175).

There are some clear signs that even her longtime friend and collaborator, E. D. Nixon, resented Rosa Parks's notoriety, but in a 1970 interview, he decried the ways the Montgomery community treated Parks. Nixon recounted, "Mrs. Parks stood up for the black community. But the community didn't stand up for her. . . . The whites wouldn't give her a job, and the Negroes wouldn't support her. . . . After the whites made it hard for her to get a job, all the doors closed on her, and the Negroes kept them closed" (Selby and Selby 1971, 64). The labor organizer and treasurer of the MIA furthered, "When Mrs. Parks finally left Montgomery, the MIA had about $400,000. They could have taken $100,000 and set up a trust fund for Mrs. Parks, and with the $5000 a year interest she could have stayed here [in Montgomery]" (Selby and Selby 1971, 64).

The economic alienation of Rosa Parks and her family by white Montgomery came as little surprise to African Americans who were used to such oppressive acts and worse on the part of white people, but the ways the black community abandoned her in her lowest moment raised questions. However, Rosa's story was familiar in an era when black organizations searched for symbols to drive their agenda while also battling incessant accusations of financial malfeasance and treasonous Communist activity. Rosa Parks was the symbol of the bus boycott and desegregation efforts in Montgomery and across the nation. As a symbol, she had to be above all reproach and devoid of any perceived weaknesses. As such, leaders of MIA likely felt it would lessen her image to disclose any financial hardships. If the icon of the movement was susceptible to economic pressures, then the boycott, too, was susceptible. The success of movements for racial equality depended in part on the perception that these efforts were unalterable, inalienable, and indelible. In other words, the movement leaders could not admit that white supremacists had any power over them. Thus, Rosa Parks could not have financial difficulties. She was secure, and the movement that she represented was equally secure.

Yes, the MIA could have funded the Parks family through this ordeal, and they should have done so. However, there were also concerns brought on by the intense scrutiny the federal government placed on these organizations. Similar to the Emmett Till lynching and other racial atrocities in this era, the Federal Bureau of Investigation (FBI) and other government entities attempted to find any excuse to shut down protests. Doubtlessly, if the MIA funded the Parks family, the FBI, and likely the Internal Revenue Service (IRS), would investigate. These investigations would not paint the MIA or Rosa Parks in a favorable light. When the NAACP collaborated with Mamie Till-Mobley to push for justice in her son's lynching, the IRS intensified its scrutiny of the organization's finances. The FBI went as far as coercing prominent civil rights figures, like photographer Ernest Withers, to infiltrate organizations and look for ways to dismantle racial uplift movements (Mace 2014, 102; Lauterbach 2019; Perrusquia 2017).

Reduced to a symbol, unsupported and perhaps even unsupportable, Rosa Parks, along with her husband and mother, decided to relocate to Detroit, where her brother lived. That city also claimed Rosa's first cousins Thomas Williamson and Annie Cruse. When he heard of her plan to come to Detroit, Williamson wired $300 to the family to fund their trip. Black Montgomery also rose to the occasion, raising $500 for the family's move. At a going-away service hosted by St. Paul's AME Church, Rosa Parks referenced her financial condition when she cautioned attendees that "they could never win unless they fought for the rights of everyone to have opportunities, and not just themselves." Having delivered her final speech as a resident of Alabama, Rosa Parks and her family moved to Detroit in August 1957 (Theoharis 2013, 149).

Financial relief came soon after the move. Alonzo Moron, president of the historically black Hampton Institute in Hampton, Virginia, offered her a job as hostess at the hotel on campus, the Holy Tree Inn. Parks and Moron met in Boston, Massachusetts while Parks was conducting a speaking engagement and Moron offered Parks a job at that time. The job was a departure from her trade as a seamstress, but Rosa welcomed the work, moving to Virginia and beginning work in October. Of this role, she described, "I would be in charge of the off-the-campus guests and also the men and women, faculty and staff, who lived there. Four women worked half days cleaning the rooms, and I would be in charge of them" (Parks 1992, 162). Initially, Rosa hoped Raymond and Leona would be able to move to Virginia along with her, but that was not the case.

These conditions proved difficult for Rosa, as they did for her husband and mother. Rosa recalled Raymond and Leona were not well, and Jeanne Theoharis pointed out that Rosa's ulcers really bothered her during her time at Hampton. Her clothes no longer fit her because she was losing so much weight due to her inability to eat. Rosa felt lonely without her family around her, and she missed them. She also found the job boring, and she felt tethered to the Inn. She inquired more than once about securing housing and a job for her husband, but she was unsuccessful each time. Hampton Institute maintained an apartment, but the college would not allow Parks to move there. She believed the Institute wanted to reserve that housing for faculty. Still, the $3,600 yearly salary was a blessing for the previously financially strapped Parks family, and Rosa stayed at Hampton as long as she could bear it. Money woes followed her family, however, and Rosa learned while she was working in Hampton that her brother Sylvester had stopped receiving pay from his employer even though he continued to work. Rosa's mother Leona McCauley wrote her daughter about seeing Sylvester's wife and children crying because there was no food to eat. Leona requested at times that Rosa send money back home to assist the family, and she was not able to save money out of her Hampton paycheck at the rate she wished to save. Rosa returned to Detroit for the 1958 Christmas holiday, and she had surgery at that time. Her husband had been hospitalized in July 1958 with pneumonia, and Rosa had worried a great deal about him, given her geographic separation from him and the poor medical conditions in black hospitals in Detroit. All of these factors compounded her own physical and psychological stress, and Rosa Parks decided not to return to Hampton in 1959. The separation, combined with her failing health and the failing health of her husband, helped solidify her decision (Parks 1992, 162–164; Theoharis 2013, 148–150).

The financial issues did not subside with Rosa's employment at Hampton or with her return to Detroit. Jeanne Theoharis recounted that Rosa Parks's nieces called her "Recycling Queen" and "Mrs. Thrifty" as she tried every means to make ends meet (Theoharis 2013, 150). It did not help that Rosa and Raymond's health issues limited their ability to work, but even when they were feeling well, there was little employment available. The Parkses felt Detroit would be a land of opportunity, but they largely encountered hardship. Rosa came to call her new city "The Northern Promised Land That Wasn't" (Theoharis 2013, 150). She had managed to save "$1,300 from her time at Hampton," but that did not last long with their persistent unemployment or underemployment (Theoharis 2013, 167). The family also had to deal with mounting medical cost that further impaired their ability to survive. The state of Michigan had very stringent licensing requirements to work as a barber, and Raymond Parks had difficulty navigating the system due in part to his failing health. Raymond did not work for most of 1959, and the family had to move out of their seventy-dollar-per-month apartment and move in to two rooms at the Progressive Civic League meeting hall. There, the Parks family paid forty dollars a month in rent while Raymond served as caretaker of the facility and Rosa as treasurer manager.

Rosa Parks's health declined steadily over the course of 1960, and she entered the hospital in the winter of that year. She lost thirty pounds due to her illnesses, and she finally had her ulcer operated on in December. Much of her weight loss was due to her inability to eat, and the stress of financial hardship further exacerbated her health condition. The surgery put the family in greater debt as they now owed $560 in medical bills. Raymond was in better health by this time, and he had secured two barbering jobs that brought in roughly fifteen to twenty dollars a week, but that money could not sustain the family and pay off the medical debt. The hospital invoice went into collections, as "they slowly chipped away at the bill, $10 a month," Jeanne Theoharis recounted (Theoharis 2013, 152). Rosa Parks also incurred medical expenses related to a tumor found on her throat in that year. Theoharis further noted that black newspapers continued to run periodic stories detailing Rosa Parks's financial struggles, but these stories failed to engender much financial support from black individuals, communities, or organizations.

In the midst of despair reminiscent of her mood immediately before she visited the Highlander Folk School, Parks once again gained energy and motivation from black youth. On February 1, 1960, four black students from North Carolina A&T staged a sit-in at the local Woolworth's store in Greensboro, North Carolina. This protest set off a national movement to challenge segregation in all public venues, and it led to the founding of the Student Nonviolent Coordinating Committee (SNCC) in 1960. Ella Baker, longtime civil rights activist, worked closely with these youths in the process. Jeanne Theoharis cited Rosa Parks's assessment of this youth movement: "We decided with these setbacks and reprisals, we still cannot afford to give up . . . we couldn't consider it a lost cause because out of [these difficulties] . . . there comes a new and young fresh group of people who have taken this action in the sit-in demonstrations and [it] seems that they have put more pressure to bear than many of us have done in the past" (Theoharis 2013, 153).

With black youth continuing to serve as her impetus for fighting racial inequity, Rosa Parks maintained her race uplift work through her physical and financial difficulties. The year 1961 proved to be a better time for the Parks family. Rosa's health improved, and both she and Raymond secured steady work. Raymond worked at Wildermere Barber Shop, and Rosa found employment at the Stockton Sewing Company. Rosa's work in particular was grueling, and she often worked ten-hour days. While not ideal working conditions, particularly for someone who had lifelong health issues, the jobs helped the Parks family climb out of debt. The family was able to use the increased income to move into an apartment in the segregated Virginia Park neighborhood near Raymond's job. Still, even a slight sense of financial security came only after nearly a decade of hardship for Rosa Parks and her family. The woman heralded as the mother of the civil rights movement found little right to economic security either in Alabama or in Michigan. The dream of a better life in the promised land of the North did not materialize, and, like many other African Americans migrating from the south, Rosa Parks "did not find 'too much difference' between . . . Montgomery and Detroit" (Theoharis 2013, 166).

From 1917 through the early 1940s, African Americans poured into Midwest cities in search of employment, housing, autonomy, and greater racial equality. Black Southerners learned of these opportunities, and they moved their families to this region. The only lull in the migration came during the Great Depression, but once the country mobilized for the war effort during World War II, African Americans again decided to make the Midwest their home. But although many black families moved to this region, they still maintained ties with relatives who remained in the South (Goodwin 1990, 27).

Numerous factors affected the migration. Push factors like racial oppression, poor economic opportunity, hate crimes, poor access to education, boll weevil infestations, and poor living conditions drove African

GREAT BLACK MIGRATION

Companies like Ford Motors actively pursued black workers. Henry Ford loved the idea of recruiting black workers. He spent time and money courting African Americans, and one of his plants housed a largely integrated workforce. Ford's loyalty to the black community, including various support and funding efforts, endeared him to African Americans and ensured that African Americans would support him in his business dealings. This support served Ford well, because the exclusion of African Americans from union activity weakened the union base at his various plants. Ford knew this, and he continued to throw his support to the black community. Corporations like Ford knew that racism directed toward black workers would create strife on the plant floor. Adding to the tension, companies used African American workers as strikebreakers. It is important to note that black workers did not cross the picket lines out of disloyalty to a union. In almost every case, African Americans were excluded from these unions. Thus, union goals did not pertain to black workers. They were simply trying to make a living. However, when black workers decided not to support the corporation, employers quickly ceased their community assistance programs. The close tie between the Ford Corporation and black workers continued until the 1941 strike. During this strike, African Americans threw their support behind the workers. This infuriated the company and alienated the black workers from the corporation. As a result, black workers had to turn to the United Auto Workers Union (UAW) for support and job security. The UAW did not feel any loyalty to African Americans, and they did little to support black union members.

Americans out of the south in unprecedented numbers during the first half of the twentieth century. Concurrently, pull factors like booming industry, war mobilization, job postings, previous migration of relatives, and hopes for more racial harmony tempted Southerners. Unfortunately, the reality of life in the Midwest was often different from the fantasy these migrants envisioned.

As the numbers of black people increased, these cities, unfamiliar with dealing with such large numbers of African Americans, endured racial turmoil and strife. Detroit as a case study epitomized this point, as the "Motor City" had the greatest housing problems (Sugrue 1996). Housing was also a major concern in Cleveland and Chicago, even though both cities contained multiple black neighborhoods, known as "black ghettoes" (Kusmer 1976 46). The majority of black people resided in Chicago's South Side because housing discrimination restricted their ability to live elsewhere; however, the West Side also housed a large percentage of black people (Goodwin 1990, 79–80). Much of the reason for the massive growth in Chicago's black population is attributable to the fact that the *Chicago*

Defender sent job postings and letters from recent migrants to black people in the South (Wolseley 1990, 53–55). Additionally, Chicago lay at the nexus of two railroads and served as a processing and distribution hub for the food industry. As the century progressed, increased hostility between races would continue to plague all Midwest cities (Trotter 1985). These issues combined into what Thomas Sugrue called, an "urban crisis" (Sugrue 1996). This "urban crisis" was clear in the workplace. Black migrants found themselves in an industrial war, and they faced frequent acts of exploitation and terrorism. Working-class white people resented the influx of black workers, and corporations used this fact to their advantage, employing cheaper black laborers to break down the power of segregated unions (Nelson 2003).

Once they left the shop, black workers encountered dismal and discriminatory conditions. After World War II, cities faced serious overcrowding issues. Exacerbating these problems was the fact that the federal government promised housing and opportunity for returning veterans. As with most policies in that era, and today, the benefit was largely seen within the white community. African American veterans were not supplied housing opportunities, and the housing they found was in the overcrowded black neighborhoods. Even with the promise of low-interest mortgages and the GI Bill, black veterans were unable to invest in property that would appreciate and increase family wealth. Redlining, or depreciation of housing values in African American neighborhoods, occurred frequently and with federal government support. Thus, people did not want to buy houses in areas where African Americans lived. This led to increased white flight. Adding to the problem, real estate agents formed pacts that intentionally excluded black people from moving into white neighborhoods, and whites made a point not to put their houses on the market for fear that blacks might try to infiltrate the "racially pure" communities. Compounding all of this was the fact that urban renewal projects destroyed housing available in the black community. Therefore, despite the lack of adequate housing, the state and local governments decided to level much of what housing already existed. Excluded from the suburban dream, black families turned to whatever government housing remained in the cities.

With growing national and international awareness of the conditions black Americans faced regardless of their locale, the climate was ripe for protest. From Montgomery in 1955 through Greensboro in 1960, blacks faced down and won public opinion against white supremacy. This is not to say that black people had not been exercising individual and collective protests beyond those covered in this text. Black people have protested their condition in overt and covert ways since the first Africans came to what would become the United States of America in 1619. As a people, African Americans faced inferior and inequitable conditions from that time forward, and they have met each oppression with resolve and depth of courage, convinced of the justice in the fight.

Such was the case in 1963 when A. Philip Randolph, founder of the largest African American labor union, the Brotherhood of Sleeping Car Porters, created the March on Washington Movement of 1963. In previous years, Randolph had organized and planned marches to protest various forms of racial oppression in the nation. None of the previous plans ended in an actual march, but each effected change in racial policies and practices; thus, each effort was successful. In 1963, however, people did march en masse on the on the nation's capital. Hundreds of thousands of protestors descended on Washington, D.C., in the summer of 1963 in the March on Washington for Jobs and Freedom.

As with so many other major events in the modern civil rights movement, Rosa Parks was at the March on Washington for Jobs and Freedom. Also reminiscent of other events, leaders minimized her efforts. In fact, one of the major critiques of this monumental march, a protest that pressed Congress to pass the Civil Rights Act of 1964, was the marginalization of the women in the movement. It was only after concerted pushback that a tribute to the women of the movement was added to the program. Jeanne Theoharis called the tribute to six women—Rosa Parks, Gloria Richardson, Diane Nash, Myrlie Evers, Prince E. Lee, and Daisy Bates—"an awkwardly brief recognition of women's roles in the struggle for civil rights" (Theoharis 2013, 161). Bates introduced the tribute and spoke the most words, 142 in total, but her speech was written for her by a man, John Morsell. Organizers selected Bates because their first choice, Myrlie Evers, was not able to attend the march. Diane Nash also did not attend (Fitzgerald 2018).

In the memo where march co-organizers A. Philip Randolph and Bayard Rustin acquiesced to a women's tribute, the two wrote: "The difficulty of finding a single woman to speak without causing serious problems vis-à-vis other women and women's groups suggest the following is the best way to utilize these women. That the Chairman would introduce these women, telling of their role in the struggle and tracing their spiritual ancestry back to Sojourner Truth and Harriet Tubman. As each one is introduced, she would stand for applause, and after the last one had been introduced and the Chairman had called for general applause, they would sit" (Theoharis 2013, 161).

As well-intentioned as it might have been, the memo raised several glaring issues that speak to the culture of gender in the civil rights movement— a culture that resigned Rosa Parks to nearly a decade of poverty while the men of the movement used her image to promote the cause.

Randolph and Rustin's memo objectified the women of the movement, suggesting that the tribute was an avenue to "utilize" rather than celebrate their effort. At nearly every turn since she refused to give up her seat on that Montgomery bus, others, mainly the MIA men, used her image to forward the cause of bus desegregation. As an object of the movement, and not a person who was the driving force behind it, Rosa Parks did not require support, nurturing, or comfort. She could be referenced without being seen or heard, and she could be hauled out at the whim of movement leaders. Moreover, the co-organizers implied that women in the movement had a higher level of pride and jealousy than the men. According to the memo, selecting one woman instead of another would create "serious problems vis-à-vis other women and women's groups" (Theoharis 2013, 161). In other words, the women who did not receive a place of honor would feel jealous of the one or ones who received acknowledgment. The solution: honor six instead of one. Yet, this very process suggested that only six women were worthy of praise that day, which was far from the truth. According to Jo Ann Robinson, MIA leader and president of the Montgomery Women's Political Council, the men, particularly the male ministers, carried a great deal of pride and jealousy. For this reason, when Robinson and her students distributed announcements about the one-day bus boycott, they left copies in the church where Montgomery's black clergy planned to meet on Friday December 2, 1955, so that "they all felt equal, included, appreciated and needed" (Robinson 1987, 53).

The idea of spiritual ancestry linked to Sojourner Truth and Harriet Tubman posed yet another issue in the memo. Although these two women's activism and impact on black lives was undeniable, foregrounding ties between the female honorees of 1963 and these historical women called into question the autonomy that each of these powerful women exhibited throughout their own lives. Yes, the historical links were important, but the black men who dominated the day and the public face of the movement were under no such restraints to conform their activism to that of historical figures. Commensurate with her treatment throughout the movement, Rosa Parks, like the other women honored that day, was expected to "stand for applause" and then sit while the men around her took the spotlight and offered their voice to lead the charge for civil rights (Theoharis 2013, 161).

It was ironic, perhaps, that a black male leader helped usher in a period of financial renewal and newfound voice for Rosa Parks. Having narrowly won the democratic nomination, Detroit resident John Conyers was elected to the United States House of Representatives in 1964. Rosa Parks was an ardent supporter of his campaign, and when Representative Conyers went to Washington, D.C., he hired Rosa as an administrative assistant in his Detroit field office. The job included a salary, much-needed health insurance, and a pension, and the Parks family saw an end to their financial strain. For her part, Rosa offered Conyers a powerful ally whose image lent credibility to his legislative actions. Theoharis surmised that "having this

Southern heroine greet constituents in his office, attend community meetings, or stand beside him at public events embodied the mix of old and
new black politics that Conyers was attempting to bring to the national
stage" (Theoharis 2013, 164). The symbiotic partnership afforded Rosa
Parks the space and security to bring her civil rights–minded energies to
bear on the pressing issues in her new home city of Detroit.

Parks and Conyers worked well together, and there was a great deal of
work to be done in Detroit and in the nation as a whole. Rosa Parks found
deep racism in her new hometown. In fact, Parks lamented that racism in
Detroit rivaled racism in Montgomery. The biggest difference was "racial
inequality in Detroit was more covert" (Theoharis 2013, 166). However,
"Like Montgomery, the city offered a decidedly second-class citizenship
for blacks. The system of racial caste and power in Detroit denied people of
color equitable education, safe policing, real job opportunities, a respon-
sive government, regular quality sanitation and health services, and due
process under the law" (Theoharis 2013, 166–167). In her autobiography,
Rosa recognized that the Civil Rights Act of 1964 "gave black people some
protection, and some way to get redress for unfair treatment," but the legislation "did not solve all our problems" (Parks 1992, 167). Of note, Rosa
took issue with the public school system in Detroit. The overcrowding in
segregated black schools, lack of good-paying jobs for blacks, and segregated housing conditions exacerbated by white flight to the suburbs were
particularly appalling to Parks. Detroit did not have the placards denoting
white and "colored"—the common term used for African Americans—
nonetheless, in hotels, restaurants, and hospitals, segregation was the
unspoken rule. That is why both Rosa and Raymond Parks had to conva-
lesce in the inferior facilities offered by black hospitals when they fell ill
during the 1960s.

Shaped by years of enduring and fighting against racial inequality in the
south and the north, Rosa Parks committed to hearing and helping people
during her time working for Congressman Conyers. Jeanne Theoharis
recounted how she traveled around Detroit visiting "constituents at
schools, hospitals, and senior citizen homes" (Theoharis 2013, 183). As
Theoharis noted, Rosa kept Conyers "grounded in community activism" by
attending meetings and rallies aimed at breaking down racial discrimination in Detroit and across the north. She worked diligently to address con-
stituent concerns, and Conyers's aides Leon Atchison and Larry Horwitz
emphasized in interviews that Parks "made her own political agenda, and
that she attended many black political events because of her own beliefs
and moral compass not because the congressman sent her or she was representing him" (Theoharis 2013, 183).

According to colleagues in Conyers's office, Rosa Parks "was a presence"
(Theoharis 2013, 185). Black constituents who visited the office stood in

awe of her, and, over the course of her tenure with Conyers, "busloads of schoolchildren came to meet her" (Theoharis 2013, 185). Yet, Rosa did real work for the congressman and for the civil rights causes that she supported. She also took time to mentor and support younger activists, something that engendered great respect and appreciation in her colleagues. Theoharis quoted Conyers staffer Jamila Braithwaite's recollection that Rosa Parks "gave us that time. If you wanted to talk, she would talk to you" (Theoharis 2013, 185). In Braithwaite's case, Rosa even suggested the junior staffer read about Malcolm X.

Born Malcolm Little on May 19, 1925, in Omaha, Nebraska, Malcolm X felt the full weight of white supremacy throughout his life. His father, a Baptist minister and devotee of Marcus Garvey, preached black self-reliance and black resistance to white supremacy. His rhetoric drew the ire of white supremacist organizations, and the Little family moved multiple times to evade violent reactions to the fiery preacher. Earl Little, Malcolm's father, died in 1931, almost definitely assassinated by white supremacists, though authorities ruled his death an accident. Malcolm's mother, Louise, suffered a nervous breakdown years after her husband's death, and Malcolm and his siblings had to live in various orphanages and foster homes. As an adult, Malcolm was convicted of burglary and spent seven years in prison. It was during this incarceration that he converted to the Nation of Islam, and he worked for that black nationalist group until 1964, the year before his assassination.

On the surface, Rosa Parks's affinity for Malcolm X might seem incongruous. The image of quietude and nonviolence commonly associated with the mother of the civil rights movement flies in the face of depictions of Malcolm X as the bombastic, brash black separatist who promoted violence as a pathway to black liberation. In fact, the juxtaposition of Rosa Parks and Malcolm X is one way scholars have delineated the lines between the civil rights and black power movements. This division of the movement for black equality is, however, false and misleading. In truth, many African Americans, including leaders like Rosa Parks, Martin Luther King Jr., and Malcolm X, embraced political rhetoric and action plans that incorporated elements of nonviolent direct action and armed self-defense. Rosa Parks appreciated Malcolm X, both his messages and his methods, and that is why she attended a number of his speeches. She recalled in her autobiography, "I met him the week before he died. He had come to Detroit to speak, and I was sitting in the front row. . . . I spoke to him and he autographed the program for me." Rosa Parks "had a lot of admiration for him," and in her estimation, "he was a very brilliant man" (Parks 1992, 177–278). Rosa Parks remembered that Malcolm X's messages resonated with her. "Dr. King used to say that black people should receive brutality with love . . . but I couldn't reach that point in my mind at all," she recalled

(Parks 1992, 178). Whites in her life had threatened and perpetrated too much violence for Rosa to agree fully with King's message, and she liked the fact that "Malcolm wasn't a supporter of nonviolence either" (Parks 1992, 178). She agreed wholeheartedly with Malcolm X's assessment of white supremacists: "Not only did they know what they were doing, but they were *experts* at it" (Parks 1992, 178).

This knowledge sustained Rosa Parks's commitment to racial justice and it informed her activism. She continued to gravitate to youth causes and the efforts young people put into the struggle for black equality. Rosa had a particular affinity for the Student Nonviolent Coordinating Committee's work, and the sit-ins at the Woolworth's in Greensboro, North Carolina, captivated her. Parks joined the Friends of SNCC (FOS) in the early 1960s, and she was active in the group for years. Jeanne Theoharis explained, "The Northern FOS organizations provided fund-raising and supported infrastructure for SNCC's Southern work and helped Northern young people who wanted to be part of the movement also take on issues closer to home" (Theoharis 2013, 190). Together with fellow Detroiter Dorothy Dewberry, Rosa Parks ran the Detroit chapter of FOS. Reprising the critical organizational and operational work Parks engaged in with E. D. Nixon, Montgomery attorney Fred Gray, the MIA, and the Montgomery and Alabama NAACP, Rosa "did mailings, collated goods to be sent south, and performed other office tasks" for FOS. The focus of the Detroit FOS in the mid-1960s was the political movement in Lowndes County, Alabama. Despite the passage of the Voting Rights Act of 1965, this county still had abysmal black voter registration numbers. In particular, black youth felt the heavy weight of disenfranchisement. Having connected with SNCC leaders during the Selma to Montgomery March of 1965, a demonstration that was full of white supremacist violence against protestors, local Lowndes County leaders moved to create an independent political party in the region. Parks had returned to Alabama to participate in the march, and she traveled to Alabama again in 1966, this time to Lowndes County to celebrate the one-year anniversary of political efforts in that locale. The crowd, some six hundred strong, listened attentively as she addressed them, Rosa having received top billing in the program.

Parks remained active in the struggle for civil rights throughout the 1960s, and she readily lent her presence, and, when the dais opened, her voice to the cause. The 1968 assassination of Dr. Martin Luther King Jr. moved Parks, as did the Poor People's Campaign in which King was engaged at the time of his death. Hearing of King's assassination, Rosa felt a sense of numbness and felt she "was lost" (Brinkley 2000, 205). She recalled, however, that she was more shocked and saddened by King's stabbing in 1958 than this 1968 shooting. The first attack left Rosa stunned that anyone would want to harm King. Ten years later, when King died by

---

Young Black Resistance Efforts

The sit-in movement was made famous by four NAACP members: Joseph McNeil, Franklin McCain, Ezell Blair Jr., and Clarence Henderson, who were students at a North Carolina historically black college, North Carolina Agricultural and Technical College. On February 1, 1960, these four students entered a Woolworth store, sat at the then-all-white lunch counter, and demanded to be served. African Americans were permitted to order food at this store; however, Southern racial norms precluded them from sitting at the counter and eating. In this example of strict white supremacist segregation, blacks were not allowed to eat with whites. The four protestors were not served, but they continued to sit at the counter until the store closed that evening. This courageous, yet seemingly simple, act ignited a groundswell of activism. The next day, other students, overwhelmingly black, joined in the sit-in, and by the fifth day, hundreds of youths crowded into the downtown Greensboro store. Emboldened by the work of these young activists, white and black people across the country began picketing and boycotting chains that upheld segregation in the South. Sit-ins sprang up across the South as people, mainly black youth, demanded equal service. They endured taunts, racial epitaphs, having food and drink dumped on them, and the constant fear of prosecution. However, following the long tradition of black activism, the protestors were relentless in their efforts. These sit-ins evolved into pray-ins at segregated churches, swim-ins at segregated pools and beaches, sleep-ins at segregated hotels, and watch-ins at segregated movie theaters. Most importantly, seeing the power of this manifestation of nonviolent direct action, Ella Baker, civil rights champion and integral part of the Southern Christian Leadership Conference (SCLC), the NAACP, and other organizations dedicated to racial uplift, helped the students coordinate their efforts. This organization process, which included a conference at Shaw University in Raleigh, North Carolina, led to the formation in 1960 of an independent student-run civil rights organization known as the Student Nonviolent Coordinating Committee (SNCC).

---

assassin's bullet, Rosa was deeply grieved and even devastated, but she was less shocked than she had been in the previous decade.

Still, troubled greatly by King's death, Rosa Parks responded with action. She and her Detroit friend Louise Tappes, who in 1976 lobbied successfully to have Twelfth Street in Detroit, Michigan, renamed Rosa Parks Boulevard, traveled to Memphis, Tennessee, to participate in a march that King, before his death, planned to lead. The march was a sign of solidarity with Memphis Sanitation Workers who were striking over deplorable working conditions, and it was all part of King's vision of a Poor People's Campaign. Parks spoke "for a few hours with a number of the striking sanitation workers," but she was so "overcome by grief" that she "accepted Harry Belafonte's invitation to ride on his plane to Atlanta with the King and Abernathy families for the funeral" (Theoharis 2013, 216; Parks 1992, 178–180). As Jeanne Theoharis recounted, at the funeral, Rosa sat on the platform next to the first speaker, actor and civil rights icon Ozzie Davis. Parks remembered that Senator Robert Kennedy and his wife Ethel Skakel Kennedy attended the service, and she met them "before the funeral at the home of Mrs. King." Later that year, an assassin killed Robert Kennedy during a campaign stop for his presidential nomination bid. A month after King's funeral, marchers descended on Washington, D.C., as part of the Poor People's Campaign, and Rosa Parks was front and center, receiving a standing ovation from the estimated fifty thousand to one hundred thousand protestors who gathered at the Lincoln Memorial for Solidarity Day (Aguilar 2017).

Rosa Parks continued to gain notoriety and accolades throughout the rest of her life, but little changed in terms of public perception of her activism. The SCLC created the annual Rosa Parks Freedom Award in 1963, and John Conyers received this honor in 1967, but the group continued to focus on her bus stand while minimizing other aspects of her lifelong activism. Rosa Parks received the Springarn Medal from the NAACP in 1979, but the group did next to nothing to provide for Parks during her decade of economic insecurity. On their website, the NAACP explicated, Parks received the 1979 Springarn Medal "In recognition to the quiet courage and determination exemplified when she refused to surrender her seat on a Montgomery, Alabama bus." There is no mention of her decades of service to the Montgomery NAACP Chapter as an impetus for her receiving the medal. Over the years, municipalities, organizations and educational institutions, to name a few, have named buildings, streets, and awards in her honor. While these all stand as a testament to the impact Parks's bus stand had on the nation, too little attention is given to the totality of her life and her work. For her part, Parks often played into this scenario. As someone who shied away from the spotlight, she rarely challenged the fact that she did not received the attention and care due her. In her biography, *Rosa Parks: My Story*, she failed to mention many of the awards and accolades that she received in her lifetime, and she skirted over her decade long economic insecurity and the lack of support she received from civil rights leaders and organizations (Theoharis 2013, 186, NAACP n.d.).

In public, Rosa Parks was the mother of the civil rights movement whose one act set off a movement, but her work before, during and after the Montgomery Bus Boycott remained largely ignored. Also ignored were her financial plights, health struggles, and other personal matters that did not fit the mold of an unbreakable—nay, untouchable—legend. Rosa Parks had an unwavering commitment to racial and gender uplift, but she was a human being with troubles and emotions that affected her life and her activism. Her legendary and mythical status left little room for Rosa Parks the person, and only recently are scholars uncovering the complexity of her life. One of the most trying times in her life came in the 1970s when she confronted the failing health of her husband, mother, and brother. Rosa Parks remembered "the 1970s as a time when I was losing the people I loved best. My husband, mother, and brother were all sick, and there was a time when I was traveling every day to three different hospitals to visit them" (Parks 1992, 180). During this time, she had to downgrade to part-time work in order to care for her family, all of whom died in the late 1970s. Raymond, her husband, passed away in 1977, and Sylvester left this world three months later. When Raymond died, Rosa had to put her mother, Leona McCauley, in a nursing home because she "wasn't able to give her the proper care and work too" (Parks 1992, 180). Rosa did bring her mother to live with her in 1978, and her mother passed away at the age of ninety-one in 1979.

For her part, Parks continued to rally to causes, attending events like the conference on Black Power in 1968 and the National Black Political Convention in 1972. She also took up causes that spoke to her the most, including cases of police brutality, the deplorable conditions in the prison system, rape and sexual assault, and the wrongful incarceration of black people. Rosa Parks also campaigned vigorously against presidential hopeful George McGovern and publicly broadcast her support of the impeachment of President Richard Nixon. Rosa Parks also threw her full weight behind the battle against apartheid in South Africa and the imprisonment of Nelson Mandela. Alongside countless others, Parks called for U.S. divestment from South Africa as a way to bring economic pressures to bear against the all-white government that maintained power by oppressing the majority black population of that African nation. She also lent public support to her friend Jesse Jackson Sr. during his run for the Democratic Party presidential nomination in 1988 (Theoharis 2013, 221–230).

Throughout her life, Rosa felt motivated by a desire to enrich the lives of black youth. In fact, citing a speech Parks delivered in Philadelphia, Pennsylvania, in 1985, Jeanne Theoharis quoted, "At some point we should step aside and let the younger ones take over. But we first must take care of our young people to make sure that they have the rights of first-class citizens" (Theoharis 2013, 230). Rosa Parks's life bore witness to this calling, and in 1987, a year after her husband died, Parks founded the Rosa and Raymond Parks Institute for Self-Development, aimed at helping young people through education, activism, and community uplift. Today, the Institute still works with youth, educating them about past struggles and empowering them for future triumphs.

Reflecting on her life in her biography, Rosa noted:

As time has gone by, people have made my place in the history of the civil-rights movement bigger and bigger. They call me the Mother of the Civil Rights Movement and the Patron Saint of the Civil Rights Movement. I have more honorary degrees and plaques and awards than I can count, and I appreciate and cherish every single one of them. Interviews still only want to talk about that one evening in 1955 when I refused to give up my seat on the bus. Organizations still want to give me awards for that one act more than thirty years ago. I am happy to go wherever I am invited and to accept whatever honors are given me. I understand that I am a symbol. (Parks 1992, 185)

As a symbol, Rosa Parks has driven a narrative of civil rights in America. It is a narrative of progress with a single woman giving birth to a cadre of mostly male movement leaders. Although this narrative makes for a neat package in history textbooks, it minimizes and marginalizes leaders like Rosa Parks. The narrative of progress also obscures the persistent racial inequities that remain in place today. As Jeanne Theoharis noted, this narrative promotes an understanding of the civil rights movement as a period that "corrected the aberration of Southern racism without overthrowing the government or engaging in a bloody revolution" (Theoharis 2013, xxiii). Yet, the revolution has been bloody for many; the movement for racial equality began in 1619 with the introduction of the first people of African descent into the colonies. Racism is an ingrained element of America, not a Southern aberration, and the battle for black liberation continues today.

Rosa Parks passed away on October 24, 2005, at the age of ninety-two. She died of natural causes on a Monday evening in her home surrounded by friends, according to a statement by family attorney Gregory Reed. National leaders responded to her death with efforts to honor her symbolic life. Her longtime employer, Congressman John Conyers, introduced a resolution for her body to lie in state at the Capitol Building in Washington, D.C. The resolution passed, and some forty thousand mourners visited her remains there. Prior to arriving in D.C., Parks's body traveled to Montgomery for a public memorial in her home state of Alabama. After lying in state, and after a public memorial service at Metropolitan AME Church in D.C., the fallen civil rights leader returned to her adopted city of Detroit for a final memorial and burial in Woodlawn Cemetery. Tens of thousands of people paid tribute to Rosa Parks at these three stops, and as Jeanne Theoharis noted, "Her body became necessary for these public rites, a sort of public communion where Americans would visit her coffin and be sanctified. This personal moment with Parks's body became not simply a private moment of grief and honor but also a public act of celebrating a nation that would celebrate her" (Theoharis 2013, xxiii–xxiv). As Rosa Parks knew so well during her life, she was a symbol, and individuals and groups use symbols at their discretion and for their own purposes.

Nearly eight years later, a nine-foot likeness of Rosa Parks was unveiled in Statuary Hall in the U.S. Capitol. She was the first African American enshrined in that august location, and the unveiling ceremony drew dignitaries from across the political spectrum. In many ways, the statue, a static figure amid other legendary American icons frozen in time in marble or bronze, memorializes her static position in American lore. Seated on a rock, even seemingly coming out of the rock, Rosa Parks's tribute statue commemorates an icon whose image is solid, immovable, and unmoved. Yet, Rosa's legacy was so much more than that December 1, 1955, bus protest, and her life was full of vigor, fight, triumph, and pain. She loved and was loved by so many, and her life was full of humanity, humility, and humanitarianism.

Why Rosa Parks Matters

Throughout her ninety-two years, Rosa Louise Parks lived a life steeped in the battle for racial justice. Certainly, her life is important to the struggle for black equality because her December 1, 1955, stand against segregation on a Montgomery bus was the symbolic launch of the modern civil rights movement. That action—choosing to take a stand by sitting down—is enough to warrant deep study of her life and legacy. Such a deep dive uncovers a treasure trove of information about her life of purpose and activism. Rosa was well versed in the historical struggles for black equality. Her family, particularly her mother and maternal grandparents, made sure Rosa and her brother had access to historical, social, political, and economic commentaries on the topic. Rosa read voraciously, and she followed the press coverage of black Americans diligently. Moreover, Rosa surrounded herself with people who were as interested and engaged in black liberation as she was. Why does Rosa Parks matter? She matters because she is the mother of the movement. She matters because her image and actions serve as props for the script detailing the national narrative of racial justice. Rosa Parks matters because her life reflects three of the major themes in black liberation, namely, the culture of gender within the civil rights movement and civil rights organizations, the movement for civil rights within the culture of white supremacy, and the cultural framework of black protest.

As a woman, Rosa Parks is an unlikely hero in the story. Men dominated the civil rights movement. Accounts of their work fill the pages of countless books, and their lives dominate the textbooks. That is not to say that the stories of black men's lives are not manipulated and distorted to fit the popular narrative. One need only look at Martin Luther King Jr. for examples of this fact. The purveyors of the national narrative on civil rights point to King as the leader of the civil rights movement and tout his adherence to nonviolence. His birthday, a national holiday, is heralded as a day of service, yet King spent the majority of his adult life engaged in protests and demonstrations. Somehow the Martin Luther King Jr. Day of Protest does not resonate in the same way as the Martin Luther King Jr. Day of Service. The national narrative of King focuses on messages of racial harmony like his "I Have A Dream" speech and ignores his demands for economic justice, his proclamations that black is beautiful, his references to black nationalism and black separatism, and his hints at the need for reparations. As a nation, Americans would rather think about King having a dream because, after all, America loves the idea of the American dream. President Barack Obama titled his first book *Dreams from My Father*, and that book resonated with the American people because it spoke of hope and progress. *The Audacity of Hope*, another book by Obama, also spoke to themes of progress and hope, as the title would imply. With his election to the presidency, many Americans felt the nation had finally defeated racism, and many began to speak of a postracial society. Yet, even with the manipulation of their narratives, King and Obama took up enough of the spotlight for enough time to demonstrate evolutions and modifications in their visions and rhetoric. This was not the case for Rosa Parks.

Rosa Parks had to be permanent, steady, immoveable, and unshakeable. So static is the national image of Rosa Parks, the first black person enshrined in Statuary Hall in the United States Capitol, that her likeness depicts her seated like a rock. In fact, her perch is a rock. Her name and her image are literally cast in the image of immobility, and that is how the nation remembers Rosa Parks, the tired and immobile seamstress among men of action in a movement for civil rights. That is the national narrative of Rosa Parks because that was the predominant image during her lifetime. To be fair, much of this perception of Rosa Parks came about because of the ways civil rights leaders framed her. Repeatedly, male leaders told Rosa to remain quiet, placating her by telling her that she had already said enough in reference to her bus stand. The women's rights movement notwithstanding, in 1950s America, there was far too little space for women to take active, visible leadership roles, even within movements for social change. At countless rallies, male leaders would acknowledge Rosa, lead the crowd in an ovation of thanks, and then ask her to return to her seat so that they could speak about the plight of black America.

Complicit with gender roles in the civil rights movement and within American culture in general, at the weekly rallies held in conjunction with the Montgomery Bus Boycott, the Montgomery Improvement Association (MIA) leadership failed to offer space for Rosa's rhetoric and vision to drive the movement. Rosa was a member of MIA's executive board, but there are no records of how her role on this body shaped the protest. Rather, Rosa's contributions, beyond her refusal to give up her seat, centered on raising funds and working as a dispatcher for the transportation committee. Men dominated leadership positions in the MIA, and the women in positions of power held largely gendered clerical positions. Rosa Parks, for her part, did not even qualify for these clerical roles, even though, before her arrest, she carried out such tasks admirably for both E. D. Nixon and Fred Gray.

When Rosa Parks joined the NAACP 1943, meeting attendees voted her in as secretary of the organization because she was the only woman present and because such work largely fell to women. Despite their deep friendship and powerful collaboration, E. D. Nixon would make disparaging and highly gendered remarks around Rosa about women's roles. Whether fully or partially joking, Nixon's references to a woman's place as in the kitchen spoke to the culture of gender within U.S. society. Nixon's words also illuminated how American gender norms permeated the civil rights movement and civil rights organizations. For all of her leadership, activism, and efforts, Rosa Parks was still a woman, and her closest male friends in the movement still felt it was appropriate to dismiss or downplay her importance.

Rosa Parks was not alone in feeling the gendered nature of the movement. Female leaders like Septima Clark and Ella Baker also labored while being obscured by the long shadows of male leaders like Myles Horton, Martin Luther King Jr., Ralph Abernathy, and Roy Wilkins. Even male leaders like Bayard Rustin, whose homosexuality did not fit the stereotypical model of masculinity, had to work in relative obscurity while the "alpha males" basked in the spotlight.

In Rosa Parks's case, even the leadership efforts she took on carried a gendered air. Rosa reprised her secretarial role for the Alabama conference, deepening her collaboration with E. D. Nixon, who served as head of the group. Despite helping to get Nixon elected to this leadership position, she was not afforded access to a more powerful and visible role in this body. Rosa worked tirelessly on efforts to bring justice in rape cases like that of Recy Taylor and Gertrude Perkins. She sought out the frequent cases wherein black women suffered sexual violence at the hands of white men, and her own personal experiences likely served as a motivating factor on this score. Rosa Parks also took an active role in working with young people, founding the Montgomery NAACP Youth Council in 1949 and revitalizing the group in 1954. Whether championing justice for women violated by rape or children marginalized and oppressed by white supremacy, Rosa Parks threw her full weight into her activism. True, she gravitated to these issues because of her own predilections, but the fact remains that these issues were largely cast as women's issues in the ranks of civil rights leadership. Even her invitation to the 1955 Highlander Folk School workshop on the *Brown v. Board of Education of Topeka, KS* hinted at the fact that youth uplift was something that concerned women more than men. In essence, women should champion issues dealing with women and children while men busied themselves with bigger issues pertaining to the general uplift of the race.

Given the gendered nature of civil rights efforts, it should come as no surprise that Rosa Parks's refusal to give up her seat on the Montgomery bus sparked the Montgomery Bus Boycott. The perception was that women were weaker and needed protection from men. Even though she was a seasoned civil rights veteran, more seasoned than most of the men in Montgomery, Parks was a woman and thus seen as vulnerable. It took the arrest of a woman to rally the community behind the boycott, because only a woman was in need of such protection. Surely, men also protested segregation and white supremacy in Montgomery, but this gendered society needed to rally around a woman who was violated. When Fred Gray filed suit on February 1, 1956, he filed on behalf of five women, Claudette Colvin, Aurelia S. Browder, Mary Louise Smith, Susie McDonald, and Jeanatta Reese. Along with Rosa Parks, these women represented a population of people who needed justice and protection. The community did not rally behind violated men; however, they did look to the male leaders to drive the fight for justice in the case of women oppressed by the long national history of white supremacy.

Since Africans first came to the land that would become the United States of America in 1619, people of African descent have battled for their civil rights. Not yet viewed as enslaved, these forced immigrants suffered longer periods of servitude, harsher treatment, and higher death rates. Those who did obtain freedom (in the years before enslavement instituted a permanence of status upon people of African heritage) endured violence, discrimination, disenfranchisement, and scapegoating, among other things. The greatest coup came when white-dominated colonies created laws of enslavement that dictated an institution in which black people could never obtain freedom. Along with this permanence of status—and, in fact, as justification for such laws—white supremacist concocted narratives of black inferiority, likening black people to animals or at least relegating them to subhuman status. Even after the ends of the institution of enslavement, the permanent condition of black inferiority plagued black people as they tried to live out their lives as free people. White supremacists created segregation as a mean of further subjugating people of African descent, and the term "Jim Crow segregation" became a sanitized way to refer to the systematic oppression of blacks. Generations of white

Americans, who only knew of black people as inferior beings and who profited greatly from this caste system, readily accepted the notion of black inferiority, and in rulings like *Plessy v. Ferguson* that instituted separate but equal as the custom and doctrine of the land, the government sanctioned white separatism and white supremacy.

This culture of white supremacy gave white people absolute, hegemonic power over black people, even denying them rights as citizens of this nation. Black inferiority was so ingrained in the ethos of the nation and the psyche of white citizens that many saw no issues with the control of black people. In their minds, as was the case in law and practice, black people amounted to animals needing the control of their white taskmasters. This power dynamic, one that minimized or ignored the humanity of people of African descent, had a grave cost, and, following the U.S. Civil War, thousands of African Americans died at the hands of lynch mobs. In many cases, the lynchers would display the corpses of their victim in full view, telegraphing to other black people the power that society afforded to white people through the culture of white supremacy. White supremacy sanctioned absolute control over black bodies, and white supremacists exercised this power in ghastly, appalling ways. Even the systems of labor that emerged following the Civil War spoke to the power. Sharecropping, tenant farming, and convict labor left black people tethered to land and labor in ways that differed little if at all from the institution of enslavement.

Rosa Parks's life demonstrates the sting of this white supremacist culture and the institutions that arose as part of this white hegemony. Although her family owned their land, as a child Rosa had to work under the eye of a white taskmaster. She recalled the brutality of this white man and the feeling that her body and her labor were not her own. She looked fondly on black people who refused to bend fully to the whims of white oppressors because those individuals gave her a sense of hope and pride in her race. Her mother spoke fondly of people like Booker T. Washington, Tuskegee Institute founder, who offered black people a place to feel some sense of racial pride, control over their condition, and avenues for uplift. The Tuskegee Institute and its founder, Washington, were not above the reproach of many blacks who felt he and the institution sanctioned white supremacy, but Leona McCauley convinced her husband to settle in Tuskegee, Alabama, for a time so that their child, Rosa, could have access to education that would instill racial pride and facilitate racial uplift. Rosa did not spend much time in Tuskegee after her birth in that town, but she did remember how important that locale was to her mother and her mother's sense of racial self-determination.

Rosa's grandfather, Sylvester Edwards, was another major influence in her development of racial pride. On multiple occasions, white supremacist in the Ku Klux Klan threatened Edwards and his family, and her grandfather's response was to stay up all night with his shotgun ready to gun down anyone who made a move on his homestead. With her grandfather as an example, Rosa connected with and eventually married Raymond Parks, a man who stood up against white supremacy and the systematic oppression of black people. When the two met, Raymond was active in the fight to free the Scottsboro Boys, nine black youths falsely accused of raping two white women. Raymond attended meetings and raised funds in support of their defense, and Rosa witnessed how these men armed themselves in defense of their right to organize and agitate for social change.

Yes, these instances of black pride and black self-reliance scared her, but that fear emboldened her to get involved in civil rights efforts. People like Rosa Parks, whose fear of white supremacy drove them to action, filled the ranks of civil rights organizations. Rosa Parks joined the NAACP in 1943 because she was determined to bring about the end of white supremacy. After her election as secretary, she worked closely and tirelessly alongside other NAACP members for that cause. She demanded justice in cases of rape, wrongful incarceration, and institutionalized oppression of black people.

Rosa Parks matters because she is a model of the best of black uplift and the power of black civil rights institutions to effect positive racial change. She learned black self-reliance and self-determination at the feet of her grandfather. Her mother taught her the importance of education and black educational institutions grounded in an ethos of civil rights. Moreover, her mother instilled in Rosa the importance of reading about and embracing the messages of black civil rights leaders and champions. From her grandmother, Rosa learned how to take these lessons of racial pride and channel them in ways that sustained the movement and protected her from the violent oppression of white supremacy.

Oppression came in many forms, from fearmongering and intimidation to physical, psychological, and sexual violence. Rosa Parks's near-rape narrative, found in her papers housed in the Library of Congress collection, speak to the power white people lorded over blacks, particularly black women. Whether real or allegorical, the narrative included a white man manipulating and cajoling a black man into providing access to a black woman. The white man, referred to in the story as Mr. Charlie, expected to have free access to the black woman's body because white supremacists' culture gave white men supreme control over black people. Mr. Charlie tried every avenue in his power, from demands to bribes, to have sexual relations with the black woman in the story, but at every turn, the black woman resisted these advances and maintained control over her person. This is not to say that black women had the power fend off white aggression. Recy Taylor's case, for example, which Rosa Parks worked on so diligently, was an instance where white men overpowered and savaged a black woman in spite of all of her efforts to fight them off. Sadly, Recy Taylor's story was the common result when white supremacists approached black women and, to a lesser reported extent, men. Rosa Parks may have been raped, or nearly raped. We do not know for certain. All we have is the narrative Rosa Parks authored and the fact that she kept that narrative closely guarded until her death. One thing is certain: the reality of rape and sexual abuse permeated the culture of white supremacy as much as, if not more than, the reality of lynching and other extralegal violence perpetrated against black people. Civil rights efforts and civil rights organizations were essential precisely because white supremacy at its very essence was about the violation of black bodies.

When Rosa Parks joined the NAACP, she was standing up and being counted as someone who would not sit idly by while these offenses went on unchallenged. She aligned herself with other conscious individuals fighting for the rights of black people to control their own bodies. In fact, corporal rights, the rights to control one's own personhood, were at the heart of civil rights, rights guaranteed as a citizen. If people were to exercise their rights as citizens, they must first be in control of what happens to their bodies. Rosa Parks understood this, and she sought out others who felt the same way.

That demand to control her own body was at the heart of Rosa's December 1, 1955, refusal to give up her seat on the Montgomery bus. White supremacy dictated that the bus driver could tell her where to sit. If she refused, the white driver could grab her and physically move her. Parks resisted this notion. She determined to place her body where she chose and in whatever way she chose. She invoked her rights as a citizen to resist white hegemony over her personhood, and her decision sparked a movement of people who chose, with great self-determination, to keep their bodies off the buses controlled by the white supremacist establishment.

By her own account, Rosa Parks thought about other black bodies when she took her bus stand. She remembered Claudette Colvin, arrested and dragged off the Montgomery bus months before. This youth faced a situation similar to Parks in that she was asked to give up her seat even though there were no other seats available to her on the bus. Montgomery law guaranteed a black person the right to remain in his or her seat if there were no other seats available, but drivers often ignored that caveat. Some thought the Colvin case would be the springboard for a citywide bus boycott, but, for various reasons, such a protest actions never came to fruition. Rosa Parks, however, knew Colvin through her work leading the NAACP Youth Council, and she thought of her as she refused to move from her seat.

Rosa Parks also thought of Emmett Till as she sat in her bus seat. The fourteen-year-old youth from Chicago traveled to the Delta region of Mississippi in the summer of 1955 to visit relatives there. Till had little experience with the Southern version of white supremacy, and he played a prank on a white woman in Money, Mississippi. Such actions on the part of African Americans, particularly black males, appeared to be a direct threat to white power and supremacy, and Emmett Till paid for his prank with his life. Three days after the incident with the white woman at a store in the whistle-stop town of Money, white vigilantes, including the woman's husband, came to the house where Till was staying and dragged him away. They beat Emmett Till without mercy in payment for his prank. Still seething with anger, and feeling the blanket validation of white supremacy, one of the vigilantes shot Emmett Till dead. The group then dumped his lifeless body in the river, weighed down by a heavy cotton gin fan. Having received permission from Emmett Till's mother, the black press published images of his brutalized body. Mamie Till-Mobley, mother of Emmett Till, wanted the world to see what they did to her boy. The black press was poised to distribute these ghastly photographs because, as an institution bent on black protest of white supremacy, they existed to print the news from a black perspective. Rosa Parks saw these photos, and the images that had haunted her since came to mind anew as she sat on that bus.

Rosa Parks's life is a stark example of the powerfully oppressive nature of white supremacy. One of the hallmarks of the culture of white supremacy is the fact that whites dictated the rules and held hegemonic control over nonwhites. As such, people of color faced arrest and worse even if they followed the written rule of law. On December 1, 1955, Rosa Parks did not violate the laws as written, but her refusal to be cowed in the face of white male authority was enough of an offense to have her arrested. Rosa did not have to get out of her seat, because the law stated that black people did not have to relinquish their seats if there were no other seats available in the black section of the bus. Yet, James Blake, the driver of the Cleveland Avenue bus that evening, did not like the fact that Rosa Parks did not obey his command. To him, as a white man in a white supremacist nation, any refusal to bend to his will was seen as an offense of the unwritten rules and customs of society. The nature of white supremacy was such that white people could interpret laws as they saw fit in any give situation. In this case, on this day, Parks was in violation even as she was following the letter of the law.

It is so important, therefore, not to miss the seemingly subtle nuances in what happened during her arrest. Rosa Parks did not move when asked to do so by the bus driver. In fact, rather than moving up out of her seat on the bus, when her seatmate relinquished the window seat next to her, Rosa moved from her aisle seat to the window seat. She moved her body deeper into the row and effectively dared the white man who was standing, waiting for a seat to open up, to sit in the row alongside her as an equal. As the police officers arrived and told her that they were going to arrest her, Rosa told them that they may do that. She did not allow the white officers the power of forceful arrest; rather, she dictated to them what they could and could not do to her person. Though seemingly subtle, these interactions demonstrated that Rosa Parks never lost control of her personage throughout the process. She grew up learning how to take control of her body, and she worked tirelessly in her adult life alongside others who experienced the violation of their personhood. This was not going to happen to Rosa Parks. As an adult, she surrounded herself with people, from her husband to her compatriots in the NAACP, who maintained control over their bodies in the face of oppressive white supremacy. Rosa Parks understood full well, and she matters because she modeled, how civil rights begin with corporal rights. White supremacists had a deep understanding of this fact, and that is why, from enslavement through lynching and segregation, they maintained hegemony by controlling the ways black people could use their bodies. Rosa Parks refused to sign on to this power structure, and her stand was a powerful lesson in confronting white supremacy.

The culture of black protest rests upon black people's control over their own bodies. In her early adulthood, Rosa Parks leaped into protest efforts that centered on white supremacist control of black personhood. She rushed to meet with Recy Taylor because Taylor's story resonated with her. A group of white men savaged and violated Recy Taylor's body, and Rosa led protest efforts singularly and as part of the Committee for Equal Justice for the Rights of Mrs. Recy Taylor. Black protest demanded equal rights and equal justice as guaranteed under the law, and civil rights protestors like Rosa Parks would stop at nothing to see these laws carried out. The pathway to justice was rarely straight and never clear, given the context of white supremacy under which these activists labored. White people made the laws and controlled the justice system designed to interpret these laws. As such, black protest required strategic mobilization and tireless activism, often under extreme duress and fear of violent retribution. White vigilantism was an ever-present fear and constant way of life for black protestors, and armed self-defense was the response in the face of such unchecked white power. That is why Sylvester Edwards stayed up at night, shotgun at the ready, during Rosa's childhood, and that is why Raymond Parks held meetings with firearms sprawled across the table in the early years of her marriage. The culture of black protest relied on armed self-defense in the face of unadulterated white oppression.

Essential, too, for the black protest was mass mobilization. Rosa began her formal work for civil rights within the structure of Montgomery's NAACP branch. Her efforts there blossomed into additional opportunities for activism at the Alabama Conference of the NAACP. At that level, too, Rosa Parks served as secretary for a time, uniting with race-conscious protestors from across the state of Alabama. After her arrest, she traveled across the country at the bequest of leaders from the national office of the NAACP located in New York City. At every point and at every level, the NAACP was effective because of their ability to mobilize en masse.

When Rosa Parks was arrested, black people in Montgomery, from both within and outside of the Montgomery NAACP, took action in protest of the violation of her rights. Leading activists like E. D. Nixon and Jo Ann Robinson went to their various civil rights–oriented organizations for action. Robinson and her Women's Political Council were ripe for action, having pushed the issues for a bus boycott earlier that year with the arrest of Claudette Colvin. For their part, the black ministers of Montgomery met regularly to discuss civil rights issues and the state of black Montgomery. At one of these meetings, the ministers discovered the announcement of a one-day boycott scheduled for December 5, 1955. Had blacks in Montgomery not been meeting regularly and discussing civil rights issues, they would not have been ready for the mass protest effort that ensued after Rosa Parks's arrest. Black churches stood ready to embrace and forward black protest efforts through mass meetings and sermons from the pulpit designed to encourage congregants in their resolve to see the protest to fruition. In the face of white supremacist violence, coercion, and intimidation, black protest required collective black action.

Although the leadership provided invaluable messaging and rallying within the context of this protest effort, the ordinary African American citizens gave the Montgomery Bus Boycott its life and longevity. Everyday people were the ones who rode the Montgomery buses on a daily basis, and it was essential that they stayed off the buses in order to bring pressure to bear against the white establishment. Many of the leaders owned or had access to cars, so it was the black masses, like Rosa Parks, who felt the weight of the oppressive practices on segregated buses. Ordinary Montgomerians came out fifteen thousand strong on Monday evening, December 5, 1955, to attend the rally at the end of the first day of the bus boycott, and they voted unanimously to find any means of travel other than the bus line. The black masses committed themselves to whatever pain, hardship, or inconvenience was necessary to break the back of segregation, and they stayed the course, refusing to ride the buses for over a year in order to bring about an end to segregation in public transportation.

Black people knew that violent reprisal faced them, and people like Martin Luther King Jr. and E. D. Nixon had their houses bombed as white supremacists tried to break the will of black protestors. Rosa Parks and her family endured constant death threats for her role as the symbol of the Montgomery Bus Boycott, but the protestors continued to stay off the buses. Arrests abounded, and white police officers harassed blacks in Montgomery with abandon, but the culture of black protest was a culture of resolve in the face of violence and oppression. Refrains of "We Shall

Overcome" and "Standing on the Promises" were oft-intoned lyrics buoy-ing black people in their protest efforts.

Institutions like the Highlander Folk School existed to support such protest efforts. Originally founded in response to labor injustices, High-lander soon focused on race and racism in the United States. Rosa Parks attended a workshop there in 1955, and she left feeling energized to protest injustices back in Montgomery. The workshop she attended focused on empowerment strategies following the Supreme Court decision *Brown v. Board of Education of Topeka, KS*. From across the country, community activists came to Highlander for fellowship, invigoration, and strategizing about how to forward black protest efforts. Similar to black churches and civil rights–minded organizations, placed like Highlander were essential incubators nurturing the culture of black protest.

Sometimes black protest involved black people relocating in hopes of finding better experiences and opportunities. In the wake of the Mont-gomery Bus Boycott, without steady work and receiving constant death threats, Rosa and her family relocated to Detroit, Michigan. She joined the ranks of millions of African Americans who left the South as part of the Great Black Migration. As was the case with the others, the North did not prove to be the promised land for the Parks family. Unemployment and underemployment plagued the family during their time in Detroit. More-over, Rosa Parks found that racism in Detroit, while less overt, resembled the racism in the South. Segregation abounded, and opportunities for black people were not readily available. She made the best of her life in her new city, and she did eventually find work in the offices of U.S. Representa-tive John Conyers, but the move to the North cast in sharp relief the harsh conditions facing black Americans regardless of who they were and where they lived.

Why does Rosa Parks matter? She matters because her life is a moving example of the life of black Americans. Born in a town that held the prom-ise of racial uplift, Parks's life showed the harsh reality of African Ameri-can lives. She learned how to stand up for herself, how to stay alive, and the importance of education in the process of black uplift during her formative years; and she carried those lessons into adulthood. Rosa Parks, like many other black people focused on racial justice, surrounded herself with posi-tive activists who wanted to bring about social change. She worked tire-lessly, despite limitations placed on her by her gender and the gender roles of U.S. society, to see racial justice. Rosa Parks directed her efforts in sup-port of black institutions and organizations bent on racial uplift, and she did what she could within the confines of gender norms to push for equal-ity. Understanding the crucial nature of education, Rosa Parks worked with youth in Montgomery, and she educated herself in many ways, includ-ing her voracious reading habits and her time at Highlander Folk School.

When it came time for Rosa Parks to take a stand in protection of her civil and corporal rights, she did so without hesitation. From her first refusal to give up her seat on the segregated buses in 1943 through her arrest in 1955 for violating segregation laws, Rosa Parks was in control of her person, because she knew that in white supremacist America, her civil rights depended on her corporal rights. After her arrest, Parks worked within the spaces afforded women to raise money and support for the Montgomery Bus Boycott, and she continued to support mass organizing efforts on the part of organizations like the MIA and the NAACP. Rosa Parks joined other black protestors in moving away from oppressive conditions in the South. While conditions in the North often mirrored those in the South, Rosa knew that removing herself from Montgomery was a way of taking control of her body and forwarding her black protest initiatives. In Detroit, she continued to work with activists on black protest efforts, in that city and around the country. Connecting with the plight of blacks in South Africa, Rosa lent her efforts to battling apartheid in that African nation.

Rosa Parks matters because hers is a story of civil rights and black protest regionally, nationally, and internationally. She matters because studying her life illuminates the cultures of gender, white supremacy, and black protest that are at the heart of the American narrative. Her story matters precisely because it is not a fable of the American dream. Rather than a fanciful American dream narrative, like the rest of black Americans, Rosa Louise Parks's story is the story of the reality of black life in America.

Timeline

1913
On February 4, 1913, Rosa Louise McCauley was born in Tuskegee, Alabama, to James McCauley and Leona McCauley (nee Edwards).

1918
Rosa McCauley began her schooling in Pine Level, Alabama. She lived with her mother; younger brother, Sylvester McCauley; and maternal grandparents, Rose and Sylvester Edwards. The family owned their house and land, something rare for black people in Pine Level.

1924–1929
Rosa McCauley attended the Miss White's Montgomery's Industrial School for Girls in, Montgomery, Alabama.

1929
Rosa McCauley had to leave school to take care of her ailing grandmother.

1932
Rosa McCauley married Raymond Parks on December 1932.

1933
Rosa Parks earned her high school diploma.

1943
Rosa Parks joined the Montgomery branch of the NAACP and was elected secretary.

Rosa Parks attempted to register to vote for the first time and was denied.

Rosa Parks was put off the bus for the first time.

1944
Rosa Parks made a second attempt to register to vote and was denied again.

1945
Rosa Parks successfully registered to vote on her third attempt.

1949
Rosa Parks became the adviser to the NAACP Youth Council in Montgomery, Alabama.

1955
July 24–August 6: Rosa Parks attended the Highlander Folk School workshop entitled "Racial Desegregation: Implementing the Supreme Court Decision," along with forty-eight people. There she met and started a friendship with Septima Clark.

August: Rosa Parks met Dr. Martin Luther King Jr. for the first time.

December 1: Rosa Parks was arrested for not giving up her seat on the Cleveland Avenue bus in Montgomery, AL.

December 5: Rosa Parks stood trial and was convicted of violating segregation laws.

Black Montgomerians staged a one-day boycott of the Montgomery buses.

Black leaders formed the Montgomery Improvement Association to spearhead the boycott efforts.

Some fifteen thousand people congregated at a mass meeting held in Holt Street Baptist Church in Montgomery and voted to launch the Montgomery Bus Boycott.

1956
Rosa Parks lost her job in January as part of a backlash against her bus protest.

January 30: White supremacists bombed the house of Martin Luther King Jr.

February 1: Montgomery attorney Fred Gray filed suit on behalf of five defendants, Aurelia S. Browder, Susie McDonald, Claudette Colvin, Mary Louise Smith, and Jeanatta Reese, under the case *Browder v. Gayle*. Reese later backed out of the filing.

February 21: Rosa Parks was indicted again, this time as a symbol of the bus boycott.

June 19: U.S. Court for the Middle District of Alabama ruled that the "separate but equal" ruling in the 1896 *Plessy v. Ferguson* violated the Constitution.

November 13: The U.S. Supreme Court upheld the lower court ruling that segregation on Montgomery buses was unconstitutional.

December 20: Montgomery city officials received the Supreme Court order to integrate the buses.

December 21: Black Montgomerians returned to the buses in force, now able to sit wherever they liked.

1956–1965
Rosa and Raymond Parks endured a period of unemployment/underemployment, often crippling debts, growing medical issues, and other economic insecurities.

1957
Rosa and Raymond Parks moved to Detroit, Michigan, with her mother, Leona McCauley.

Rosa Parks participated in the Prayer Pilgrimage for Freedom.

1957–1958
Rosa Parks worked as hostess at the Holly Tree Inn, Hampton Institute, Hampton, Virginia.

1958
Rosa Parks left her job at Hampton Institute and returned to Detroit, Michigan.

1963
Rosa Parks was one of five women recognized at the March on Washington for Jobs and Freedom.

1965
Rosa Parks met Malcolm X.

Rosa Parks returned to Alabama to participate in the Selma-to-Montgomery March.

1965–1988
Rosa Parks worked in Congressman John Conyers's district office in Detroit, Michigan.

1968
Rosa Parks flew to Memphis, Tennessee, after Dr. Martin Luther King Jr. was assassinated, and she then attended his funeral in Atlanta, Georgia.

Continuing with plans King laid out before his murder, Rosa Parks joined tens of thousands of others in Washington, D.C., at demonstrations planned as part of the Poor People's Campaign. On June 19, she attended a rally at the Lincoln Memorial as part of Solidarity Day events.

1977
Raymond Parks, Rosa's husband of forty-two years, died after a five-year battle with cancer.

Sylvester McCauley, Rosa's brother, died three months after her husband, having also succumbed to cancer.

1979
Rosa Parks was awarded the NAACP Spingarn Medal.

Leona McCauley, Rosa's mother, died at the age of ninety-one.

1984
Rosa Parks famously participated in a march protesting apartheid in South Africa. Photos of her carrying a picket sign reading "Freedom Yes Apartheid No!" graced the news.

1987
Rosa Parks founded the Rosa and Raymond Parks Institute for Self Development.

1988
Rosa Parks backed Reverend Jesse Jackson's run for the Democratic nomination for president of the United States. She appeared at the party's national convention that year in support of Jackson.

1992
Rosa Parks published *Rosa Parks: My Story* with Jim Haskins.

1994
Rosa Parks published *Quiet Strength: The Faith, the Hope, the Heart of a Woman Who Changed a Nation* with Gregory J. Reed.

1996
Rosa Parks was awarded the Presidential Medal of Freedom.

Rosa Parks published *Dear Mrs. Parks: A Dialogue with Today's Youth* with Gregory J. Reed.

1999
Rosa Parks was awarded the Congressional Gold Medal.

2005
On October 24, Rosa Parks died in Detroit, Michigan. Her body lay in honor in the U.S. Capitol Rotunda.

2013
On February 27, President Barack Obama and other dignitaries joined in the ceremonial unveiling of a nine-foot bronze statue in Statuary Hall of the Capitol Building. She became the first African American enshrined in that august location.

2014
On August 28, the Howard G. Buffet Foundation purchased the Rosa Parks Archives for $4.5 million after the materials languished for years in storage.

2015
On February 4, the Rosa Parks Archive opened to the public. The Buffet Foundation entrusted the materials to the Library of Congress on a ten-year loan.

Bibliography

Aguilar, Louis. "Site Where 1967 Uprising Began Sees New Signs of Life." *The Detroit News*, July 20, 2017. https://www.detroitnews.com/story /news/local/detroit-city/2017/07/20/detroit-rising-ashes/103840222/.

Alabama State University. "About." n.d. https://www.alasu.edu/about-asu /about-asu.

"Arrest Report for Claudette Colvin." Police Department City of Montgomery. http://okra.stanford.edu/transcription/document_images /undecided/550302-001.pdf.

Bates, Beth Tomkins. *Pullman Porters and the Rise of Protest Politics in Black America, 1925–1945*. Chapel Hill: University of North Carolina Press, 2001.

Bernstein, Barton J. "Plessy v. Ferguson: Conservative Sociological Jurisprudence." *The Journal of Negro History* 48, no. 3 (1963): 196–205.

Berry, Mary Frances. *Black Resistance White Law: A History of Constitutional Racism in America*. New York: Penguin Books, 1971.

Biko, Steve. *I Write What I Like: Selected Writings*. Chicago: University of Chicago Press, 1978.

Blackmon, Douglas A. *Slavery by Another Name: The Re-Enslavement of Black People in America from the Civil War to World War II*. New York: Doubleday, 2008.

Borstelmann, Thomas. *The Cold War and the Color Line: American Race Relations in the Global Arena*. Cambridge, MA: Harvard University Press, 2003.

Brinkley, Douglas. *Rosa Parks: A Life*. New York: Penguin, 2000.

Brundage, W. Fitzhugh. *Lynching in the New South: Georgia and Virginia, 1880–1930*. Urbana: University of Illinois Press, 1993.

Buni, Andrew. *Robert L. Vann of the* Pittsburgh Courier*: Politics and Black Journalism*. Pittsburgh: University of Pittsburgh Press, 1974.

Carson, Clayborne. *In Struggle: SNCC and the Black Awakening of the 1960s*. Cambridge, MA: Harvard University Press, 1981.

Carter, Dan T. *Scottsboro: A Tragedy of the American South*. Baton Rouge: Louisiana State University Press, 1969.

Cash, Wilbur J. *The Mind of the South*. New York: Vintage Press, 1991.

City of Montgomery Police Department. "Arrest Report for Claudette Colvin." King Institute, 1955. https://kinginstitute.stanford.edu/king-papers/documents/arrest-report-claudette-colvin.

CNN. "Town Honors an African-American WWII Veteran Blinded in a 1946 Police Beating." *CNN*, February 11, 2019. https://www.cnn.com/2019/02/11/us/isaac-woodard-blinded-historical-marker-trnd/index.html.

Cobb, James C. *Redefining Southern Culture: Mind and Identity in the Modern South*. Athens: University of Georgia Press, 1999.

Cody, Cheryll Ann. "There Was No 'Absalom' on the Ball Plantations: Slave-Naming Practices in the South Carolina Low Country, 1720–1865." *The American Historical Review* 92, no. 3 (1987): 563–596.

Cohen, William. *At Freedom's Edge: Black Mobility and the Southern White Quest for Racial Control, 1861–1915*. Baton Rouge: Louisiana State University, 1991.

Collier-Thomas, Bettye, and V. P. Franklin, eds. *Sisters in the Struggle: African American Women in the Civil Rights-Black Power Movement*. New York: New York University Press, 2001.

Cone, James H. *A Black Theology of Liberation*. New York: Orbis Books, 1970.

"Conflicts and Mobilization." *In Motion*. n.d. http://www.inmotionaame.org/gallery/detail.cfm;jsessionid=f8306702415756406333378?migration=9&topic=8&id=486636&type=image&bhcp=1.

Cornish, Samuel, and John Russwurm. "Editorial." *Freedom's Journal*, March 16, 1827. https://web.archive.org/web/20150209163534/http://www.wisconsinhistory.org/pdfs/la/FreedomsJournal/v1n01.pdf.

Dailey, Jane, Glenda Elizabeth Gilmore, and Bryant Simon. *Jumpin' Jim Crow: Southern Politics from Civil War to Civil Rights*. Princeton: University of Princeton Press, 2000.

Daniels, Peter. *Lost Revolution: The South in the 1950s*. Chapel Hill: University of North Carolina Press, 2000.

D'Emilio, John. *Lost Prophet: The Life and Times of Bayard Rustin*. Chicago: University of Chicago Press, 2004.

Detweiler, Frederick German. *The Negro Press in the United States*. Chicago: University of Chicago Press, 1922.

Dittmer, John. *Local People: The Struggle for Civil Rights in Mississippi*. Urbana: University of Illinois Press, 1995.

Dudziak, Mary L. *Cold War Civil Rights: Race and the Image of American Democracy.* Princeton: Princeton University Press, 2002.

Durr, Virginia Foster. "The Emancipation of Pure, White, Southern Womanhood." *New South* 26 (1971): 46–54.

Fitzgerald, Joseph R. *The Struggle is Eternal: Gloria Richardson and Black Liberation.* Lexington: University Press of Kentucky, 2018.

Fitzgerald, Michael W. "'We Have Found our Moses': Theodore Bilbo, Black Nationalism, and the Greater Liberia Bill of 1939." *The Journal of Southern History* 63 (1997): 293–320.

Frederickson, Kari A. *The Dixiecrat Revolt and the End of the Solid South, 1932–1968.* Chapel Hill: University of North Carolina Press, 2001.

Gallagher, Gary W., and Allan T. Nolan, ed. *The Myth of the Lost Cause and Civil War History.* Champaign: Illinois University Press, 2010.

Gavins, Raymond. "March on Washington Movement (MOWM)." In *The Cambridge Guide to African American History.* Cambridge: Cambridge University Press, 2016.

Giddings, Paula J. *IDA: A Sword among Lions.* New York: Amistad, 2008.

Gilmore, Glenda Elizabeth. *Defying Dixie: The Radical Roots of Civil Rights, 1919–1950.* New York: W. W. Norton, 2009.

Goodman, James E. *Stories of Scottsboro.* New York: Pantheon Books, 1994.

Goodwin, E. Marvin. *Black Migration in America from 1915 to 1960: An Uneasy Exodus.* Lewiston: Edwin Mellon Press, 1990.

Green, Laurie B. *Battling the Plantation Mentality: Memphis and the Black Freedom Struggle.* Chapel Hill: University of North Carolina Press, 2007.

Griffin, Larry J., and Don H. Doyle, ed. *The South as an American Problem.* Athens: University of Georgia Press, 1995.

Gutman, Herbert G. *The Black Family in Slavery and Freedom, 1750–1925.* New York: Vintage Books, 1976.

Hale, Grace Elizabeth. *Making Whiteness: The Culture of Segregation in the South, 1890–1940.* New York: Vintage, 1999.

Halpern, Rick. *Down on the Killing Floor: Black and White Workers in Chicago's Packing Houses, 1904–1954.* Urbana: University of Illinois Press, 1997.

Hanson, Joyce Ann. *Mary McLeod Bethune and Black Women's Political Activism.* Columbia: University of Missouri Press, 2003.

Harlan, Louis R. *Booker T. Washington: The Making of a Black Leader, 1856–1901.* New York: Oxford University Press, 1972.

Harmon, David. "Montgomery Industrial School for Girls." *Encyclopedia of Alabama.* n.d. http://www.encyclopediaofalabama.org/article/h-1162.

"Harper Councill Trenholm, Jr." *King Encyclopedia.* https://kinginstitute
.stanford.edu/encyclopedia/trenholm-harper-councill-jr.

Harris, J. William. *Deeps Souths: Delta, Piedmont, and Sea Island Society in the Age of Segregation.* Baltimore, MD: The Johns Hopkins University Press, 2001.

Hendrickson, Paul. "Montgomery." *The Washington Post,* July 24, 1989. https://www.washingtonpost.com/archive/lifestyle/1989/07/24/montgomery/72b9733d-81fc-4367-9f84-b4471f507d74/.

Hirsch, Arnold. *Making the Second Ghetto: Race and Housing in Chicago, 1940–1960.* Chicago: University of Chicago Press, 1998.

"History & Culture." *National Park Service.* n.d. https://www.nps.gov/brvb/learn/historyculture/index.htm.

hooks, bell. *Black Looks: Race and Representation.* Boston: South End Press, 1992.

hooks, bell. *We Real Cool: Black Men and Masculinity.* New York: Routledge, 2004.

Hoose, Phillip. *Claudette Colvin: Twice toward Justice.* New York: Melanie Kroupa Books, 2009.

Houck, Davis W. "From Money to Montgomery: Emmett Till, Rosa Parks, and the Freedom Movement, 1955–2005." *Rhetoric and Public Affairs* 8 (2005): 175–176.

Jackson, Rev. Jesse L., Sr. "Appreciation." *Time,* July 11 2005. http://content.time.com/time/magazine/article/0,9171,1124307,00.html.

Jacobs, Ronald N. *Race, Media, and the Crisis of Civil Society: From Watts to Rodney King.* Cambridge: Cambridge University Press, 2000.

Jonas, Gilbert. *Freedom's Sword: The NAACP Struggle against Racism in America, 1909–1969.* New York: Routledge, 2004.

Jones, Jacqueline. *Labor of Love, Labor of Sorrow: Black Women, Work and the Family from Slavery to the Present.* New York: Vintage Books, 1985.

Kelly, Robin. *Race Rebels: Culture, Politics and the Black Working Class.* New York: Free Press, 1994.

King, Martin Luther, Jr. "There Comes a Time When the People Get Tired." Address at opening meeting of the Montgomery Bus Boycott, Montgomery, AL, December 5, 1955.

Klarman, Michael J. "How Brown Changed Race Relations: The Backlash Thesis." *The Journal of American History* 81, no. 1 (1994): 81–118.

Kleppner, Paul. *Chicago Divided: The Making of a Black Mayor.* Kalb: Northern Illinois University Press, 1985.

Kusmer, Kenneth L. *A Ghetto Takes Shape: Black Cleveland, 1870–1930.* Urbana: University of Illinois Press, 1976.

Lauterbach, Preston. *Bluff City: The Secret Life of Photographer Ernest Withers.* New York: W. W. Norton, 2019.

Lemire, Elsie Virginia. *"Miscegenation": Making Race in America*. Philadelphia: University of Pennsylvania Press, 2002.

Levine, Daniel. *Bayard Rustin and the Civil Rights Movement*. New Brunswick: Rutgers University Press. 2000.

Litwack, Leon F. *Trouble in Mind: Black Southerners in the Age of Jim Crow*. New York: Vintage Books, 1998.

Lubin, Alex. *Romance and Rights: The Politics of Interracial Intimacy, 1945–1954*. Jackson: University of Mississippi Press, 2005.

Mace, Darryl. *American History through Its Greatest Speeches*. Vol. 2. Jolyon P. Girard, series editor. Santa Barbara: ABC-CLIO, 2016.

Mace, Darryl. *In Remembrance of Emmett Till: Regional Stories and Media Responses to the Black Freedom Struggle*. Lexington: University Press of Kentucky, 2014.

McEnaney, Laura. "Atomic Age Motherhood: Maternalism and Militarism in the 1950s." In *Women's America: Refocusing the Past*, 5th ed., edited by Linda Kerber and Jane Sherron De Hart, 448–454. New York: Oxford University Press, 1999.

McGuire, Danielle L. *At the Dark End of the Street: Black Women, Rape and Resistance—A New History of the Civil Rights Movement from Rosa Parks to the Rise of Black Power*. New York: Vintage, 2011.

Meier, August. *Negro Thought in America, 1880–1915: Racial Ideologies in the Age of Booker T. Washington*. Ann Arbor: University of Michigan Press, 1963.

Meier, August, and John H. Bracey, Jr. "The NAACP as a Reform Movement, 1909–1965: 'To Reach the Conscience of America.'" *The Journal of Southern History* 59 (1993): 3–30.

Meier, August, and Francis L. Broderick, ed. *Black Protest Thought in the Twentieth Century*. Indianapolis: Bobbs-Merrill, 1971.

Meier, August, and Elliott Rudwick. *Black Detroit and the Rise of the UAW*. New York: Oxford University Press, 1979.

Meier, August, and Elliott Rudwick. *CORE: A Study in the Civil Rights Movement, 1942–1968*. New York: Oxford University Press, 1973.

Meier, August, and Elliott Rudwick. *From Plantation to Ghetto*. New York: Hill and Wang, 1976.

"Montgomery Bus Boycott: Biographical Sketches." n.d. https://www.crmvet.org/info/mbbbios.htm.

Morris, Aldon D. *The Origins of the Civil Rights Movement: Black Communities Organizing for Change*. New York: Free Press, 1984.

Morris, Willie. *The Ghosts of Medgar Evers: A Tale of Race, Murder, Mississippi, and Hollywood*. New York: Random House, 1998.

"Most Unfortunate." *Birmingham News*, February 21, 1945, p. 6.

Muller, Will. "New 'Klan in Tuxedos' Fights Desegregation." *Detroit News*, January 9, 1955, A:49.

National Association for the Advancement of Colored People. "Springarn Medal Winners: 1915 to Today." *NAACP.* n.d. https://www.naacp .org/awards/spingarn-medal/winners/.

Nelson H. Viscount. *The Rise and Fall of Modern Black Leadership: Chronicles of a Twentieth Century Tragedy.* Lanham: University Press of America, 2003.

"Our History." Highlander Center. n.d. https://www.highlandercenter.org /our-history-timeline/.

Ownby, Ted, ed. *The Role of Ideas in the Civil Rights South.* Jackson: University Press of Mississippi, 2002.

Pacifico, Michele F. "'Don't Buy Where You Can't Work': The New Negro Alliance of Washington." *Washington History* 6 (1994): 66–88.

Papers of the NAACP. Bethesda: University Publications of America, 1995.

Parks, Rosa. "Account of a Near Rape, ca. 1956–1958." Autograph manuscript. *Rosa Parks Papers*, Manuscript Division, Library of Congress (082.00.00).

Parks, Rosa. *Dear Mrs. Rosa Parks: A Dialogue with Today's Youth.* New York: Lee and Lowe Books, 1996.

Parks, Rosa. *Rosa Parks: My Story.* New York: Puffin Books, 1992.

Parks, Rosa, Myles Horton, and E. D. Nixon, radio interview by Studs Terkel, June 8, 1973, transcript. https://www.npr.org/templates/story /story.php?storyId=4973548.

Parks, Rosa, excerpts from radio interview by Lynn Neary. 1992. https:// studsterkel.wfmt.com/programs/rosa-parks-and-myles-horton -discuss-importance-highlander-folk-school-montgomery-bus.

Payne, Charles M. *I've Got the Light of Freedom: The Organizing Tradition and the Mississippi Freedom Struggle.* Berkeley: University of California Press, 1995.

Payne, Charles M., and Adam Green, eds. *Time Longer than Rope: A Century of African American Activism, 1850–1950.* New York: New York University Press, 2003.

Perrusquia, Marc. *A Spy in Canaan: How the FBI Used a Famous Photographer to Infiltrate the Civil Rights Movement.* New York: Melville House Publishing, 2017.

Pfeffer, Paula F. *A. Philip Randolph, Pioneer of the Civil Rights Movement.* Baton Rouge: Louisiana State University Press, 1990.

Pollard, Sam, Sheila Curran Bernard, Laurence Fishburne, Jason L. Pollard, Andrew L. Young, Michael Bacon, and Douglas A. Blackmon. "Slavery by Another Name." 2012. http://www.pbs.org/tpt/slavery -by-another-name/home/.

Purnell, James, Jeanne Theoharis, and Komozi Woodard, eds. *The Strange Career of Jim Crow North: Segregation and Struggle outside of the South.* New York: New York University Press, 2019.

Reeves, Jeremiah, Jr. "Condemned" *Birmingham World*, n.d. http://digital
.archives.alabama.gov/cdm/ref/collection/voices/id/6378.

Robinson, Jo Ann Gibson. *The Montgomery Bus Boycott and the Women Who Started It*. Knoxville: University of Tennessee Press, 1987.

"Rosa Parks." *National Women's Hall of Fame*. n.d. https://www.women ofthehall.org/inductee/rosa-parks/.

Rouse, Jacqueline A. "'We Speak to Know . . . in Order to Speak the Truth': Nurturing the Seeds of Discontent—Septima P. Clark and Participatory Leadership." In *Sisters in the Struggle: African-American Women in the Civil Rights-Black Power Movement*, edited by Bettye Collier-Thomas and V. P. Franklin. New York: New York University Press, 2001.

Selby, Earl, and Miriam Selby. *Odyssey: Journey through Black America*. New York: G. P. Putnam's Sons, 1971.

Sharp, Joanne P. *Condensing the Cold War: Reader's Digest and American Identity*. Minneapolis: University of Minnesota Press, 2000.

Silver, James W. *Mississippi: The Closed Society*. New York: Harcourt, Brace & World, 1966.

Sitkoff, Harvard. *The Struggle for Black Equality, 1954–1992*. New York: Hill Wang, 1993.

Smith, John David. *The Ticket to Freedom: The NAACP and the Struggle for Black Political Integration*. Gainesville: University of Florida Press, 2005.

Spratling, Cassandra. "2 Other Bus Boycott Heroes Praise Parks' Acclaim." *Chicago Tribune*, November 16, 2005. https://www.chicagotribune .com/news/ct-xpm-2005-11-16-0511160360-story.html.

Squires, Buddy, Jean Tsien, Daniel Anker, Barak Goodman, Andre Braugher, and Edward Bilous. *Scottsboro: An American Tragedy*. Alexandria: PBS Home Video, 2005.

Sugrue, Thomas J. "Crabgrass-Roots Politics: Race, Rights, and the Reaction against Liberalism in the Urban South, 1940–1964." *The Journal of American History* 82 (1995): 551–578.

Sugrue, Thomas J. *The Origins of the Urban Crisis*. Princeton: Princeton University Press, 1996.

Theoharis, Jeanne. *A More Beautiful and Terrible History: The Use and Misuse of Civil Rights History*. Boston: Beacon Press, 2018.

Theoharis, Jeanne. *The Rebellious Life of Mrs. Rosa Parks*. Boston: Beacon Press, 2013.

Trotter, Joe William, Jr. *Black Milwaukee: The Making of an Industrial Proletariat, 1915–1945*. Urbana: University of Illinois Press, 1985.

U.S. Bureau of Census. *Anderson McCauley*. Washington, D.C.: Bureau of the Census, 1900.

U.S. Bureau of Census. *Anderson McCauley.* Washington, D.C.: Bureau of the Census, 1910.

U.S. Bureau of Census. *James Pursavill.* Washington, D.C.: Bureau of the Census, 1870.

U.S. Bureau of Census. *Lelar Percival.* Washington, D.C.: Bureau of the Census, 1930.

U.S. Bureau of Census. *Rosa McCauley.* Washington, D.C.: Bureau of the Census, 1920.

U.S. Department of Justice. *Federal Enforcement of Child Support.* Washington, D.C.: U.S. Department of Justice, 1950.

Vogel, Todd, ed. *The Black Press: New Literary and Historical Essays.* New Brunswick: Rutgers University Press, 2001.

Wolseley, Roland Edgar. *The Black Press, U.S.A.* Ames: Iowa State University Press, 1990.

Woodham, Rebecca. "Southern Conference for Human Welfare." *Encyclopedia of Alabama.* n.d. http://www.encyclopediaofalabama.org /article/h-1593.

Yarborough, Tinsley E. "Julius Waties Waring." *South Carolina Encyclopedia.* n.d. http://www.scencyclopedia.org/sce/entries/waring-julius -waties/.

Young, Jasmin. "Strapped: A Historical Analysis of Black Women and Armed Resistance, 1959–1979." Ph.D. dissertation, Rutgers University, New Brunswick, 2018.

Index

About the Author

Darryl Mace is professor and chair of the history and political science department at Cabrini University. He studies cultural history, the civil rights movement, the experiences of Africans in the diaspora, media studies, popular culture, and gender theory. Mace authored *In Remembrance of Emmett Till: Regional Stories and Media Responses to the Black Freedom Struggle* (2014) and edited *American History through Its Greatest Speeches*, vol. 2 (2016). Darryl Mace earned his PhD in history and a graduate certificate in women's studies from Temple University.